OSCAR WILDE
THE GREAT DRAMA OF HIS LIFE

THE UNIVERSITY OF
WINCHESTER

*In memory of Edna, for ever my love
and my inspiration.*

OSCAR WILDE
THE GREAT DRAMA OF HIS LIFE

How His Tragedy Reflected His Personality

ASHLEY H. ROBINS

sussex
ACADEMIC
PRESS
Brighton • Portland • Toronto

2 4 6 8 10 9 7 5 3

First published 2011 in hardcover, reprinted 2012 in paperback in Great Britain by
SUSSEX ACADEMIC PRESS
PO Box 139
Eastbourne BN24 9BP

and in the United States of America by
SUSSEX ACADEMIC PRESS
920 NE 58th Avenue, Suite 300
Portland, Oregon 97213-3786

and in Canada by
SUSSEX ACADEMIC PRESS (CANADA)
8000 Bathurst Street, Unit 1,
PO Box 30010,
Vaughan, Ontario L4J 0C6

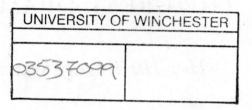

British Library Cataloguing in Publication Data
A CIP catalogue record for this book is available from the British Library.

Library of Congress Cataloging-in-Publication Data
Robins, Ashley H.
   Oscar Wilde—the great drama of his life : how his tragedy reflected his personality / Ashley H. Robins.
      p.   cm.
   Includes bibliographical references and index.
   ISBN 978-1-84519-434-5 (h/c : alk. paper)
   ISBN 978-1-84519-541-0 (pbk : alk. paper)
      1. Wilde, Oscar, 1854–1900. 2. Wilde, Oscar, 1854–1900—Health.
3. Wilde, Oscar, 1854–1900—Imprisonment. 4. Wilde, Oscar,
1854–1900—Relations with men. 5. Wilde, Oscar, 1854–1900—Trials,
litigation, etc. 6. Queensberry, John Sholto Douglas, Marquis of,
1844–1900—Trials, litigation, etc. 7. Great Britain—Social life and
customs—19th century. 8. Authors, Irish—19th century—Biography.
9. Gay men—Great Britain—Biography. I. Title.

PR5823.R63   2011
828'.809—dc22 [B]   2010022926

MIX
Paper from
responsible sources
FSC
www.fsc.org   FSC® C013056

Typeset and designed by Sussex Academic Press, Brighton & Eastbourne.
Printed by TJ International, Padstow, Cornwall.
This book is printed on acid-free paper.

CONTENTS

LIST OF ILLUSTRATIONS

Cover Illustrations and Their Sources

Front cover, Forefront: Oscar Wilde in his heyday and shortly before his downfall (photograph courtesy of Sotheby's London); Lord Alfred Douglas ("Bosie"), youngest son of the Marquess of Queensberry, with Oscar Wilde, partially obscured, to his right (private collection). Background: Theatre programme for *The Importance of Being Earnest* (private collection); Queensberry's fateful calling card with its notorious misspelling, presented as "Exhibit A" at the Old Bailey trial (courtesy of The National Archives, Kew, Surrey); and the prison door spyhole through which Wilde was observed by warders at Reading Gaol (courtesy of Donald Mead, Chairman of The Oscar Wilde Society).

Back cover: Constance Wilde in 1892, some years before she first learned of Oscar's extramarital homosexual affairs (photograph courtesy of Sotheby's London). Background: Door of Wilde's cell at Reading Gaol and its spyhole (courtesy of Donald Mead, Chairman of The Oscar Wilde Society).

Source information is provided at the illustration placement in the text.

ACKNOWLEDGEMENTS

I was introduced to Oscar Wilde by my late mother during my childhood in Southern Rhodesia (now Zimbabwe). She read me his fairy tales, and it was obvious as she did so that she was thoroughly enchanted by them. But whenever she spoke about Wilde I detected sadness in her demeanour. Without divulging any details, she would shake her head, intimating that life had treated him cruelly and that he had died a broken man. Her reactions induced in me a mixed sense of delight, pathos and curiosity: sentiments that became entrenched with the passage of time. The writing of this book is the product of a sixty-year-long journey of incubation, contemplation and exploration – decidedly aided by my later training in clinical psychiatry – of which my mother's gentle but pervasive influence was the *fons et origo*.

I am indebted to Groote Schuur Hospital, Cape Town, South Africa, and the Provincial Government of the Western Cape for granting me the sabbatical leave in which to write this book. I also acknowledge the support I received from the Health Sciences Faculty of the University of Cape Town.

I have spent most of my professional life in Cape Town, and this has isolated me from the mainstream cultural and literary activities associated with Oscar Wilde. In the earlier days of my research, and before the advent of the Internet, I was dependent on two people who kept me abreast of major developments in the field and gladly offered their advice: Joy Melville and Don Mead. To both I express my warmest gratitude.

My thanks go to Merlin Holland, grandson of Oscar Wilde, who showed an encouraging interest in my work and generously gave information and input, especially about the illnesses that afflicted his grandmother Constance and, of course, Oscar himself.

The most important source of my data on Wilde's imprisonment was the Public Record Office (now The National Archives, Kew, Surrey). It was there that I had the exciting (and emotional) experience of examining the original

Home Office and Prison Commission files, which had only a short time before come into the public domain. I thank Nigel Taylor for helping me to locate esoteric documents and records. It has been a privilege, of which I have taken full advantage, to be able to reproduce substantial excerpts of Crown copyright material.

The William Andrews Clark Memorial Library, Los Angeles, supplied me with photocopies of the entire and copious correspondence between Adela Schuster and More Adey, together with letters from Constance Wilde and others.

The following additional institutions and their staff assisted me in my research, and if a specific person there had made a special effort on my behalf I have named, with appreciation, him or her in parentheses: Berkshire Record Office (Peter Durrant); Bibliothèque Interuniversitaire de Médecine; Bodleian Library, Oxford University; British Library, including Colindale Newspaper Library; British Medical Association Library; Greater London Record Office; H.M. Prison Service (Chris Jowett and Peter Davies); House of Commons Library, London (Chris Pond); King's College Library, Cambridge University; Lincoln's Inn Library (Guy Holborn); Magdalen College Library (Janie Cottis); Reading University Library (Michael Bott); Sotheby's London; United States Library of Congress (Abby Yochelson); and University of Cape Town Libraries (Marion Konemann, Tanya Barben and Celia Walter).

Throughout the many years that I have been engaged on the Oscar Wilde project, the following people have given me advice, information or shared their opinions: Anne Clark Amor, Davis Coakley, Owen Dudley Edwards, Deborah Hayden, Ludvig Heiberg, Melissa Knox, Tony Lacey, Solly Leeman, Rohase Piercy, Richard Pine, Felix Pryor, Peter Raby, Michael Seeney, Sean Sellars, Douglas van der Horst and Peter Vernier. I am most grateful to Frederick Mostert, who generously gave his time and legal assistance to resolve an issue related to this book.

I greatly appreciate the cooperation and efforts of those who contributed to the questionnaire study described in the Appendix. Their participation made it possible to test an innovative tool for assessing Oscar Wilde's personality. Although I had initially intended to acknowledge each one of the respondents by name, there was resistance to this idea from several quarters, and I eventually decided on ethical grounds to maintain anonymity for all.

My special thanks go to Anthony Grahame, Editorial Director of Sussex Academic Press, for his support, guidance and wisdom. He is a true professional and it has been most gratifying to work with him.

I have acknowledged the source of the illustrations after the caption to each item. I am grateful to HarperCollins Publishers Ltd for permission to reproduce quotations from *The Complete Letters of Oscar Wilde* (2000), edited by Merlin Holland and Rupert Hart-Davis.

Dale Taylor readily and patiently rescued me from my computer woes – however trivial – and, when the occasional, real problem did arise, he promptly restored order. Michael Wyeth constructed the graphs in the Appendix and did some of the photography. Louise Cohoe meticulously typed the manuscript from my handwritten pages, and Faldiela Clark assisted with secretarial tasks over many years.

Finally, I owe a tremendous debt to my late wife, Edna. Her abiding love and unstinting support sustained my focus and morale throughout all stages of the work. My deep sorrow is that she did not live to see the finished product. This book is dedicated to her memory.

ABOUT THE AUTHOR

Born in Salisbury, Southern Rhodesia (now Harare, Zimbabwe), Ashley Robins graduated in medicine at the University of Cape Town in 1963. He then embarked on postgraduate training in psychiatry in London (Maudsley Hospital), Oxford and Johannesburg. He obtained his specialist qualification in 1967, a doctoral degree in 1971, and foundation membership of the Royal College of Psychiatrists, London, in 1973.

He was senior specialist and senior lecturer in clinical pharmacology and psychiatry at Groote Schuur Hospital and the University of Cape Town, where he was awarded the title of Distinguished Teacher in 1984. He is the author of *Biological Perspectives on Human Pigmentation* (1991), a well-received book that explains the physiological basis of skin colour, its sociological implications and the possible evolutionary factors determining its variation among human populations.

Ashley Robins has been researching the life and personality of Oscar Wilde for many years, and has lectured and written about his subject – notably in a much-publicized paper by himself and Professor Sean Sellars in *The Lancet* (2000), which reinterpreted Wilde's final illness and scotched the syphilis theory.

Ashley Robins is widowed, has three children and lives in Cape Town. Although retired, he continues to teach and advise in an honorary capacity.

"I am in constant correspondence now with a Radley schoolboy . . . He seems to read nothing but my books, and says his one desire is to 'follow in my footsteps'! But I have told him that they lead to terrible places."

Oscar Wilde, in a letter to Reginald Turner, January 1899

"For please let us hear no more of the tragedy of Oscar Wilde. Oscar was no tragedian. He was the supreme comedian of his century, one to whom misfortune, disgrace, imprisonment were external and traumatic. His gaiety of soul was invulnerable . . . Even on his deathbed he found in himself no pity for himself, playing for the laugh with his last breath, and getting it with as sure a stroke as in his palmiest prime."

George Bernard Shaw, preface to Frank Harris's
Oscar Wilde (1938)

INTRODUCTION

OSCAR Wilde once asked André Gide in rhetorical vein: "Would you like to know the great drama of my life? – It's that I've put my genius into my life; I've put only my talent into my work." This admission was made in Algiers in January 1895, the month before Wilde received the Marquess of Queensberry's insulting calling card; and he may well have added that he put his personality into his downfall. Hence the subtitle of this book, "How his tragedy reflected his personality", which refers to the phase of Wilde's life that climaxed in his disgrace and ruin at the hands of Queensberry, an outcome that in large measure emanated from his extraordinary character and temperament.

In this volume I have set out to examine in detail the events surrounding the Queensberry episode and its devastating aftermath, and attempt to address one of the besetting questions: why did Oscar Wilde prosecute the Marquess of Queensberry for criminal libel? It was an action that led swiftly and predictably to his own arrest and prosecution. Why did he choose to slide down that slippery slope to disaster? My arguments differ from those that are customarily presented. The decisions facing Wilde were more complex than previously believed, and the notion that he should have withdrawn from the lawsuit (once it had been instituted) is largely unrealistic.

Considerable attention is given here to a review of Wilde's imprisonment and his subsequent life in exile. The machinations resorted to by the authorities regarding Wilde's health and welfare during imprisonment are uncovered. I dwell at some length on his mental state as a prisoner and make my own appraisal of the quality of the medical reports and the treatment administered. I have been cautious to make this appraisal through the prism of late Victorian medical and psychiatric practice and not on the basis of present-day standards. Wherever possible, fuller biographical information on some of the medical practitioners who interacted with Wilde have been provided in order to cast his case within a broader professional perspective.

1

All the official papers relating to Wilde's imprisonment are available on open access at The National Archives, Kew (formerly the Public Record Office). I made the rather awkward discovery that Montgomery Hyde's *Oscar Wilde: The Aftermath* (1963), which purported to be a comprehensive documentary record of Wilde's imprisonment, omits most of the sensitive but crucial Prison Commission communications. For example, the entire section dealing with Wilde's alleged sexual activities and the resultant intercession of Richard Haldane (later Viscount Haldane) has been deleted from the book. At the time that Hyde inspected the relevant prison files, he did so by special permission of the Home Secretary (obtained in November 1954): the material had not yet been released into the public domain and nor would it be until decades later. One of the conditions made by the Home Secretary was that Hyde had to submit for approval the excerpts that he wished to publish. It is possible that the Home Secretary vetoed the seemingly indecent and compromising contents, but it is more likely that Hyde himself exercised the censorship in view of the prevailing moral climate in Britain at the time.

The life interest of Mrs Constance Wilde's marriage settlement became a major bone of contention during Oscar Wilde's imprisonment. The misunderstandings and conflicts over this issue wreaked havoc with Wilde's marital relationship. It is possible that had this business been handled more delicately, the outcome may have been more positive in terms of family reconciliation. The protracted and extensive correspondence between Adela Schuster and More Adey, lodged at the William Andrews Clark Memorial Library in Los Angeles, has been invaluable in giving me insight into the behind-the-scenes discussions between these two friends of Wilde's. This is an area which has not been sufficiently exposed in the literature, and I have tried to remedy the shortcoming by devoting a full chapter to it, including a brief introductory commentary on the evolution of women's property and matrimonial rights in Victorian Britain.

The debate on whether Wilde suffered from syphilis continues. In order to mark the centenary commemorations of Oscar Wilde's death in November 2000, I wrote a paper for *The Lancet*, together with Professor Sean Sellars, entitled "Oscar Wilde's terminal illness: reappraisal after a century". In it we exploded the belief that Wilde had died of syphilis or even shown clinical signs of it during his lifetime. Instead, we presented what we considered to be the best retrospective diagnosis. Our paper generated a surprising wave of international publicity; we were inundated with requests for newspaper, radio and television interviews. Owing to the fervent interest in this topic, a chapter is allocated to a detailed (and, I hope, intelligible) discussion of Wilde's medical history, with special emphasis on the syphilis controversy.

The issue of Wilde's homosexuality is obviously central to any exposition of his life story. However, I did not want to examine the subject without first contextualizing it within a historical framework and have therefore sketched the societal and legal attitudes to homosexuality in Britain (including the infamous Section Eleven of the Criminal Law Amendment Act of 1885) – highlighting the reactionary approach of the medical profession towards it and the tardy movement for legislative reform, which only really became effective from the mid-1950s. Following Chapter Eight's background discussion, I embark on an assessment of Oscar Wilde's sexual orientation and especially his decision to marry. There is no consensus from the plethora of available biographies whether Wilde was homosexual before his marriage or whether he was initiated into the practice some years afterwards. I try to resolve this question, and the timely appearance of Neil McKenna's *The Secret Life of Oscar Wilde* (2003) was a valuable resource for this purpose.

In the last chapters of the book, attention is given to an analysis and evaluation of Oscar Wilde's personality – the personality that, as my title and subtitle suggest, was ultimately the driving force of his downfall and tragedy. This task was undertaken with the aim of achieving an objective and reliable clinical assessment. I first portray Wilde's personality as perceived by others: his behaviour towards them and their reaction to him. Then I interrogate the nature and quality of his very close personal involvements; in particular, I inquire into the conduct of his marriage and family life and also his capacity to nurture and sustain relationships with his long-standing and devoted friends. Finally, I use well-established diagnostic instruments in order to make a clinical diagnosis of Wilde's personality.

The Appendix describes an unorthodox and controversial experimental project in which a group of Wilde scholars and experts were invited to complete a recognized and widely applied personality questionnaire as if they were doing so on *Oscar Wilde's behalf*. Although this account has a statistical basis (hence its location in the Appendix), I have endeavoured to explain the material in simple terms for the benefit of the uninitiated. Therefore, I would urge readers not to overlook it as its contents are both original and revealing, and they give cause for reflection.

Home Office (Prison Commission) documents are quoted from extensively and to a much lesser extent Adela Schuster's unpublished letters to More Adey. In all cases contents of letters and documents are reproduced with the exact wording intact; the only changes made in the transcription have been to correct misspellings, remove abbreviations and alter punctuation (where this provided greater clarity).

As has become the practice recently, the names "Wilde" and "Oscar" are used interchangeably throughout the text. I have generally done so naturally and spontaneously, although in those passages and sections relating to official or formal matters I have tended to avoid the use of his first name.

The reference section has been compiled according to the format used in medical and scientific journals, and the following numbering convention adopted. Every reference is numbered sequentially the *first* time it appears in the text. Where the same item is referred to subsequently in that chapter, then the *original* number allocated to it is repeated so that the reader recognizes that it pertains to an already cited source.

Gordon Allport, the eminent American psychologist, once wrote that "the same flame that melts the butter hardens the egg": in other words, exactly the same stimulus can have diametrically opposite effects on different individuals and, presumably, on the same individual in different situations. My intention has been to show that this maxim applied to Oscar Wilde. The very genius and personality that catapulted him into fame and glamour also plummeted him into infamy and ruin. But that genius and personality have done something else: they have galvanized generations of scholars and biographers into a frenzy of activity trying to unravel and come to terms with the truth – "rarely pure and never simple" – about the character of Oscar Wilde.

I

"PURSUED BY A PUGILIST OF UNSOUND MIND"

THE most disastrous decision of Oscar Wilde's life was to sue the ninth Marquess of Queensberry (John Sholto Douglas) for criminal libel. In brief, on 18 February 1895 Queensberry left his calling card at the Albemarle Club with the infamous words scribbled on it: "For Oscar Wilde posing as somdomite [*sic*]". Wilde was handed the card by the hall porter when he visited the Club on 28 February. By the next day he had instituted the action.

Merlin Holland, Oscar Wilde's grandson, has written: "If there is one thing I would like to ask my grandfather it is this: 'Why on earth did you do it?'" It has been a long-standing matter of debate why Wilde embarked on that lawsuit, which he was subsequently forced to abandon during the trial itself. The result was that he himself was arrested, tried on charges of gross indecency (homosexual offences) and ultimately convicted and sentenced to two years' imprisonment with hard labour. Various hypotheses have been mooted: that he was under the irresistible sway of Lord Alfred ("Bosie") Douglas, the Marquess's son, whose passion to prosecute his father was overwhelming; that he relished the opportunity of a theatrical interlude at the Old Bailey with himself on centre stage. Certainly the former weighed heavily on Oscar and in *De Profundis* he accused Bosie Douglas of propelling him into the débâcle:

> To see him 'in the dock', as you used to say: that was your one idea . . . Well you had your desire gratified . . . and feasted your eyes with the spectacle of your father standing in the dock of the Central Criminal Court. And on the third day I took his place.[1]

The universal consensus is that Wilde was foolhardy and reckless in prosecuting Queensberry – a viewpoint that Wilde himself later endorsed when he referred to his conduct as "a combination of absolute idiocy and vulgar bravado".[2] But it is all too easy to look through the "retrospectoscope" and blame Wilde entirely for what he did. It is necessary to cast a colder eye on the whole question and make a more balanced assessment.

A major consideration is that in the year preceding the receipt of the offensive card Wilde had experienced a series of abusive interventions by Queensberry, who was defiantly opposed to his son's intimate friendship with Wilde and was determined to destroy it. In a letter to Bosie on 1 April 1894 he had written as follows:

> I am not going to analyse this intimacy, and I make no charge; but to my mind to pose as a thing is as bad as to be it. With my own eyes I saw you both in the most loathsome and disgusting relationship as expressed by your manner and expression. Never in my experience have I seen such a sight as that in your horrible features. No wonder people are talking as they are. Also I now hear on good authority, but this may be false, that his [Wilde's] wife is petitioning to divorce him for sodomy and other crimes. Is this true or do you not know of it? If I thought the actual thing was true and it became public property, I should be quite justified in shooting him at sight.[3]

Then on Saturday 30 June 1894 the Marquess and an accomplice arrived uninvited at Wilde's Tite Street house and deliberately provoked an angry and intimidating confrontation, which Wilde terminated by expelling Queensberry. This surprise and hostile encounter on his own territory unnerved Oscar, who decided then and there that he had to halt Queensberry's belligerence by legal action. However, the Queensberrys (and particularly Lady Queensberry) urged him to desist from this course in order to avert the publicity of a family scandal. On the Wednesday following the Tite Street incident, Wilde met with Bosie's maternal cousin, the Member of Parliament George Wyndham, who made the insipid proposal that Oscar should drop Bosie. But Oscar was not persuaded and he sought the advice of the eminent solicitor Sir George Lewis. Lewis had already been engaged by Queensberry and so Wilde turned to Charles Humphreys, who was Robert Ross's solicitor. On 11 July 1894 a letter was sent to the Marquess by Humphreys, stating that Queensberry had "most foully and infamously libelled" Wilde in letters to his son; it then gave him the opportunity of retracting his assertions and insinuations, with an apology for having made them: if not, then Wilde would be advised to pursue litigation to vindicate his character.[4] Queensberry responded promptly (13 July) and emphatically that he would not tender any apologies and he urged them to take any steps they wished. He maintained that he had made no direct insult but had merely informed Wilde that to pose as a certain thing was as bad as the actual thing.[5]

Figure 1 *Oscar Wilde's nemesis: John Sholto Douglas, the 9th Marquess of Queensberry. Taken the year after Wilde's trials and conviction, this photograph shows the Marquess (then in his early fifties) still eager to demonstrate his athleticism.*

(From *The Cycling World Illustrated*, May 1896)

Unfortunately, no further steps were taken, presumably out of respect for the wishes of the Queensberry family. Wilde was shortly afterwards to regret the inaction. In a letter to Douglas some weeks later he remarked that the Marquess was on the rampage again at the Café Royal: "I think now it would have been better for me to have had him bound over to keep the peace, but what a scandal! Still, it is intolerable to be dogged by a maniac."[6]

It was Hyde's view that had Wilde prosecuted the Marquess for criminal libel in mid-1894 instead of eight months later – when much more damning evidence had accumulated against him – Queensberry might have been convicted and imprisoned.[7] But the silence from Humphreys, after Queensberry had thrown down the gauntlet in his responding letter, must have given the Marquess a feeling of triumph and renewed confidence in his vendetta against Wilde.

From August 1894 until February 1895 there was no further incident between Queensberry and Wilde. This did not betoken a cessation of hostilities between the parties. Various circumstances intervened during that period.

During August and September 1894 Oscar, Constance and the two children spent the summer holidays at a seaside house on the Esplanade at Worthing, where Oscar wrote *The Importance of Being Earnest*. During the first half of October Oscar moved to Brighton with Bosie. He was therefore out of range of Queensberry's prying and prowling for about twelve weeks. Then, just as Wilde was returning to London towards the latter part of October 1894, two events struck in quick succession, both of which had a devastating effect on Queensberry.

The first was the death of Francis, Viscount Drumlanrig (Queenberry's eldest son and heir) at the age of twenty-seven on 18 October. Drumlanrig was out with a shooting party at Quantock Lodge in Somerset where he was invited to meet the family of his fiancée, Alexandra Ellis. He left the group and a few minutes later a shot was heard. Drumlanrig was found dead in a field with the gun lying across his stomach. An inquest determined the cause as "accidental death", but this was clearly a cover-up because the medical evidence pointed strongly to suicide. He had died instantaneously from a single charge of his gun which had entered his mouth, fracturing the lower jaw and penetrating the roof of the mouth – a highly improbable point of entry for an accidental shooting.[8]

Drumlanrig had been private secretary to Lord Rosebery, then Foreign Secretary under Gladstone. In 1893 it was decided to elevate him to the British peerage under the title of Baron Kelhead so that he could sit in the House of Lords in the junior office of Lord-in-Waiting to the Queen. This was the start of a schism between Queensberry and his heir that lasted until Drumlanrig's death. In 1881 Queensberry himself had not been re-elected as one of the sixteen Scottish representative peers to the House of Lords on account of his

Figure 2   *The familiar photograph of Oscar Wilde and Lord Alfred Douglas ("Bosie"), youngest son of the Marquess of Queensberry. Oscar was 38 and Bosie 22 at the time, and it was their intimate relationship that precipitated the Marquess's vendetta against Wilde.*

(Private collection)

confessed atheism. Before accepting the peerage, Drumlanrig approached his father for his approval, which was given graciously by Queensberry. But within a month the tide had turned and the Marquess launched a campaign of sending hate letters to Rosebery, Gladstone and even Queen Victoria for the way he had been humiliated by his exclusion from the House of Lords. In August 1893 he followed Rosebery to Homburg, threatening to thrash him with a dog-whip. It required the intercession of the chief of police to send Queensberry on the next train to Paris. "It is a material and unpleasant addition to the labours of Your Majesty's service to be pursued by a pugilist of unsound mind," wrote Rosebery to the Queen some time after the incident.[8,9]

This aggression against the Foreign Secretary was fuelled not only by the peerage issue but by Queensberry's belief that Rosebery was a bad influence on Drumlanrig. In fact, Queensberry suspected a homosexual relationship between the two. A fortnight after his son's death the Marquess informed his ex-father-in-law, Alfred Montgomery, that he blamed "the snob Queers like Rosebery" for Drumlanrig's fate. "I smell a Tragedy behind all this and have already *got Wind* of a more *startling one*."[10] Indeed it was generally rumoured that Drumlanrig's suicide was associated with a suppressed scandal involving an affair with Rosebery. In certain quarters it was whispered that Rosebery was a practising homosexual, but there is actually no reliable evidence either to corroborate this or to suggest any sexual intimacy between him and Drumlanrig.[9]

It must also be recognized that there was a strong history of suicide and mental illness in the Queensberry line. The Marquess's father had died in a shooting accident (presumed to be suicide) under circumstances remarkably similar to Drumlanrig's. Queensberry's brother Jim, Lord James Douglas, was a manic-depressive and alcoholic who slit his throat with a razor. Queensberry's grandson Raymond (Bosie's son) was diagnosed with a psychotic illness, certified and committed to a psychiatric hospital from 1927 until his death in 1964.[11] And, in 2009, the twelfth Marquess's son, a manic-depressive, killed himself by jumping from a building. This familial pattern is key to understanding Drumlanrig's suicide. There is a tendency to seek explanations for an individual's suicide whereas, in a person who has a hereditary predisposition to psychiatric disorder and suicide, there may not necessarily be a specific causal event. Thus the attribution of Drumlanrig's misadventure to a supposed sexual involvement with Rosebery may be entirely erroneous. He may have developed a severe depressive state (unrelated to any particular environmental stress) and committed suicide as a consequence of that illness.

The second blow to befall Queensberry was the annulment of his second marriage. This took place six days after his son's tragic death. Queensberry had been divorced from his first wife, Sybil Douglas, in Edinburgh in January 1887, and on 7 November 1893 in Eastbourne he had married Ethel Weeden, a woman of about twenty-one. On 24 October 1894 this marriage was "pronounced and declared to have been and to be absolutely null and void . . . by reason of the frigidity, impotency and malformation of the parts of generation of the said Respondent [the Marquess of Queensberry]".[12]

Owing to the sensitive nature of the proceedings, the case was heard *in camera*. The papers of the Queensberry versus Queensberry divorce (with Sir George Lewis acting for the Marquess and Day Russell for the Marchioness) were only released into the public domain in 1996.[12] According to Ethel Douglas, Queensberry had been unable to consummate the marriage, from its very beginning, by virtue of frigidity and impotence.

In terms of the law at that time, the court would not grant a decree of nullity on the part of the husband for impotence unless both he and his wife were medically inspected: in his case to determine whether he was capable of performing the act of generation and, if incapable, whether his impotence was remediable or curable; in her case whether she was or was not a virgin or had any impediment to prevent consummation of the marriage. The registrar of the Divorce Court appointed two medical practitioners to act as inspectors, and Queensberry and his wife were duly examined. The outcome was that the young Marchioness was declared to be *virgo intacta*. This gave Queensberry no defence, and the nullity decree was granted uncontested and with costs against the Marquess. The news was leaked to Wilde, who wrote to Bosie: "I heard all the details of the divorce of the Scarlet Marquess the other day: quite astonishing."[13]

The experience of having to face a nullity decree was undoubtedly one of outright mortification for Queensberry. Here was a man who in his prime proudly sported his athletic and pugilistic prowess; a man who had no difficulty in siring several children and was known as an inveterate womaniser who flaunted his numerous extramarital conquests.[14] He regarded himself as a fine specimen of machismo and virility and, at the same time, he virulently detested effeminacy and homosexuality. It must therefore have been humiliating for him to fail sexually with a wife thirty years his junior. He was fortunate that the case was held *in camera* because public exposure of his incapacity would have made a mockery of him in the light of his previous reputation. Ironically, had the hearing been conducted in open court with the press having their field day, Queensberry might have been so sensitized to the gossip and ridicule that he would have gone into hiding over the Wilde–Douglas relationship. Instead he channeled his sense of personal disgrace and discomfort into a fierce assault on Oscar and Bosie.

In the late nineteenth century impotence (nowadays referred to as "erectile dysfunction") was regarded as a shameful defect because it vitiated procreative function. Attitudes since then have been transformed and today there is a compassionate and optimistic approach to the problem with several effective treatments available. Impotence is common, as was observed in the Massachusetts Male Aging Study, which found that fifty-two percent of men aged between forty and seventy reported some degree of impotence.[15] Impotence is associated with conditions such as diabetes, obesity, high blood pressure and arterial disease. It is often an early indication, and indeed a warning sign, of subsequent heart and brain complications, as was the case with Queensberry. He was forty-nine at the time of his second marriage and he died in January 1900, aged fifty-five, after having suffered a stroke that partly paralysed him and left him in a semi-conscious state.[16]

By February 1895 Queensberry, having recovered somewhat from the calamities of the previous autumn, was on the warpath again, but with an added vengeance. His eldest son had killed himself, supposedly over a homosexual affair with Rosebery, and now his youngest son was immersed in a homosexual relationship with Oscar Wilde. Wilde had not heeded his warnings to break the friendship and the Marquess was determined to ruin him.

In November 1882 Queensberry had attended a performance of Tennyson's *The Promise of May* at the Globe Theatre in London. One of the leading actors, Hermann Vezin, was cast as the atheist and radical villain of the piece and, as soon as he began to speak, Queensberry leapt to his feet and protested, on behalf of the Freethinkers, at the travesty of an interpretation given by Tennyson to atheism. Pandemonium broke out in the house and Queensberry was eventually evicted, delighted at the sensation he had created.[17] It was now time for an encore – a bigger and better one, and with Oscar Wilde as the target.

The Importance of Being Earnest was due to open at the St James's Theatre on 14 February 1895, and Queensberry had hatched a plan. He would reserve a seat for the *première*, disrupt the play to address the audience with offensive remarks about the author, and then hurl a bunch of vegetables onto the stage, possibly when Wilde took a curtain call at the end. Fortunately for Wilde, the Marquess in a moment of intoxication and bravado revealed his scheme and, on being apprised of this, Wilde arranged for Queensberry's ticket to be cancelled and the money refunded. He also wisely informed Scotland Yard, who posted a posse of twenty policemen to guard the theatre and bar Queensberry's entrance. After prowling around for some hours, Queensberry departed but not before depositing his bundle of vegetables (the "phallic bouquet", as Sherard so aptly called it) at the box office.

Wilde was deeply disturbed at Queensberry's attempt at a public assassination of his character. At the end of that first performance, he disappointed the enthusiastically applauding and expectant audience by (uncharacteristically) declining to make a speech. The tensions and malice surrounding

Queensberry's behaviour that night had obviously taken their toll of Wilde's self-confidence.

The truth is that, had Queensberry's mission succeeded, there would have been devastating consequences. The run of *The Importance of Being Earnest* might well have been aborted at its inception and Wilde's reputation and career would have been instantly blighted. There was no other course open to him but a prosecution. He returned to his solicitors, Humphreys, Son and Kershaw, whom he had last consulted seven months before, with instructions to press charges against Queensberry. It is important to note that this decision was made by Wilde in the absence of any influence from Bosie Douglas, who was abroad in Algeria at the time. Wilde recognized immediately that this was his opportunity to nail the Marquess without any embarrassment or reference to the wider Queensberry family. He expressed this advantage in his letter to Bosie a few days after the incident: "I feel now that, without your name being mentioned, all will go well."[18]

Humphreys set about garnering first-hand evidence from George Alexander and the staff of the St James's Theatre about Queensberry's foiled mischief on the night of 14 February, but to no avail. Alexander steadfastly declined to cooperate in any way with the request for statements and assistance. He had decided that he and his theatre were not becoming involved in any lawsuit between Wilde and Queensberry. Alexander, who had never been particularly sympathetic to Oscar during his troubled times, was not prepared to compromise his business interests or alienate the goodwill of his patrons by joining forces against the Marquess. Ironically, in November 1895 George Alexander's own reputation received a blow in a manner entirely unrelated to the Wilde–Queensberry feud. Alexander was charged with indecent conduct with a prostitute to whom he had given money in Chelsea. He testified that the encounter was innocent: she had begged from him, pleading starvation, and he had merely assisted with a contribution. Arthur Pinero, the dramatist, was called as a character witness. Alexander was acquitted, and two days later he appeared on his theatre stage amid applause from the audience.[20]

By coincidence, on the same day that Wilde received Queensberry's insulting calling card (28 February 1895), Humphreys had written to him advising that there was no prospect of a prosecution for the St James's Theatre incident owing to Alexander's non-compliance. But, in an impressive touch of prescience, he added that "the only consolation we can offer to you now is that such a persistent persecutor as Lord Queensberry will probably give you another opportunity sooner or later of seeking the protection of the Law . . .".[19]

It is intriguing to ponder whether Wilde had first received Humphrey's letter and then the card, or vice versa. I suspect the former. It was established in court that Wilde visited the Albemarle Club between five and six o'clock on the evening of Thursday 28 February,[21] thus giving him virtually the whole working day to have received the letter. Being an important private communication, it was probably not posted but delivered by messenger from the solicitors' offices. The gist of Oscar's reaction to the card "with hideous words on it" was conveyed almost immediately in a note to Robert Ross which reached him by hand at 6:40 that evening. "I don't see anything now but a criminal prosecution. My whole life seems ruined by this man."[22] If Oscar had already heard from Humphreys on the negative outcome of the St James's Theatre matter, he would have been even more convinced of the need for a criminal action. Again it is necessary to emphasize that this idea of a prosecution was entirely his own; there was no pressure from Bosie. Thus the argument generally advanced by biographers, and by Wilde himself in *De Profundis*, that he was virtually coerced into litigation by Douglas needs to be reconsidered.

With the failure of his two previous applications to Charles Humphreys to bring Queensberry to book, Wilde recognized *a fortiori* that on this occasion he had no alternative but to silence the Marquess. He realized – and with good cause – that if he did not curb Queensberry's hate campaign without delay he was in danger of future and potentially more vicious strikes. Furthermore, the possibility of violence was real. Queensberry had written in the previous year (see above) that he would be justified in shooting Wilde. He confirmed this sentiment a year later in a letter to his daughter-in-law Minnie, Percy Douglas's wife:

> [Y]ou will find the whole town has been reeling with this hideous scandal of Oscar Wilde for the last three years . . . If I were to shoot this hideous monster in the street, I should be perfectly justified, for he has almost ruined my so-called son.[23]

And on his acquittal in the criminal libel trial, Queensberry is reported to have told Oscar Wilde through newspaper reports: "If the country allows you to leave, all the better for the country. But if you take my son with you, I will follow you wherever you go and shoot you like a dog."[24] Queensberry was an aggressive man with paranoid tendencies, as exemplified by his bid to assault Lord Rosebery in Homburg in 1893.

Therefore, on the evening of 28 February 1895, Wilde instinctively knew that if he wanted to preserve his reputation, his personal safety and his intimacy with Bosie he had no option but to neutralize his "persistent persecutor". The hour had come: the card "with hideous words on it" was the *casus belli*. Oscar arranged to meet with Ross at 11:30 that night and with Bosie the next day, preferring in the first instance to seek the more sober opinion of the former. But in fact circumstances dictated a reversal of the order and Bosie was already with

Oscar when Ross arrived at 11:30.[22] Some biographers have maintained that Bosie, with his zeal to have his father convicted and sentenced, would have browbeaten Oscar into submission before Ross's supposedly wiser counsel could prevail. There is no doubt that Bosie did exert considerable pressure on Oscar but, as argued, Wilde had earlier decided in principle to sue Queensberry and so Bosie was in effect preaching to the converted.

The upshot of the trialogue was that the next day (1 March 1895) Wilde, accompanied by Ross and Douglas, went to his solicitor, Charles Humphreys, to initiate proceedings against Queensberry. A warrant for the latter's arrest was issued at Marlborough Street Police Court on the same day and the Marquess was apprehended at nine o'clock the next morning.

The sequence of events occurred with rapidity and in the context of high emotion. The card was in Wilde's possession at about six o'clock on Thursday evening; the meeting with Douglas and Ross ended in the early hours of the following morning; the interview with Humphreys took place hours later; and the warrant for arrest was secured shortly thereafter. Within less than twenty-four hours of the receipt of the card Wilde had signed and sealed his fate. What is regrettable is that Oscar had no opportunity for a cooling-off period of a few days in which to review his momentous decision. That would have enabled him to deliberate on the possible consequences and get advice from other close friends.

Bosie Douglas was ecstatic that at last his *bête noire* had got his just deserts and was to stand trial. He wanted the good tidings to be spread far and wide, and no sooner had the warrant been served on his father than he planned a press notice for James Nicol Dunn, editor of the *Morning Post*, announcing Queensberry's arrest that morning on the charge of defamatory libel of Oscar Wilde.[25]

There is another issue that is repeatedly raised. When Humphreys took instructions to prosecute the Marquess for criminal libel, he asked Wilde whether there was any truth in Queensberry's allegation. Wilde declared that there was not and the matter went ahead. But he later admitted in *De Profundis* to "telling serious lies to a bald man".[26] While he certainly lied to his lawyers on that score subsequently, was he lying to Humphreys during that first consultation on 1 March 1895? The answer is that he was probably not.

An examination of Queensberry's card is revealing (Figure 3). The first line of the handwriting ("For Oscar Wilde") is clear; and on the second line "somdomite" is clearly written albeit misspelled. The difficulty arises with the first word of that line. Anyone unfamiliar with Queensberry's scrawl would have had a problem deciphering it. The hall porter at the Albemarle Club, Sidney Wright, testified at Marlborough Street Police Court on 2 March that the words read "For Oscar Wilde ponce and sodomite", at which point Queensberry interrupted and stated that the words were "posing as sodomite".[21] (Ellmann revealed in his 1987 biography that what was actually written was "For Oscar Wilde posing somdomite [sic]".) [27]

The question is: How did Wilde or Ross or Douglas read the second line of the card? If as "ponce and sodomite", as did Sidney Wright, then this clearly imparted a different and much more serious message from the one that Queensberry intended. My view is that Wilde interpreted it in exactly the same way as did the hall porter. On the basis of this assumption, two significant implications arise. First, Wilde was not and never had been a ponce (a word with a very similar meaning to "pimp" – namely, a man who solicits for a prostitute and lives off her earnings). Second, Wilde had never admitted to committing the act of sodomy; nor was that charge ever brought against him or proved in his two criminal trials. For these reasons, Oscar felt amply justified in denying both accusations when he was specifically challenged by Humphreys. And, in so doing, he was not strictly lying.

It must have come as a surprise when, the next day in court, Oscar heard the Marquess announce the intended, and thereafter accepted, version – namely, "posing as sodomite". (To Queensberry, posing as something was as bad as the actual thing.) This more cautious wording must have given Wilde a frisson of doubt as to the wisdom of his course of action. What initially had seemed an indefensible position for Queensberry now became an eminently defensible one. But it was too late to reverse the process. It is germane that, at the adjourned hearing at the Police Court a week later, Wilde testified that he had read what was on the card *as well as he could*.[21] This was an admission of ambiguity, and it suggests that what he initially assumed he had read was not what Queensberry intended.

Biographers have been consistently puzzled as to why Wilde, having committed the blunder of instituting the prosecution, did not subsequently withdraw from it. He was strongly advised by friends who predicted the outcome to drop the case. During the oft-quoted meeting at the Café Royal between Frank Harris, George Bernard Shaw and Wilde, Oscar was sternly warned by both men that his best move would be to go to Paris with his wife and write a letter to *The Times* explaining that, although insulted by Queensberry, he realized that no jury would give a verdict against a father. Douglas then joined the trio and, when he heard what had been discussed, he was furious and stormed out, followed sheepishly by Wilde. At that stage it is probably true that Douglas's influence over Wilde was paramount. Bosie had invested so heavily emotionally in the forthcoming trial – and with keen anticipation of giving evidence against his father – that he could not tolerate any endeavour to dissuade Oscar from continuing. Bosie was convinced that Oscar would win, and the fantasy of his father behind bars was irresistible.

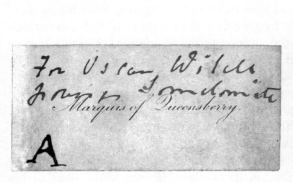
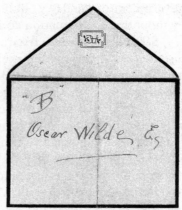

Figure 3 *Queensberry's fateful calling card with its notorious misspelling (presented as "Exhibit A" at the Old Bailey trial). The hall porter at the Albemarle Club put the card in the accompanying envelope ("Exhibit B") and addressed it to Oscar Wilde. Was the choice of a black-edged envelope fortuitous or did it reflect prescience on the hall porter's part?*

(Courtesy of The National Archives, Kew, Surrey)

What has not been debated by biographers is the question of Wilde's legal position had he withdrawn his action for criminal libel against Queensberry. The matter is far from simple and certainly any disengagement from the proceedings might have elicited a number of potential consequences.

At the conclusion of the Marlborough Police Court hearing on 9 March 1895, the magistrate committed Lord Queensberry to trial at the next sessions of the Central Criminal Court, and Oscar Wilde was bound over in the sum of £40 to attend and prosecute.[21] The minimum penalty for withdrawal of the prosecution would have been forfeiture of the £40 together with payment of Queensberry's legal costs to date. But there were several more ominous legal scenarios.

In the first place, although Wilde himself might have decided to halt the lawsuit, the Crown would have had to decide whether or not to continue with it. Criminal libel was a criminal offence (as opposed to a civil action) and, if it considered that sufficient grounds existed, the Crown prosecuting authority might have deemed it appropriate and in the public interest to sustain the charge and take it to trial. Wilde would then have been subpoenaed as a witness for the prosecution. However, against the backdrop of Queensberry's erstwhile harassment and vilification of the political leadership (Gladstone and Rosebery in particular) over the Drumlanrig saga, it seems unlikely that the Liberal government of the day would have risked further provocation of the Marquess by mounting a prosecution against him.

Secondly, Queensberry would have had recourse to legal remedies to clear his name. One was that he could have instituted an action for malicious prosecution: that is, he would have been entitled to sue Wilde for subjecting him to the disgrace of unfounded legal proceedings. In order to recover damages in such an action the plaintiff would have had to prove that injury resulted to him either in person, reputation or pocket. Alternatively, but along similar lines, Queensberry might have brought his own action of defamatory libel against Wilde on the grounds that the aborted but vexatious prosecution, and its associated public humiliation, had denigrated his good name and dignity.

I do not believe that the Marquess would have allowed Wilde to withdraw the case without exacting retribution from him. He was at the peak of his vindictiveness and he was hell-bent on exposing Wilde for his homosexual activities and crushing the relationship with Bosie. In fact, part of Queensberry's cunning scheme (the "booby trap", as he described it) was to goad Wilde into litigation. Wilde had already sought legal advice seven months previously and the Marquess realized that another bout of strong provocation from his side would inveigle Oscar into a legal reprisal. When the St James's Theatre plan foundered, he embarked on the Albemarle Club strategy. The message on his calling card was carefully contrived (possibly with professional assistance) to arouse Wilde's ire but yet to cushion the insult by using the weasel word "posing". Queensberry did not mail the card to Wilde or present it to the hall porter, Sidney Wright, in a closed envelope. Instead he made a personal visit to the Club, wrote out the card *in the presence* of Wright (misspelling "sodomite" in the excitement of the moment) and handed it to him to give to Oscar Wilde.[21] Wright read it, wrote the time and date on the back of the card, and then inserted it in an unsealed envelope, which, prophetically, happened to be black-edged (Figure 3). It is obvious that Queensberry took these steps to establish that the libel was published to a third party. Criminal libel did not require publication to a third person, but for a *civil* libel action to succeed such publication was a prerequisite.[28] The Marquess was taking no chances!

Wilde fell headlong into Queensberry's craftily laid trap. As the Marquess told the *New York Herald* at the time of his arrest:

> I wished to assault him [Wilde] so that he should be forced to bring an action again me and thus give me an opportunity of stating what I believe to be the truth about the matter. I am delighted at the result of my action in leaving that card, and I feel much easier in my mind now.[29]

The fact that Queensberry was laying the ground for his own arrest and prosecution meant that he was confident of a successful defence. Under Lord Campbell's Libel Act of 1843, criminal libel carried a statutory maximum sentence of two years', or one year's, imprisonment, depending on whether the accused was proved to have known the falsity of the libel, or not, respectively.[28] As the Marquess was certainly not so foolhardy as to risk his own freedom, this presupposes that by February 1895 he had collected enough damning material to win the case. The impression is created in the literature that Queensberry and his solicitor only really set their detectives to work after his arraignment at the Police Court in early March. That may have been so in the formal sense but Queensberry was by then well informed of Wilde's numerous liaisons with the rent-boys and was secure in the knowledge that the latter would be available as (paid) witnesses. The Marquess's insight into Wilde's sexual exploits is evident in a letter he wrote to his daughter-in-law, Minnie Douglas, on 26 February, two days before the receipt of his card.

> [I]f he [his son Percy] is still so obstinate to refuse to recognise what the character of this man [Wilde] is, with which the whole of London is ringing, let him go and speak to Cook the detective . . . He knows more about him (O.W.) than I do . . .[30]

But even the year before (April 1894) Queensberry had sent the inflammatory warning to Bosie which made insinuations about Wilde's possible participation in sodomy (see above). He had obviously had his ear to the ground for a considerable time and was well prepared for any offensive from Wilde.

Unfortunately Oscar was naïve enough to accept that Queensberry had little ammunition of substance against him other than some of his controversial literary contributions. This attitude may have encouraged him at the start but he was speedily disabused and astounded when he was confronted with the Marquess's Plea of Justification on 30 March 1895, which itemized the dates and venues of his alleged homosexual encounters with various rent-boys between February 1892 and September 1894. If Wilde had opted to withdraw at that juncture (days before the trial began) he would not only have had to contend with the possibility of Queensberry's personal action for damages but also with a criminal indictment for homosexual offences. When Wilde's prosecution of the Marquess failed on 5 April, Charles Russell, Queensberry's solicitor, forwarded their witnesses' statements (together with the shorthand notes of the trial) to the Director of Public Prosecutions. This led to Wilde's arrest later in the day. It is almost certain that exactly the same procedure would have been followed had Wilde capitulated prior to the commencement of the trial.

And if Wilde had withdrawn the action before it came to trial, it would have been perceived by society as an admission of guilt: that is, that Queensberry's words were true. On that account alone he would have had to suffer the vituperation of the press, the denunciation of the public and the damage to his career and reputation.

In short, the advice given by Oscar's friends, namely, that he abandon the case, was not sound. On the contrary, I have tried to show that such a move would have been counter-productive. By February 1895 Wilde was in a typical "catch-22" situation, as he later admitted in *De Profundis*: "[I]f I retaliated I would be ruined, and if I did not retaliate I would be ruined also."[31] Had he thrown Queensberry's malicious card into the fire, he would merely have postponed the Marquess's revenge to another day – and when that day came the assault might have been more brutal and destructive than the message on a calling card. Had he withdrawn the prosecution there were the potentially dire consequences outlined above. The recommendation that he leave England for France was not a solution. If he had done so with Bosie in tow, the Marquess would undoubtedly have carried out his threat to follow him there and harm him. Moreover, relocation would have been a highly disruptive course for Oscar and his family and very prejudicial to his professional interests. And, above all, he himself abhorred the idea of being an escapee or a fugitive from justice and of sacrificing the success and acclaim he had achieved in London.

Many of Wilde's friends accused Bosie of selfishness because he did not urge Oscar to go abroad after he had begun his action against Queensberry. Decades later Bosie challenged George Bernard Shaw on the consequences if Wilde had taken his and Frank Harris's advice to flee the country after initiating the lawsuit against Queensberry:

> Where would he have gone? How would he have lived? Would he have even escaped prosecution? All the evidence would have been handed to the Public Prosecutor, and his failure to go on with his proceedings against my father would have been a complete admission of guilt. How would he have benefited?[32]

Ultimately the only step Wilde could have taken to remove the Marquess of Queensberry from his orbit would have been to terminate, decisively and permanently, his association with Bosie. In the London of 1895 he was resolutely opposed to that option: in Reading Goal two years later he expressed with great bitterness how grossly mistaken he had been.

2

IN DURANCE VILE:
PENTONVILLE

SATURDAY, 25 May 1895 was a day of contrasting emotions for British theatre. It was the day that Oscar Wilde was formally and decisively ostracized from society, never to return. His sentence of two years' imprisonment was his personal punishment but, in a more general sense, it was not only he but his plays and literary works that were sentenced – sentenced to withdrawal from production and from circulation, respectively. It would be many years, even decades, before the name of Oscar Wilde was restored to a position of rightful recognition.

On the other hand, that particular Saturday was a glorious occasion for Henry Irving. The news of his knighthood was proclaimed amid huge fanfare far and wide. He was the first person of the theatre in Great Britain to receive the honour of knighthood. Thus 25 May 1895 marked the beginning of a new era in the history of the actor. Acting had come of age and from then onwards it lost its perceived status of inferiority; it had achieved equality with the other arts such as music and painting. As *The Theatre* of 1 July 1895 commented:

> [T]he manner in which the distinction has been welcomed by the press
> at large shows that Lord Rosebery [the Prime Minister] has done one
> of the most popular and graceful acts of his administration.

By coincidence, a knighthood was announced at the same time for Thornley Stoker, the distinguished Irish surgeon and brother of Bram Stoker. The latter happened to be Henry Irving's business manager at the Lyceum, and two years later he became famous for his novel *Dracula*.

But while Sir Henry Irving was cheered at the Lyceum, Oscar Wilde was jeered at the Old Bailey. It was a grim weekend for him. He was incarcerated in a cell at Newgate Gaol, adjoining the Central Criminal Court, until his transfer to Pentonville Prison on the Monday afternoon. A medical examination conducted there passed Wilde as fit for "light labour", thereby sparing him the ordeal of hard labour, which was actually imposed on him by Mr Justice Wills. (Alfred Taylor, Wilde's co-accused, was deemed fit for "hard labour".)

The conditions of Wilde's imprisonment at Pentonville have been described in detail by Montgomery Hyde.[1] He was confined to a small, poorly ventilated cell for twenty-three hours a day. The diet was stringent and inadequate (often producing severe diarrhoea and weakness), the sanitary arrangements deplorably primitive, and the hard plank bed caused marked discomfort and sleepless nights. The general penal principle of the day was the "silent system", where inmates were barred from communicating with one another during their shared exercise time so as to prevent contact with undesirable and corrupting influences. Letters and visits from family and friends were rationed to once a quarter, respectively. Indeed the sentence of two years' imprisonment in a local gaol was generally regarded as more rigorous than penal servitude in the convict establishments which, from 1891, was imposed for sentences of three years or longer. Penal servitude allowed for the remission of sentences ("tickets-of-leave") and for far freer association between fellow convicts during their labour outdoors.

Wilde's reception weight was 190 lbs, but this must not be taken as his "true" (pre-trial) weight. He had been an awaiting-trial prisoner at Holloway for about a month before his release on bail. During this time it was noted that he had lost a great deal of flesh. *The Illustrated Police News* (20 April 1895) commented: "The fortnight's confinement in Holloway Gaol has told severely on Wilde. He has lost a great deal of flesh. His face looked almost bloodless, and his eyes heavy and weary."

In a sense Wilde was unfortunate because his term of imprisonment antedated the 1898 Prison Act, which gave effect to the recommendations of the Departmental Committee on Prisons (known as the Gladstone Report). This was a landmark document which ushered in a new era in penal reform and introduced more progressive attitudes on prison administration. The overriding concern of the old order was the achievement of uniformity.[2] Each individual prisoner was treated exactly alike with regard to the application of regulations and discipline. As Sir Edmund Du Cane, the conservative and reactionary chairman of the Prison Commission, put it in 1885: "The previous career and character of the prisoner makes no difference in the punishment to which he is subjected." This philosophy was clearly inimical to the welfare of an individual like Oscar Wilde because it ignored his cultural and intellectual background as well as his personal sensitivities. It was support for the reformist provisions of the proposed new Prison Act that motivated Wilde to contribute a remarkably cogent account of the adversities of his imprisonment in a letter to the *Daily Chronicle* in March 1898.[3]

But Wilde was not entirely disadvantaged because, although he served his sentence prior to the 1898 Act, he did benefit from the impact of the Gladstone Report, which appeared in April 1895. A mood of transformation began to permeate the Prison Commission as from mid-1895, and in fact the Home Office issued a circular in 1895 instructing prison governors to implement some of the Report's recommendations. More significant – and certainly from Wilde's standpoint – was the appointment of Evelyn Ruggles-Brise (1857–1935) as Du Cane's successor at virtually the same time as he commenced his term at Pentonville.

Ruggles-Brise was soon to be involved in the Wilde prison saga, as will be discussed below, and there is no doubt that his open-mindedness and insight played a major role in the alleviation of Wilde's plight. In June 1896 Frank Harris sought an interview with Ruggles-Brise, on Oscar's behalf, and as he later remarked: "Sir Ruggles-Brise's attitude was extraordinary, sympathetic at once and high-minded: another true Englishman at the head of affairs: infinite hope in that fact, and solace."[4] Herbert Asquith, then Home Secretary, had appointed Ruggles-Brise to head the Prison Commission because he knew that he had the ideological disposition and the drive to liberalize the prison system and individualize the treatment of prisoners. With Ruggles-Brise at the helm, therefore, Wilde secured privileges and a relaxation of rules that would not have been possible under the former regime.

Before we proceed, it is worthwhile to reflect on events which led to the establishment of the Departmental Committee on Prisons. This was a sequel to an outburst of public protest against the inefficiencies and backwardness of a prison administration that was overburdened by bureaucracy and devoid of transparency and accountability. This campaign was catalysed by a series of censorious articles and editorials in the *Daily Chronicle* during January 1894 under the title of "Our Dark Places".[5]

Although these pieces were written anonymously, it was believed that they may have emanated from the pen of Reverend William Douglas Morrison, who was subsequently to engage in considerable behind-the-scenes activity during Wilde's confinement in Wandsworth Prison.

The government was unable to ignore these denunciations of its prisons and their management, and it responded by the appointment in June 1894 of the Departmental Committee on Prisons, chaired by Herbert John Gladstone, son of the Liberal leader. Among its members was Richard Burdon Haldane, Q.C., M.P. The Committee held thirty-five sittings in which it interviewed Ruggles-Brise, Du Cane, a selection of prison governors and prison medical officers, and others including William Morrison and Michael Davitt (the Irish Socialist Member of Parliament who was tried at the Old Bailey for treason in 1870 and sentenced to fifteen years' penal servitude). The Committee presented its report to Parliament in April 1895.[6] In essence, the upshot of the Report was to promote a greater awareness of the individual needs of prisoners and to develop special methods and skills to "reclaim" them, the great majority of whom were curable. It also emphasized the value of personal and moral influences in effecting reformative treatment.[7] Ultimately, prisons should aim to change their inmates so that they left as better people than when they came in.

When Morrison appeared before the Committee in July 1894 he was assistant chaplain at Wandsworth Prison, having joined the prison service in 1883 after ordination in the Church of England. In his evidence he expressed very progressive views on the ways and means of improving the lives and welfare of prisoners. He was a courageous man who did not hesitate to expose the inhumanities he observed at first hand in his daily round. In this respect he was regarded with suspicion and even animosity by the authorities, who held that he was out of order in publicly criticizing an administration in which he himself was an officer. However much he antagonized his superiors, Morrison was one of the most influential and successful prison reformers of the period. He left the service in 1898 and in 1908 became Rector of St Marylebone in London, a position he occupied until 1941, two years before his death aged ninety-one. Morrison wrote two books and numerous articles on criminology, and his pioneering work in this field is discussed elsewhere.[8]

Although Wilde was derogatory in his comments about prison chaplains,[3] he must surely have found an exception in Morrison, who befriended him and took up his cause energetically at Wandsworth. Little did he know how instrumental Morrison was in shaping the course of his imprisonment, as will be revealed in the following chapter. However, he was sufficiently impressed by Morrison's scholarship to have requested copies of his work on his release from Reading Gaol and sufficiently appreciative to have sent him a complimentary first edition of *The Ballad of Reading Gaol* on its publication in 1898.

I return now to Oscar Wilde at Pentonville Prison. The press keenly focused on his health, and particularly on his mental condition. This was understandable as it was generally anticipated that, owing to his temperament, he was likely to develop some kind of adverse psychological reaction to the rigours of imprisonment. Indeed, barely a week had passed after his reception when the *Pall Mall Gazette*, in a special edition on 4 June 1895, stated:

> According to a news agency the mental condition of Oscar Wilde, who is at present in Pentonville prison, is causing much anxiety to the officials . . . and it is said that he has become insane. The last account of the prisoner was that he was confined in a padded room.

A similar notice appeared in the *Daily Chronicle* of 5 June. The news created a wave of consternation in the Home Office, and Asquith sent the following message to the Prison Commissioners:

> Please inquire whether there is any foundation for the statement in today's Chronicle that Oscar Wilde – said to be in Pentonville – has become mentally disordered. Where is he, and to what prison is he ultimately to be removed?[9]

The response to the latter question was that Wilde would serve out his sentence in Pentonville; and as to the former, the matter was referred to Dr C.A. Innes, the medical officer, who replied: "I beg to report that the person [Wilde] has not been in hospital or padded cell, and has given no anxiety to any of the officials here... he is in good health and perfectly sane."[9]

An opportunity for outside corroboration of Dr Innes's opinion arose with the visit to Wilde, exactly a week later, by Richard Haldane (later Viscount Haldane and Lord Chancellor under Asquith). Haldane was a man of independent mind and strong social conscience. He came from a remarkably gifted family: his sister, Elizabeth, was a notable social reformer; his brother John Scott a brilliant physiologist and philosopher; and his nephew (the latter's son) became the world famous biologist J.B.S. Haldane, known for his outspokenness and uncompromisingness.

Haldane interviewed Wilde privately in a special room. Although Oscar was silent initially, he burst into tears when Haldane offered to procure books and writing materials for him. This broke the ice and thereafter he conversed spontaneously and cheerfully about his choice of books. Certainly Haldane was reassured about his sanity. He kept his word about the books and in due course Wilde received fifteen volumes from him.

During the month of June two petitions were submitted to Queen Victoria on Oscar Wilde's behalf. One was from Lord Alfred Douglas (Bosie) asking her to exercise her power of pardon; the other from his solicitors (Humphreys, Son and Kershaw) praying for a remission of the whole or part of his sentence on various legal grounds relating to the conduct of the criminal trials. Both were refused out of hand.[9] And then, as a *bonne bouche* to end the month, the Marquess of Queensberry's solicitors applied to the Prison Commissioners for a visiting order to Pentonville to serve Wilde with a bankruptcy petition. This was granted on 29 June, and Wilde was visited two days later.[9]

But perhaps the most surprising turn of events occurred on 26 June, when an application was made for a warrant to transfer Wilde from Pentonville to Wandsworth Prison. The result was that on 4 July 1895 he was moved to Wandsworth. (At the same time Alfred Taylor was also withdrawn from

Pentonville but dispatched to Wormwood Scrubs.) As mentioned above, three weeks earlier the Prison Commissioners had conveyed their intention of retaining Wilde at Pentonville for the duration of his sentence. Why therefore was there this sudden change of policy? Various suggestions have been advanced but the truth lies in a message on a narrow and elongated sheet of paper concealed in the Home Office files. It reads as follows:

> Mr Ruggles-Brise — Capt Stopford informs me that he received a verbal message from the late Secretary of State [Asquith] that there was suspicion that the Officers of Pentonville were being *tampered with* [my italics] by O Wilde's friends. The Prisoner was, for this reason, removed to Wandsworth. No papers passed on the subject.[10]

The note was dated 30 September 1895 and it appears to have been initialled by E.G. Clayton, secretary of the Prison Commission. It was an unexpected and off-the-record disclosure and it insinuates that, during the already turbulent first month of Oscar's imprisonment, there was "interference" from his friends. Interestingly there is a letter from Bosie Douglas to his brother Percy exhorting him to use the family's political connections to help Oscar and to bribe the warders at Pentonville to get food sent in.[11] This letter is dated 11 July 1895, by which time Wilde had already been relocated to Wandsworth. Moreover, as will be described in a later chapter, Adela Schuster and More Adey were attempting to infiltrate the prison personnel network (through various contacts) in order to effect Wilde's early release. These potential outside influences do add some weight to the suspicions of the Home Office.

It seems as though Wilde was endeavouring to adapt to prison conditions at Pentonville, but the transfer to Wandsworth had a definite destabilizing effect on him. Sherard was the first of his friends to visit him in gaol (26 August 1895), and he was struck by Oscar's obvious depression, coupled with his markedly undernourished state.[12]

The weight problem had come to assume grave significance. Oscar's reception weight at Pentonville was 190 lbs but, as indicated above, this was lower than his weight at the time of his arrest nearly eight weeks before. His leaner condition during his detention in Holloway Prison was noticeable not only to the press but to Max Beerbohm, who observed Oscar during his first trial at the Old Bailey. In his letter to Reginald Turner on 3 May Beerbohm remarked: "Hoscar [*sic*] is thinner and consequently finer to look at."[13] Wilde had been fat and flabby before the trials, and one would have estimated his weight then to be in excess of 200 lbs.

Wilde was examined by the medical officer at Wandsworth, Dr Quinton, on 18 September 1895. It must be mentioned that Quinton was an Irishman and, like Oscar, had attended Portora Royal School, Enniskillen. He enjoyed the reputation of being a competent and committed doctor, and he showed a deep interest in criminology on which he later published two major books, *Crime and Criminals* (1910) and *The Modern Prison Curriculum* (1912). After Wandsworth he became governor and medical officer at Holloway Prison. In his report to the Prison Commissioners, Quinton wrote:

> Oscar Wilde is in good general health at present. Although he is on extra diet he has lost a great deal of weight (22 lbs) since reception. He was then very fat. His reception weight was 190 lbs and today it is 168. He makes no complaint of his health or treatment, says he sleeps better lately than at first, but complains of feeling very hungry, especially in the evening. I am recommending a further increase in diet in consequence of his loss of weight.[10]

The governor, Captain Helby, added the following comment about Wilde's weight:

> I may observe that he lost weight principally during the earlier part of his sentence (which accords with general experience). Since his transfer here (4th July) he has only lost 8 lbs. The Medical Officer has taken cognizance of this and has ordered him some additional diet.[10]

What emerges from the above is that Wilde's weight loss was severe and disturbing. If his pre-trial weight is established at 200 lbs plus, then this recorded weight of 168 lbs signifies about a twenty per cent loss of body weight, an alarming reduction. Insufficiency of food was the principal explanation but the chronic diarrhoea that Oscar experienced (a common complaint of the prison diet) aggravated the problem. Wilde's friends who saw him during this period were distressed at the alteration in his appearance.

Arthur Clifton, as Wilde's trustee, was allowed to see Oscar at the Bankruptcy Court on 24 September 1895. "I was very much shocked at Oscar's appearance . . . he looked dreadfully thin . . . and was very much upset and cried a good deal."[14] It was a short time after this meeting that Oscar collapsed and was admitted to the Wandsworth infirmary.

Robert Ross had an interview with Oscar on 12 November, also at the Bankruptcy Court. Oscar had then spent a month's convalescence in the infirmary under a markedly improved diet. Notwithstanding this, Ross was appalled. "Physically he was much worse than anyone had led me to believe. Indeed I really should not have known him at all . . . His clothes hung about him in loose folds and his hands are like those of a skeleton." Ross added that the only subject on which Oscar spoke calmly, and without breaking down, was death.[15]

What followed from mid-September onwards in the Oscar Wilde drama was a series of interventions which disconcerted the authorities and sent them into a frenzy of defensive postures and face-saving manoeuvres.

3

HALDANE AND MORRISON vs. THE HOME SECRETARY

T HE Reverend William Douglas Morrison was the assistant chaplain at Wandsworth during Oscar Wilde's confinement there. Richard Haldane, who had served on the Gladstone Committee, was well aware of Morrison's championship of prison reform and had heard, and been impressed by, his evidence before the Committee the year before. Taking advantage of Morrison's presence on the scene, Haldane asked him to observe Wilde and to report to him any regression in his general health. This is exactly what Morrison did and, in a letter to Haldane dated 11 September 1895,[1] he dropped a minor bombshell and send perturbations throughout the Prison Commission. The salient features of that letter are reproduced here:

He is now quite crushed and broken. This is unfortunate, as a prisoner who breaks down in one direction generally breaks down in several, and I fear from what I hear and see that *perverse sexual practices are again getting the mastery over him* [my italics] . . . The odour of his cell is now so bad that the officer in charge of him has to use carbolic in it every other day.

As regards his mental state generally I must tell you that he has no delusions and is quite rational . . . I need hardly tell you that he is a man of a decidedly morbid disposition. He likes getting into morbid grooves of thought, and his life has from what I gather and as we know has been of a very unhealthy character. Prolonged and continuous cellular imprisonment is certain to make such a man more morbid, and to accentuate his original weaknesses. In fact some of our most experienced officers openly say that they don't think he will be able to go through the two years.

The practical question is what should be done? If he were to go off his head under cellular discipline it is almost certain to arouse a good deal

of indignation in the public mind . . . Had he pleaded guilty it is probable that medical evidence would have been put in to mitigate the
sentence. The Home Secretary would then have had something to go
by. As he pleaded not guilty no medical evidence was forthcoming and
the authorities are in the dark as to the man's mental condition. It
seems to me that it would be prudent in case of trouble to have Wilde
examined by a first class medical expert.

Certain comments arise in respect of this letter. Morrison was unambigu-
ously of the opinion "that Wilde had broken down" although he was not
psychotic ("he has no delusions and is quite rational"). However, Morrison
prognosticated that Wilde would continue to deteriorate mentally; hence he
urged referral to a specialist. He also raised the interesting point (that has not
been debated since) that, had Wilde pleaded guilty at his trial, psychiatric
evidence might have been led in mitigation of sentence.

But the provocative focus of Morrison's report was the mention that
Wilde's "perverse sexual practices are again getting the mastery over him", an
opinion based on the offensive odour of Wilde's cell. Although the word itself
is not mentioned, masturbation was obviously the concern.

In the nineteenth century "self-abuse", especially in the adolescent, was
perceived as a sinister phenomenon with deleterious consequences such as
acne, idiocy, epilepsy and insanity. In the 1860s the Scottish psychiatrist
Daniel Skae had delineated the entity of "masturbatory insanity" and Henry
Maudsley, the most eminent British psychiatrist of his generation, had
supported and enlarged on the concept in his writings, highlighting the
mental derangement and characteristic insanity that masturbation produced.
He depicted the masturbator as prey to antisocial impulses, as a violator of
middle-class male behaviour, and ultimately as a species apart, a degeneration
of mankind.[2]

Towards the end of the nineteenth century there had been some change in
attitude, and even Maudsley, by 1895, was arguing that masturbation was only a
symptom (and not the cause) of an insanity that was brought on by the process
of adolescence. However, against this harshly prejudiced historical background,
allegations of masturbation by prison officials were taken seriously, and
certainly so in the case of Oscar Wilde ("a man of decidedly morbid disposition", as Morrison put it).

On receipt of Morrison's letter, Haldane immediately wrote (13 September
1895) to Evelyn Ruggles-Brise, chairman of the Prison Commission:

Mr Morrison (the deputy chaplain at Wandsworth) has now sent me
his private opinion about Oscar Wilde's condition. You may remember

I said that I should ascertain it and let you know. Please treat it as private.

P.S. I believe there is some bookbinding done at Wandsworth – this might be good work to put Wilde to. [1]

The Prison Commissioners were uneasy about Morrison's explicit reference to Wilde's masturbatory activities, even though this was based solely on the tenuous evidence of a "bad odour" in Wilde's cell. It may well have been true that Wilde was masturbating, and under different circumstances that would have been far from surprising. But at that stage of his imprisonment Oscar was depressed and physically debilitated, and it is questionable whether he would have had the sexual drive and vigour to sustain what Morrison implied was frequent masturbation. All these considerations led Ruggles-Brise to summon the Medical Inspector to Prisons, Dr R.M. Gover, to investigate.

On 23 September Gover submitted the following report to Ruggles-Brise:

At my visit to Wandsworth last Friday [20 September] I took particular pains to ascertain whether there were any grounds for the statement made by Mr Morrison. There is not the slightest reason to suppose that Wilde is 'yielding to perverse sexual practices'. On the contrary, there is strong reason to think that *under the prison regime he is becoming altogether more healthy, both in body and mind* [my italics].

Self-abuse is not common among prisoners of his class, as Mr Morrison alleges. It is very incorrect to speak of Wilde's condition as being one of 'cellular isolation'. On the contrary, he receives quite as much attention and quite as many visits as are good for him. As to the 'odour' of his cell being so 'bad' through his indulgence in such habits as to necessitate the use of carbolic acid, I can only say that this most extraordinary allegation is not only false but worse than false – it is a vile and malignant misinterpretation. [1]

It was an astounding assertion to claim that prison had strengthened Wilde's health, in body and mind, when the descriptions given by Sherard and Clifton, who saw Oscar in late August and late September, respectively, attested to the very opposite. Ruggles-Brise realized that Gover's report was inappropriate for official purposes; and he therefore requested him to revise and formulate his opinion in a more restrained form that could be forwarded to the Home Office and to Mr Haldane. This was duly done by Gover on 28 September:

I write to inform you that I visited Oscar Wilde on the 20th of this month and had a long interview with him in his cell. There was nothing whatever in his manner, appearance or conversation to indicate that he is 'crushed and broken', as alleged by Mr Morrison. On the contrary, he conversed cheerfully and freely, and manifested no sign of mental depression. He appeared to be reconciled to his lot, and described himself as improving both in mental and bodily health. He sleeps well, has an excellent appetite and disposes with relish of his very abundant diet. In my opinion, Mr Morrison's fear that 'these perverse sexual practices are again gaining mastery over him' is absolutely groundless and his suggestion that *in consequence of such practices* the odour of his cell is now so bad as to necessitate the use of carbolic acid is most unjustifiable and exceedingly unfair to the prisoner. It is one of Wilde's duties to clean his cell utensils and to wash the floor of his cell: but, like many other prisoners of his class, he is at present clumsy at this kind of work, so that these cleaning functions are at present performed somewhat imperfectly. A little of Jeyes' purifying fluid has accordingly been served out to him, and to other prisoners who fail in the same way, to mix with the water used for washing his floor. This is a common practice, and if Mr Morrison never before noticed the odour of a disinfectant in a cell, he must be strangely unobservant. After a little more practice, Wilde will become more expert in keeping his cell clean and tidy, and the Jeyes' fluid will then be unnecessary.

Notwithstanding Mr Morrison's suggestions and insinuations, some of which appear to me to be of an unworthy character, Wilde is now in good mental and bodily health, and he is in thoroughly good hands. He stated to me that he had a horror of fresh faces, and he did not indicate any desire to be placed in association. He appeared rather to prefer to remain in his cell. It may nevertheless, after an interval of a few weeks, be advisable, as a precaution, to allow him to work at some interesting employment, as book binding, in association with others; but for this some special arrangement will be necessary. It would not be to his advantage to place him in association with the London thieves and other low criminals who form the bulk of the population of Wandsworth Prison. With reference to this matter, I propose shortly to pay another visit to the prisoner, and to submit a recommendation for your consideration.[1]

I have quoted the above letter in full to show the lengths Gover went to in order to rebut Morrison's allegations. There are also some elements in the report which do not ring true. Given that Wilde was not deemed to be depressed, it seemed most unlike Oscar to want to remain in solitary confinement in his cell and avoid association. Furthermore, it was pointedly disingenuous to remark on the gusto with which he consumed his "very abundant diet" when the man had suffered relative food deprivation for months, with a consequent weight loss of about 40 lbs.

Just at the time of this correspondence, the *Daily Chronicle*, one of the few newspapers concerned about Wilde's welfare, alerted the public to his poor health and weight loss, and used this fact as an illustration "of the way in which our prison system destroys the mind and enfeebles the body of its victims".[3] It directed the attention of the Home Secretary, Sir Matthew Ridley White, to these inhumanities of a system which "in spite of its root and branch condemnation by an impartial committee, remains to this day absolutely unreformed".[4]

The next instalment was a memorandum from Ruggles-Brise to the Home Office, dated 1 October 1895:

I think that the Secretary of State should see the enclosed correspondence that has taken place 're' Oscar Wilde. The best medical advice at our disposal disproves Mr Morrison's allegations.

I have seen Mr Morrison: he adheres to his statement, but can bring no evidence. I have also seen the warder in charge of Oscar Wilde's ward. It is the fact that he told Mr Morrison that he suspected Wilde of masturbation on account of the odour of his cell. This odour you will see the doctors account for otherwise. I am afraid that *Morrison is a dangerous man* [my italics] who is trying to make Wilde a peg whereon to hang his theories of the brutality of our prison system. I have spoken very seriously to him and told him it was his duty to report matters affecting prisoners and the prison system to me as the responsible head of the department and not to outside agencies and persons. I told him that I relied on his loyalty to do this in the future, and he promised that he would but *I do not trust him* [my italics]. If the Secretary of State concurs I propose to send the medical evidence to Mr Haldane. It is my opinion and from personal inquiries that I have made conclusive against Mr Morrison's allegations.[1]

On receipt of the above by the Home Office, a senior official there had added these comments on 1 October:

This case appears to have been most judiciously managed by Mr Ruggles-Brise. It originated in a letter sent by Mr Morrison to Mr

Haldane and forwarded to Mr Ruggles-Brise who personally sifted the whole matter to the bottom. Mr Morrison is apparently desiring to make capital out of this matter, and the investigations made sufficiently demonstrate the falseness of his information. I would advise:

(a) that Mr Ruggles-Brise be informed by the Secretary of State that he is at liberty to inform Mr Haldane as to the inquiry, and the results of it;
(b) I believe it is in contemplation to advise the Secretary of State to transfer Wilde to a country prison. His conduct seems to have been good. As to this say the Secretary of State will be prepared to consider any suggestions made by the Prison Commissioners as to future dealing with Oscar Wilde. It would probably be better not to remove him at once as Mr Morrison might then say that this had been done to remove him from observations, but it might be done later? [1]

When the Secretary of State had read Ruggles-Brise's explanatory account and the above addendum, he penned his opinion: "I agree – Mr Morrison's letter is disgraceful."[1]

The striking and consistent tenor of these communications is the bitter, contemptuous and mistrustful attitude shown towards Morrison by the authorities. Apart from his perceived act of disloyalty in operating as an "inside informer" for Haldane, he had queered his pitch previously by openly challenging the penal system while he was serving as an official within it. Furthermore, during his evidence to the Gladstone Committee, Morrison had allowed himself to become over-emotional, making wild statements regarding the brutality practised within prisons. For this display of passion he was sternly rebuked by Sir Algernon West, a member of the Committee.[5]

But the most revealing insight from these papers is that the plan to transfer Wilde out of London to a country prison had *already* been contemplated and for no other apparent reason than to distance him from Reverend Morrison, who was supposedly intent on exploiting Wilde's fate to buttress his own reformist cause. This is a new perspective on the real reason for Wilde's move to Reading. It had previously been assumed that that action was prompted purely in the interests of Wilde's health and welfare. Indeed, there were distinct secondary advantages for Oscar to be placed in a smaller country prison, and these not only rendered the decision an easy one to defend administratively but also gained it the support of the medical specialists who were subsequently consulted on the case. Moreover, removal to a prison out of London had the added benefit of making Wilde far less accessible to the attentions of the press.

This was certainly the view of the governor of Wandsworth who, when Wilde was admitted to the infirmary, became apprehensive lest news of his condition would be leaked to outside agitators by visitors and discharged inmates.[1]

On 7 October Ruggles-Brise sent a private letter to Haldane, informing him of the outcome of his investigations:

> I have been at great personal pains to investigate the truth of Mr Morrison's allegations as to the mental and physical state of Oscar Wilde.
>
> I enclose for your information a copy of a letter from Dr Gover – our Medical Inspector – which to my mind absolutely disposes of these allegations. Of course I do not for a moment believe that Mr Morrison made them otherwise than in perfect good faith and out of a sincere anxiety for the welfare of the prisoner.
>
> I have seen Mr Morrison, who adheres to his statement in spite of the medical evidence which is supported also by that of the prison doctor, Dr Quinton, who enjoys a very high reputation for professional acumen. The warder in charge of Oscar Wilde's cell tells me that he had noticed a curious smell, and that he had mentioned it in conversation with the chaplain. You will see that Dr Gover accounts for this smell by the issue of Jeyes' purifying fluid. Dr Gover is to see Wilde again shortly, and I think that his suggestion as to moving Wilde into association, where he would not be associated with the London criminal population, is worthy of consideration.[1]

Ruggles-Brise had done his duty meticulously: he had acted on Haldane's original request, instituted an inquiry and then provided him with the follow-up. He must have sighed with relief and satisfaction at the conclusion of this task. But his complacency was not to last long. Three days later (10 October) the next blow fell, with a sharp rejoinder from a disconsolate Haldane:

> I did not myself lay any stress on the physical results of sexual malpractices notion of Mr Morrison. Probably he is wholly wrong about this. But what I do lay great stress on is his description of Wilde's mental condition. I had two interviews with Wilde – one in Pentonville and the other in Wandsworth. The difference in his condition on the second occasion was very striking. I rely, not on Mr Morrison's evidence, but what I saw myself, and as for Wilde 'conversing cheerfully and freely' and manifesting 'no sign of mental depression' as Dr

Gover optimistically phrases it, I can only say that I myself was painfully struck with the exact contrary. Unless Wilde has altered since I last saw him for the better, I should think, judging as a layman, that his mind is showing symptoms of danger. His utterance was indistinct and confused with what I found on the former occasion and he was extremely depressed.

[The] observation not only of Mr Morrison but of Mr Pigott [the chaplain] (I do not observe that Dr [Gover] states that he made any inquiry of either of them) confirms this impression.

My own belief is that since various unlucky little incidents in connection with the evidence before the Prison Committee for which I am far from holding Mr Morrison blameless, Dr Gover has been so set up that he is not a reliable judgment on any observation made. The tone of his report on the present occasion reminds one of last year's controversies.

If you are examining Wilde's condition further I believe it would be best to have it done by an outsider of eminence in mental disease, who would form his own judgment.

I do not know whether it would be practicable to allow Wilde to have writing materials after a time, the Governor keeping what he wrote, but I feel pretty sure that this would help him most. It would be settling him to the occupation which could be of use to him.[1]

Haldane was not one to mince his words. He was not prepared to accept what he believed to be a bureaucratic denial of Wilde's deteriorating mental state. Although his sense of fairness led him to dismiss Morrison's preoccupation over the alleged masturbatory activities, he did not hesitate to imply (quite correctly as it turned out) that there was something of a conspiracy against Morrison, whose assessment of Wilde's health was therefore rejected *ad hominem*. Ruggles-Brise, of course, was within his rights to have expected Morrison (qua prison officer) to approach him as head of the service and not to engage with outside parties. But, in Morrison's defence, he had perhaps not regarded Haldane as an outsider but rather as part of the extended network of prison administration, namely, as a Member of Parliament who had served on the Gladstone Committee on Prisons.

What was most disturbing was Haldane's unreserved repudiation of the medical inquiry and his call for an independent examination by a mental specialist. Ruggles-Brise was clearly unsettled by Haldane's displeasure, and without delay (11 October) he communicated with Sir Kenelm Digby, Permanent Under-Secretary at the Home Office:

> I am not quite easy in my mind as to the attitude taken up by Mr Haldane who, as you will see in the enclosed letter, declines to accept the testimony of our medical advisers.

> Of course it is possible for a man of Wilde's abnormal disposition to go mad and perhaps not unlikely – though from causes quite unconnected with prison life. Still it would not be wise for us to expose ourselves to the charge of not having taken any necessary precautions. As a matter of prudence, therefore, and having regard to Mr Haldane's position, I should be in favour of a special inquiry into Wilde's mental state and would suggest that this should be conducted by Dr Brayn and Dr Nicolson. I only recommend this as a *exceptional* case, having thorough confidence in Dr Gover and Dr Quinton and presumably should be prepared to abide by their reports, but the Secretary of State may desire to be protected by an outside expert opinion.[1]

Ruggles-Brise subsequently held a meeting with Digby, as a result of which the latter briefed the Home Secretary, Sir Matthew White Ridley, on the same day (11 October):

> I have had a conversation with Mr Ruggles-Brise upon the question raised in Mr Haldane's last letter of the 10th instant. You will see from Mr Brise's note to me that he thinks it would be on the whole safer to have an independent inquiry into Wilde's mental condition and also as to whether any special mode of treatment is desirable. He wishes you clearly to understand that he does not himself consider this necessary. He is quite satisfied with the report of Dr Gover and Dr Quinton, but feels that under the circumstances it would probably be the wiser course having regard to the attitude which Mr Haldane will probably take when Parliament meets. I think Mr Haldane's statement as to the impressions he himself received on his visit to Wilde is on the whole sufficient justification for the inquiry suggested by Mr Brise and that probably on the whole it is wise to hold it. If there were nothing to be considered but the simple requirements and medical treatment of the case itself I should be satisfied with Dr Gover and Dr Quinton's report, but it is necessary to take into consideration *the attacks which will probably be made in Parliament and in the press* [my italics] and to be provided

beforehand with the best possible information as to the real facts of the case. I fear that Dr Gover will be rather sensitive on the matter, but if you should think the inquiry might be held, this cannot be helped.[1]

When Ridley had read this memo, he appended his own comments (13 October):

I agree. But will the doctors named [Drs Brayn and Nicolson] be accepted as satisfactory by Mr Haldane? Do you think Mr Brise could write to Mr Haldane in reply to his of 10th, and tell him what we propose to do and whom to send as an *exceptional measure* – thereby giving him an opening to express satisfaction or the reverse, and I hope it will not be difficult to satisfy Dr Gover.[1]

These pieces of correspondence between the Prison Commission and the Home Office demonstrate the underlying anxiety and uncertainty felt by the Conservative government on the Oscar Wilde case. These feelings were accentuated by the image of the redoubtable Liberal Member of Parliament Haldane crossing swords on the issue from the Opposition benches and accusing the Home Office of a cover-up. It is not apparent from the existing documents whether Ruggles-Brise did write to Haldane, as suggested by Ridley, but Drs Nicolson and Brayn were duly instructed, in the words of Digby, "to visit Wilde and furnish a full report on this matter and on the question whether any special mode of treatment would be desirable".[6]

As if all these contretemps were not enough, the ill-starred Home Office was beset by another development, which occurred in early October 1895, shortly before Nicolson and Brayn were about to be summoned. Oscar Wilde's health declined to an extent that necessitated admission to the infirmary at Wandsworth. This is the notorious and oft-quoted episode described by Frank Harris.[7] According to him, on one Sunday morning Wilde could not rise from bed; he was chided by the doctor for malingering, threatened with punishment, and forced to get up and attend chapel. While standing in chapel in a state of extreme weakness, he became dizzy and fell, injuring his ear which ached and bled for months afterwards.

There are two embellishments in Harris's story which require correction. First, it is hardly credible – and especially in the midst of the furore provoked by Morrison and Haldane – that the doctor (presumably Dr Quinton) would have dared to call Wilde a malingerer or threaten him with punishment. Second, it has become lore among biographers that Oscar's chronic ear trouble originated in the fall at Wandsworth. This is incorrect, as will be discussed in detail in Chapter 7.

The nearest approximation one can make to what happened at Wandsworth is that Wilde suffered a severe attack of diarrhoea which, superimposed on his already precarious and enfeebled state, led to dehydration and marked physical weakness. It is highly probable that he collapsed on attempting to walk or stand because, in Wilde's own words, he "had to be carried into hospital".[8]

Independent confirmation of this diagnosis comes from Lily Wilde, Oscar's sister-in-law, who visited him at the Wandsworth infirmary on 17 October, some time after his admission there. The following day she wrote to More Adey: "He is suffering from dysentery brought on I should say by great bodily weakness . . . Mentally he is very unhappy . . ."[9]

The stage was now set for the entry of Nicolson and Brayn. These gentlemen arrived at Wandsworth on the afternoon of Tuesday 22 October 1895. Nicolson had expected the examination of Wilde to take an hour but it actually lasted nearly three hours.[10] This is an indication not only of the complexity of the problem but also of the thoroughness with which the two specialists pursued their mandate. Apart from the interview with Wilde, it was necessary for them to be briefed by the medical officer Dr Quinton and possibly the governor. Indeed Nicolson himself had testified to the Gladstone Committee the year before that the psychiatric assessment of any individual case for a special report might take up to an hour or two at least and might require a follow-up visit.[11]

Who were Nicolson and Brayn, and why were they selected by the Home Office? In today's terms we would have referred to them as forensic psychiatrists: that is, specialists in the diagnosis, treatment and management of psychiatric disorder as it pertains to criminal behaviour and its medico-legal implications. In the late Victorian era they were considered as mental specialists who worked with the "criminally insane".

In 1895 David Nicolson (1844–1932) was medical superintendent of the State Criminal Lunatic Asylum, Broadmoor, and had served in that position since 1886, having previously been deputy superintendent from 1876. Nicolson was an efficient and benevolent administrator of Broadmoor, noted for his humane and caring attitudes towards the criminally insane. He was held in high esteem as a psychiatrist and was elected president of the Medico-Psychological Association of Great Britain and Ireland for 1895–1896. In 1896 his vast experience and sound judgement led to his appointment as the Lord Chancellor's Visitor in Lunacy, which established him as the medical adviser to the Home Secretary in criminal mental cases. A year later he was created Companion of the Order of the Bath.[12]

A fascinating cameo on Nicolson recently emerged with the publication of *The Surgeon of Crowthorne* by Simon Winchester.[13] This is a compelling narrative of the life and fate of Dr William Chester Minor, an American surgeon who came to London, where he committed a murder. He was diagnosed as mentally disordered (paranoid schizophrenia) and was committed to Broadmoor Asylum (situated at Crowthorne in Berkshire). It was while he was an inmate there that Minor became involved with the compilation of the *Oxford English Dictionary*; and for more than three decades he made an astounding personal contribution to the *Dictionary*'s contents. It was only in the latter period of his confinement that Minor eventually came to meet the editor of the *Dictionary*, Dr James Murray, and the two of them subsequently became firm friends. This relationship between the surgeon-inmate and the editor was facilitated and nurtured by Dr Nicolson who, as superintendent of Broadmoor, adopted a sympathetic and kindly approach to Minor. He accorded him many privileges and allowed him maximum opportunities for reading, writing and receiving visitors. Minor's remarkable input (tens of thousands of entries) into the *Oxford English Dictionary* was in no small measure assisted by Nicolson's active support and cooperation.

Nicolson's colleague who was sent to accompany him to Wandsworth to report on Oscar Wilde was Richard Brayn (1850–1912). Brayn was then governor and medical officer at the Female Convict Prison at Woking, having been in the service since 1875. But in 1896, when Nicolson was promoted to the position of Lord Chancellor's Visitor in Lunacy, Brayn succeeded him as medical superintendent of Broadmoor and held that position for over fourteen years. During his tenure there he was the acknowledged expert in criminal lunacy and was frequently consulted by the Home Office on intricate and difficult questions of criminal responsibility. In fact, he and Nicolson were frequently engaged jointly in statutory medical inquiries on the psychiatric status of certain prisoners who faced the death penalty. The stress and gravity of the work affected Brayn's health and he retired from Broadmoor in 1910. He was knighted in 1911 (the Coronation Year) and died in 1912, aged sixty-one.[14]

During his governance of Broadmoor, Brayn earned the reputation of being a highly competent administrator and one who was dedicated to its patients and staff. He also oversaw the considerable structural developments and improvements that the institution underwent during his term of office. But to William Minor, the surgeon-turned-lexicographer, it was a different matter. The resignation of Nicolson as medical superintendent and the installation of Brayn in 1896 brought a reversal of fortune for Minor. Nicolson had been gentle, charitable and accommodating, and Minor had flourished. Brayn, on the other hand, was perceived as a martinet and he treated Minor with sternness, insensitivity and, at times, with outright rejection. His most devastating action was to transfer Minor to the infirmary from his two-roomed suite in the cell block which, together with his desk, books and writing materials, had been his home and comfort zone for nearly thirty-eight years. This decision incensed Dr Murray (now Sir James Murray), the *Dictionary's* editor, and arrangements were promptly made to have Minor sent back home to America and, in the words of Simon Winchester, "out of the clutches of this monstrous Dr Brayn" and "away from a hospital that no longer seemed the benign home of harmless scholarship".[13] It is therefore intriguing to view Sir Richard Brayn from these two diametrically opposed angles – the widespread public acclaim for his professional achievements, and yet the private disdain and bitterness of a mentally ill, but gifted inmate.

We return to Oscar Wilde in the Wandsworth infirmary in October 1895. The descriptions given above of the careers of both Nicolson and Brayn dispel any ideas that they were mediocre doctors called in by the Home Office to submit another opinion on Wilde's state of health. They were indeed the two most accomplished and knowledgeable forensic mental specialists in the country. Oscar therefore had the benefit of the best available expertise. For this reason I am reproducing their psychiatric evaluation in full. Although it is lengthy, it has been composed with a reasonable degree of objectivity and, being one of very few detailed medical records on Wilde, it represents a valuable historical document that deserves more careful analysis than it has hitherto enjoyed.

The report was addressed to the Under-Secretary of State: Home Office.[15]

Broadmoor Criminal Lunatic Asylum
Crowthorne, Berks
29th October 1895

Sir,
We have the honour to report for the information of the Secretary of State that on the 22nd instant we visited Prisoner Oscar Wilde in Wandsworth Prison and held a lengthy inquiry into his mental condition, and that we have carefully considered the further question submitted to us as to whether any special mode of treatment would be desirable in his case.

As the case is in many ways an exceptional one we feel that with the view of fully and clearly describing his condition, mental and otherwise, it will be necessary to consider it under the following heads:

1. His history before trial and imprisonment.
2. His condition since the commencement of his imprisonment.
3. His present mental (and physical) condition.
4. His possible and probable condition during the remainder of his imprisonment.
5. Suggestions as to management and treatment.

1. His history before imprisonment shows that he had the birth and education of a gentleman, and that his intellectual capacity was of a high order as evidenced by the success which his novels, plays, and other writings met with. He busied himself in seeing to the rehearsal and proper stage rendering of his own plays; he possessed a great fund both of general information and of worldly knowledge. He also posed as the apostle of art and culture, more especially as seen in an aestheticism which was the outcome of an almost childish vanity.

   On the other hand, with all his ability and while he gloried in being, as he was, in some sort, a social pet and pattern, he lived a life of the grossest self-indulgence and practised the most disgusting and odious of criminal offences with others of his own sex and that too not with one or two individuals of a better station in life, but apparently with the most casual acquaintances of comparatively low social position. He exhibited these depraved tastes and lived this double life for years before his arrest and trial: and whatever estimate we may put upon these facts as evidences of his normal mental condition, there is no doubt that the habits were of long standing, and that there was no sudden or recent alteration in the cast of his mind prior to his imprisonment.

2. After spending some portion of his imprisonment in Pentonville prison where he lost weight to some extent, he was transferred to Wandsworth, where in spite of being put on extra diet he continued to lose weight, the maximum recorded loss being 22 lbs. As he was a man of bulky and flabby physique and weighed originally 190 lbs this loss under the circumstances is not surprising: nor is it necessarily an unmixed evil, especially as there was no corresponding loss of 'condition', the prisoner himself informing us that he had never accustomed himself to walking or physical exercise of any sort and found no pleasure in either.

In the early part of the present month he appears to have developed a tendency to diarrhoea due possibly to the proportion of oatmeal and brown bread in the dietary. For this he was removed for treatment to an infirmary cell and afterwards placed in association in the infirmary, upon hospital diet with white bread and extras. Up to this time he had been employed making canvas bags for the post office in the ordinary prison cell.

3. With regard to the prisoner's present condition, when we first saw him he was unaware of our presence and he was smiling and conversing apparently in a friendly and cheerful way with the other inmates of the ward. During our interview with him he entered freely into the circumstances of his past history, more especially as they had relation to his present position which he appeared to feel acutely, and upon which he dilated with great fervour and some amount of emotional depression, occasionally accompanied by tears. This display of feeling was no doubt referable, as he himself gave us to understand, to remorseful and bitter thoughts of the blasting of his future by the abominable follies of the past, and we do not regard it as being either unnatural or as indicating mental derangement. The display was possibly accentuated by the sympathetic nature of our inquiries, and by the knowledge that friends were agitating on his behalf, a fact which he is quite capable of taking advantage of.

He expressed himself as being quite satisfied with his present treatment and as being comparatively happy in the associated infirmary ward, signifying his intense dislike of the thought of having to return to the ordinary prison cell. He has gained 6 lbs in weight during the past week or two, and says he has much improved during that time. He struck us as being a man of indolent and lethargic temperament: and the medical officer informed us that he is very careless and slovenly in his habits and unwilling to take exercise. He does not appear to sleep very well at night, but in other respects his present bodily condition is satisfactory, and he complains of no bodily illnesses. He has a most excellent appetite and enjoys all the food he now gets and says he 'could do with more'. This we regard as being a valuable and healthy sign.

So far as his mental condition is concerned we found no indications of disease or derangement and we have explained that any tokens of mental depression which manifested themselves were, up to the present at least, due to the natural and not unhealthy operation of circumstances, and to the existence of a limited circle of thoughts which are unusually active in their character. He answered all our questions rationally and sensibly, and if at times he responded slowly the reply always showed that careful consideration had been given to it.

It is own opinion that, taking imprisonment for what it is and what it is intended to be, its operation upon the mind of prisoner Oscar Wilde has not been such as to give rise to anxiety or alarm.

4. As to what may happen in a mind constituted as his is during the remainder of his imprisonment, we can only hazard an opinion: but so far as our inquiry has enabled us to judge, we have no reason to think that with the consideration which has, and will be, given to the circumstances of his case, any untoward or undesired result of a detrimental kind is likely to occur.

5. *Further treatment.*

   (a) As some difficulty will be found in again locating him in an ordinary cell at Wandsworth after his stay in the associated infirmary, it would be well, under all the circumstances, to select a suitable prison in the country or away from London to which he should be transferred in the course of a week or two when his further associated treatment is uncalled for and his health still further improves.

   (b) Location in a cell larger than the usual size.

   (c) To be allowed such association with other prisoners as may be deemed advisable or desirable or convenient. It would not however be right to allow a man with his proclivities and with his avowed love for the society of males, to be in association *except under the continuous supervision of a warder.*

   (d) Variation of employment by giving him some bookbinding or other work which would be the means of enabling the time to pass in a less uninteresting way than a man brooding on the past.

   (e) The continuation of such minor relaxations of the full rigour and discipline of prison life as have already been sanctioned, especially should a freer range of books be allowed and a larger supply.

   (f) A country prison would suit well for insisting on the prisoner taking outdoor exercise *with some garden work*, with a view of a more wholesome state of his tissues being induced and his mind being thereby roused to more healthy action so far as the subjects of his thoughts are concerned.

   (g) Points referring to the maintenance of his physical health. He appears to require additional food: and an increase in this and an allowance of the Admiralty cocoa would be advantageous if thought to be necessary.

In conclusion we desire to bear testimony to the judicious care and treatment with which the Medical Officer of Wandsworth Prison has managed this difficult case.

Dav. Nicolson
Rich. Brayn

Judged by the 1895 perspective, the above psychiatric report was commendable and based on a thorough examination of Wilde's past history and present situation. And even from a modern psychiatric standpoint, Nicolson and Brayn had presented a fair and balanced appraisal and arrived at an accurate diagnosis. Wilde showed no signs of confusion (disorientation); there was no evidence of a psychotic disorder (that is, no delusions, hallucinations or disturbances of thinking). But there were features of a depressive state (with ruminative thoughts, tearfulness and sleep impairment), although this was not pervasive because, when Oscar was initially observed, he was engaged in friendly and cheerful conversation with the other prisoners. The so-called "excellence" of his appetite was not compatible with severe depression, in which there is usually a marked loss of appetite.

In short, the psychiatrists ruled out a *serious* depressive illness. They attributed the depressive symptoms that Wilde showed to the impact of adverse circumstances, chiefly relating to past events. There was no cause for alarm and certainly no reason to release him from prison on medical grounds. On the contrary, they boldly but cautiously predicted that he would complete the remainder of his sentence without detrimental effects. To this end they recommended a series of constructive proposals for further management. As it turned out, their prognosis was not entirely correct since Wilde did experience a prolonged interlude of emotional instability and vulnerability during the first half of his custody in Reading Gaol (see Chapter 4).

It is interesting to note that the remarks made by the doctors on the situational nature of Wilde's depression echoed in part the evidence that Nicolson had given to the Gladstone Committee in December 1894:

[T]here may be a number of individuals, especially people of a better class of life, whose moods are more sensitive to the changes in their surroundings; they may for some time feel some amount of depression, not necessarily from the prison itself, but in connection with the whole circumstances which have brought them there.[11]

The most disconcerting passage in their report is the second paragraph under section 1. Here the psychiatrists dispensed with their otherwise moderate tone and launched into an unnecessarily forthright invective against Wilde's prior sexual behaviour, using such phrases as "a life of the grossest self-indulgence" and "the most disgusting and odious of criminal offences with others of his own sex". *O tempora! O mores!* These words, by today's standards, would be considered outrageous. But the fact that they were contained in an official communication by the two most highly respected (and presumably enlightened) specialists of the time underscores the latters' deep-seated personal prejudice against homosexuality. One might have expected leading psychiatrists a century ago to have adopted a more progressive and less hard-line attitude or, if not that, to have been more controlled in their language. They also referred to Wilde's liaisons with social inferiors – a theme harped on *ad nauseum* by Carson in the Queensberry trial – and in this respect they identified strongly with the British ethos regarding the inviolability of class barriers.

In Britain in the 1890s homosexuality was not regarded as a pathological state or a medical condition (as it was in some European countries), and therefore doctors had no inclination to incorporate it into a disease model. On this score, it is regrettable that the medical profession historically has not only been resistant to changes in social and intellectual paradigms but also obstructive to movements for reform. The subject of homosexuality was a conspicuous example, but there were others such as menstruation, birth control and masturbation, in all of which the medical community had clung onto reactionary and non-scientific beliefs. Thus Nicolson and Brayn, however esteemed in their professional capacities, were creatures of their age in ideological terms.

There is an additional aspect of the report which was offensive. In their third recommendation for further treatment (section 5), they suggested that Wilde should be allowed limited association with other prisoners but with the caveat that "a man with his proclivities and with his avowed love for the society of males" must be *"under the continuous supervision of a warder"*. This admonition evoked a brisk reaction from the Prison Commissioners, who feared that Wilde might be driven to abuse his fellow inmates. Major Clayton, secretary of the Commission, promptly sent the following order to the governor of Wandsworth on 6 November 1895:

Be so good as to make arrangements at once to ensure an officer being present at all times both by day and by night in the room in which the prisoner Oscar Wilde is located. Officers in whom you have complete confidence should be selected for this duty and they must be instructed to put a stop to all conversation in this ward.

46

If your present staff will not permit you to do this, the Commissioners will, as a special case, authorize the employment of temporary officers in place of those selected for this special duty.[16]

The outcome was that, by the same afternoon, Governor Helby had requisitioned two temporary officers to replace those who had been detailed to mount a vigil on Wilde.

The opinion of Nicolson and Brayn was that Wilde would not easily readapt to cellular confinement in Wandsworth. Accordingly, they recommended that he should be transferred to a country prison where there would be opportunities for salubrious outdoor exercise and gardening. As mentioned above, the plan to place Wilde in a prison outside London had been made about a month earlier, not in the primary interests of his health but to separate him from the machinations of Morrison and to distance him from the paparazzi of the day. I suspect that when the medical officer Dr Quinton was interviewed by the psychiatrists, he proposed that it would be to everybody's advantage if Oscar were to be sent to a country prison.

On receipt of the psychiatric report, the Home Office requested the Prison Commission to advise on the choice of prison. Reading Prison was designated, and the governor thereof, Lieutenant-Colonel Henry Isaacson, was informed. On 9 November 1895 Isaacson replied to the Commissioners with this positive and encouraging response, which seemingly augured well for the succeeding phase of Wilde's imprisonment:

I shall be very glad to do anything I can to carry out the Commissioners' wishes as regards prisoner Oscar Wilde.

In fine weather he can be employed daily for about three hours in the garden. He can also be employed with the schoolmaster in sorting, repairing, and distributing books and he can have such relaxation as regards a greater range of reading as is desired.

In the event of his being transferred here I will call the Medical Officer's careful attention to him and as the Commissioners have kindly granted me three days' leave I shall be glad if the prisoner is not sent before Thursday night [14 November].[17]

Wilde had to attend the Bankruptcy Court on 12 November, on which date his bankruptcy examination was concluded. However, he was required to return to the Court on 19 November to read over the notes of his Public Examination, verify them and sign that they were correct. On his return from Carey Street to

Wandsworth on that day, the deputy governor notified the Prison Commission that Wilde would not be needed again at the Bankruptcy Court. Consequently, on 19 November, the secretary of the Commission forwarded a warrant for the removal of Oscar Wilde to H.M. Prison Reading, subject to the medical officer's report that he was fit for transfer. The latter, signed by Dr. Quinton and dated 20 November, declared that Wilde was indeed fit.

Ruggles-Brise must have felt a weight lifted from him as he wrote on 19 November:

> The Bankruptcy Proceedings have now come to an end. Oscar Wilde will be removed tomorrow to Reading Prison where suitable occupation in the way of gardening and bookbinding and library work will be found for him. I have so informed Mr Haldane privately, sending copy of medical report [from Nicolson and Brayn].[18]

And so on a grey London Tuesday, 20 November 1895, Oscar Wilde was sent on his way to Reading – via Clapham Junction.

4

THE BATTLE OF READING GAOL

LIEUTENANT-COLONEL Isaacson (1842–1915) felt complimented by the Prison Commissioners' choice of Reading Prison for Oscar Wilde. His optimistic letter to the Commission (see page 47) gave some indication of his enthusiasm; and, in addressing his staff subsequently, Isaacson told them to be proud that Reading had been singled out as being the most suitable for the famous prisoner.[1] One would have hoped that these expressions of goodwill would have alleviated Wilde's plight. Unfortunately this was not the case, and Isaacson's seemingly benevolent commitment to the Commissioners did not translate into a betterment of Wilde's situation. On the contrary, Isaacson became Oscar's *bête noire*, and I can only conjecture that from the very outset of their association there was not only a failure of rapport but a mutual mistrust and animosity.

Isaacson had been appointed deputy governor of Reading Prison in 1890 and promoted to the governorship in 1895. He had reached the rank of lieutenant-colonel in the Royal Marines in 1883.[2] He was essentially a military man who had been reared in the strict Victorian tradition of discipline and regimentation. He was driven by rules and regulations and was quick to punish those who infringed them. His inflexibility and authoritarianism were anathema to Wilde. Isaacson was unable to make allowance for the latter's needs and sensitivities, and he expected the same conformity from him as from any other prisoner. He had no mind for the individualization of penal management.

Indeed, Isaacson was the kind of governor who resisted the new era of reform that the Gladstone Report had heralded. A Home Office circular of 1895 had been distributed to all prison governors after publication of the Report, advising them to give effect to some of its recommendations prior to the advent of the Prison Act of 1898.[3] There is nothing to suggest that Isaacson ever honoured that instruction or conceded any privileges to Wilde.

A telling example of his mean-spiritedness occurred when the brother of Adela Schuster wrote to Isaacson in January 1896, enclosing an open letter addressed to Wilde from M. Larochelle, director of the Théâtre Libre in Paris, with a request for Oscar's authorization to perform *Salome*.[4] Isaacson returned the enclosed letter with a curt note that the prisoner was not entitled to receive it.[5] This was a heartless refusal to impart an important business communication seeking permission to direct the play. More distressing was the fact that it denied Wilde the small measure of pleasure he would have derived from that message. (As it turned out, Lugné-Poe produced the first public performance of *Salome* at his theatre in Paris in February 1896, much to Oscar's satisfaction.)

Wilde was scathing about Isaacson: "a 'mulberry-faced Dictator': a great red-faced bloated Jew who always looked as if he drank, and did so".[6] (In fact, Isaacson was not a Jew and his father was minister and rector of Bradfield St Clare, Suffolk.) [2] Frank Harris, who visited Wilde at Reading in June 1896, interviewed Isaacson and, although he refused to divulge the details of the conversation, he unmistakably associated him with "Man's inhumanity to man".[7]

The Prison Commissioners had required a full medical report on Wilde's condition after two months' confinement at Reading. This report was dated 20 January 1896 and signed by the medical officer at the prison, Dr Oliver Maurice:

> I certify that I have today examined Oscar Fingal O'Flahertie Wills Wilde, a Prisoner in this Gaol; that I find him in good health both bodily and mentally. The only complaint he makes is that he has rest-less nights.[8]

This is barely the *full* report that the Commission had sought. It is so terse that one wonders how thoroughly the examination was conducted. There is no mention of Wilde's weight or his emotional state (other than his disturbed sleep). There is also no reference to any ear signs or symptoms that became such a problem shortly afterwards. It would have been more meaningful for Maurice to list the various components of his examination, even if these were negative. One would then have been satisfied that the relevant body regions had been examined, e.g., chest, abdomen, ears.

Dr Maurice came in for considerable criticism from Wilde on the neglect-ful way in which he had treated him during the prolonged period of his ear infection. (This matter is discussed in detail in Chapter 7.) Oscar was referring particularly to Maurice when he wrote in a letter to the *Daily Chronicle* (24 March 1898):

> As a class I regard, and have always from my earliest youth regarded, doctors as by far the most humane profession in the community. But I

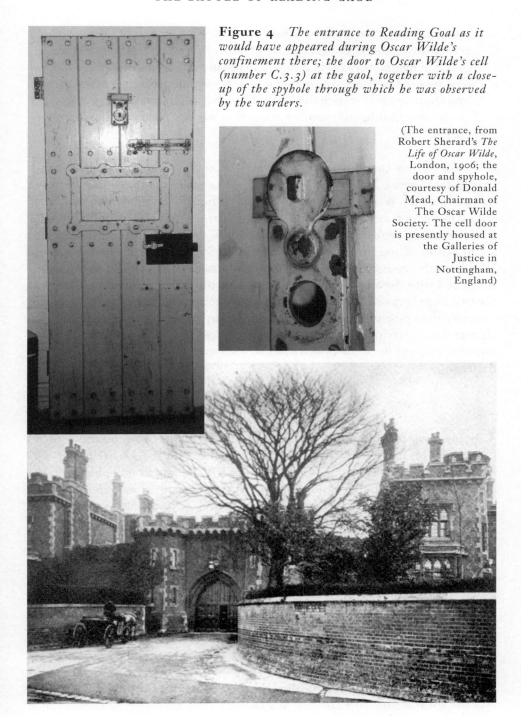

Figure 4 *The entrance to Reading Goal as it would have appeared during Oscar Wilde's confinement there; the door to Oscar Wilde's cell (number C.3.3) at the gaol, together with a close-up of the spyhole through which he was observed by the warders.*

(The entrance, from Robert Sherard's *The Life of Oscar Wilde*, London, 1906; the door and spyhole, courtesy of Donald Mead, Chairman of The Oscar Wilde Society. The cell door is presently housed at the Galleries of Justice in Nottingham, England) must make an exception for prison doctors. They are, as far as I came across them, and from what I saw of them in hospital and elsewhere, brutal in manner, coarse in temperament, and utterly indifferent to the health of the prisoners or their comfort. If prison doctors were prohibited from private practice they would be compelled to take some interest in the health and sanitary condition of the people under their charge.

Maurice was aged fifty-seven, and he had worked in the prison service for twenty-three years. Unlike the medical officers and assistant medical officers in Pentonville and Wandsworth, who were all in full-time employment, Maurice served in a part-time capacity and had no assistants. This was common practice with doctors in smaller prisons. According to the 1893–4 statistics, Reading had a population of 164 inmates compared with 1086 and 1080 at Pentonville and Wandsworth, respectively. Maurice's salary in 1894 was £150 per annum compared with the £450 per annum earned by the full-time medical officers at the two larger prisons.[9] Wilde was insightful enough to grasp the disadvantages of a part-time position for the health and welfare of the prisoners. He was also correct in specifying sanitation, because the duties of the medical officer included inspection of the prison's sanitary system and attention to any defects therein.

A momentous blow to Wilde during the winter of 1896 was the death of his mother, Lady Jane Wilde ("Speranza"), on 3 February at the age of seventy-five. Against the kaleidoscope of Oscar's life there was one unchanging element, the unconditional love and devotion for his mother. He adored her, and her death (although not unexpected) sent him into a spiral of grief in the midst of his already miserable circumstances. It was decided by Willie Wilde and others that Oscar's wife, Constance, should be the bearer of the news. One reason was that this action might help to reconcile the couple. Lily Wilde (Willie's wife) wrote to Constance, who replied from Italy that she would journey to Reading, despite her ailing health, in order to bring the news sympathetically to Oscar. Constance accordingly wrote to Haldane, who arranged with Ruggles-Brise for her to see her husband in a private room. The visit took place on 19 February. Constance was shocked at his appearance – "an absolute wreck compared with what he was," she told her brother.[10] She decided then and there to come again, and she informed the governor that she intended applying for a visiting order when it fell due in three months' time. Unfortunately that was never to happen, and the meeting on 19 February was the last time they ever saw each other.

Oscar was greatly moved by Constance's remarkable effort in travelling "ill as she was, all the way from Genoa to England to break to me herself the tidings of so irreparable, so irredeemable a loss".[11]

During the first half of 1896 Wilde's friends were seriously concerned about his physical and mental state. Several of them (Sherard, Clifton, Ross and Lily Wilde) had seen him during his confinement at Wandsworth and all had been distressed at his marked deterioration. In May, the next quarterly visit fell due, the one that Constance had intended to make. But it was Robert Ross and Robert Sherard who applied, and both were invited. Ross was meticulous in recording his impressions of that visit, which he conveyed in a long letter to More Adey (original in Clark Library). This has been published in full by Margery Ross[12] and reproduced also by Hyde.[13] The special significance of the Ross document is that it presents a lucid and objective appraisal of Oscar at the halfway stage of his imprisonment. In summary, Ross portrayed him as leaner, with vacant eyes and thinning and greying of his usually thick, abundant hair. He hardly talked and he cried the whole time. He showed no interest in literary and artistic news, had difficulty concentrating on his reading, and was fearful of losing his mind. He complained that he was still not allowed writing materials. Ross's conclusion was ominous: that imprisonment had made Wilde "temporarily *silly*" and that he would not be in the least surprised if Oscar died within the following few months – not so much for physical reasons but because "he is simply wasting and pining away . . . sinking under a broken heart". In his turn, Sherard reported thus to More Adey: "I thought Oscar very bad indeed. All elasticity and resistance seem to have gone out of him, and his state under the circumstances is really alarming. It was very 'terrible'." [14]

Ross's account is graphic enough to enable one to make a comparison with the Nicolson-Brayn report of seven months earlier. One is obviously comparing the casual descriptions of a layman with the professional findings of two medical specialists. However, notwithstanding this reservation, I maintain that Wilde was definitely no better than he had been at Wandsworth in October 1895, despite his participation in a wider range of activities at Reading such as gardening and binding, sorting and distributing books. If anything, he appears to have been worse psychiatrically, as witnessed by his withdrawn and uncommunicative demeanour (very uncharacteristic of Oscar), his lack of interest in the outside world, his loss of concentration, and his recurring anxiety about losing his mind.

It was a thoroughly disillusioning outcome. The transfer of Wilde to the healthier environment of a country prison had backfired: instead of leading to an improvement in his general situation, as reasonably expected, he showed a palpable decline in his state of health and morale. There were two main reasons for this which could not have been foreseen. First, Wilde's experience of hostility from the governor and medical officer; and, second, the bereavement reaction to his mother's death. It is conceivable too that Wilde's removal to Reading may have contributed to a sense of isolation, a feeling of separation from the familiarity of London with his friends and acquaintances in the vicinity.

The disturbing visit by Ross and Sherard stirred up a wave of apprehension amongst Wilde's circle. Ross's premonition that Oscar might soon be dead set the alarm bells ringing. The upshot was that Frank Harris was approached for assistance. Not only was Harris a good friend of Wilde's but, as the editor of the *Fortnightly Review*, he was perceived to have influence with the authorities. He agreed to intervene and was granted an interview with Ruggles-Brise. Harris has recounted the subsequent events in his biography.[15] Ruggles-Brise listened carefully to the lugubrious reports about Oscar emanating from Reading. As mentioned earlier, he was a man of compassion and one with a finely tuned approach to prison administration. He impressed Harris with his empathy for Wilde's predicament, and then surprised him by proposing that Harris himself go to Reading to meet with Oscar and bring back his own report and recommendations.

On 13 June 1896 the Prison Commission sent the governor of Reading notice that "an order has been granted to Mr Frank Harris to have an interview of one hour's duration with the prisoner Oscar Wilde in the sight but not within hearing of an officer".[16] The visit was set for 16 June, but just before it took place the Prison Commissioners asked the governor for a confidential report on Wilde's mental condition. The reply came back (predictably) that this was satisfactory.

Harris found Oscar to be greatly changed: he had aged, his hair was streaked with grey, and he had lost thirty-five to forty pounds in weight. With his trimmer figure, though, he looked physically better than he had done for years before his imprisonment except that his face bore signs of nervousness and depression. Oscar gave vent to a litany of grievances about prison life: the governor, the unnecessary punishments meted out to him, the hunger and so on.[15] It was on this occasion that Wilde apparently informed Harris of the events surrounding his fall in the Wandsworth chapel (see page 38). On his return to London, Harris briefed Ruggles-Brise on his impressions of Wilde and made recommendations for further management.

The mid-point of Wilde's imprisonment (May–June 1896) also marked the nadir in his health and adjustment. But Harris's intervention had given Oscar hope: he realized that pressure was being exerted on his behalf and that Ruggles-Brise was sympathetic. Shortly after the visit from Harris, Wilde submitted on 2 July 1896 a remarkably poignant petition to the Home Secretary. As this was the first petition from Oscar in the thirteen months since his sentence began, I suspect that it was Harris who suggested such a step.

The sole justification for the release of prisoners before expiry of their term was medical. It was the practice to discharge inmates with grave or terminal illnesses but only if they had somewhere to go. Cynics doubted the humanitarian motive for this policy and saw it instead as a way of reducing the prison death rate and avoiding a public inquest (compulsory on the death of every prisoner), which was sometimes embarrassing for the medical officer if his competence was in question.[17]

Frank Harris probably advised Wilde (their interview was out of the hearing of a warder) to submit a petition which focused heavily on his psychological torments and bodily illnesses so as to incline the authorities towards a medical discharge. This is what Wilde did in a long and carefully reasoned document, which has been published in its entirety elsewhere.[18]

In the first part of the petition Wilde tendered a blanket confession as to the truth of "the terrible offences of which he was rightly found guilty". He then went on to characterize these offences as "forms of sexual madness", "the most horrid form of erotomania", and "the most revolting passions". He informed the Home Secretary that certain European countries had decriminalized these practices in the recognition that they were aberrations that belonged with physicians and not with judges. In this context he cited the work of Lombroso and Max Nordau as being of direct relevance to him.

An overriding preoccupation was his fear of insanity, and here he raised the spectre of solitary cellular confinement and its aggravating effects on his mental stability. The deprivation of books, the silence and the solitude all led to a vicious cycle of morbid and loathsome ruminations (especially of a sexual nature) which he could no longer bear. It was therefore imperative, before he lapsed into full insanity, that he be freed, taken abroad and restored to health under appropriate medical treatment.

The last section dealt with his physical ill health, and in it he complained about his deafness, the perforation of the right eardrum and the continuing discharge from that ear, all of which had been unsuccessfully managed by the doctor (see Chapter 7). Finally, he mentioned his failing eyesight and the photosensitivity he experienced in sunlight.

It has surprised scholars that Wilde was so explicit about his homosexual behaviour (to which he had pleaded not guilty in court), using terms of outright condemnation in referring to it. The latter has aroused criticism from present-day gay activists who believe that that kind of denunciation from the pen of Wilde was a betrayal of the cause. Moreover, his identification with the philosophies of Lombroso and Nordau was considered retrogressive.

Cesare Lombroso (1836–1909) was an Italian criminologist who popularized the theory that criminals were degenerate beings, biological throwbacks who could be recognized by their peculiar facial structures. He also promoted the idea that genius and insanity were intimately linked.

Max Nordau (1849–1923), a middle-class conservative *pur sang*, built on the concepts of Lombroso but went even further by specifically attacking artists and authors for their degenerate status. He expounded his philosophy in his book *Entartung* (1893), which was translated into English as *Degeneration* and published in February 1895, just before Wilde's trials. It captured the public imagination and was favourably reviewed in the *Weekly Sun* (16 June 1895) as book of the week.[19] It was a *succès de scandale* and it elicited both acclaim and disgust, the latter notably in a bitter attack by George Bernard Shaw. As stated by Wilde in his petition, Nordau had targeted him for special comment on account of his outrageous dress and reckless egocentricity (see Chapter 12).

It would be a mistake to put too serious a construction on certain aspects of the petition or to regard Wilde's extraordinary repudiation of his homosexuality as a true reflection of his viewpoint. At the time he wrote this, he was in a very low state and becoming desperate about the onset of insanity. His remarks about solitary confinement were accurate and persistent. Although the subject has been discussed in the media for many years, there was a dearth of adequate research until recently.

It is interesting that when Dr David Nicolson appeared before the Gladstone Committee in December 1894 he was asked to state his position on solitary confinement. He answered that he could not recall any harm, physical or mental, that had resulted therefrom.[20] One is baffled that the leading forensic psychiatrist in the country – even though more than a century ago – was prepared to deny the detrimental outcome of this punishment. Nicolson is vindicated to an extent because there is currently debate about the consequences of solitary confinement (as opposed to imprisonment without solitary confinement), and there are some researchers who find no evidence that solitary confinement *per se* is consistently damaging to inmates.[21] But there is a far larger, and more recent, literature which supports the contrary proposition, namely, that it is harmful and productive of a multitude of deleterious psychological reactions. A review in 2003[22] established that the most common psychopathological effects of prolonged isolation, occurring in over eighty per cent of prisoners, were ruminations or intrusive thoughts, irrational anger and irritability, an over-sensitivity to external stimuli, confused thought processes, difficulties with attention and memory, and a tendency to introspection and social withdrawal. Seventy per cent of prisoners felt themselves to be on the verge of an emotional breakdown.

On the basis of Ross's description of Wilde's behaviour, Oscar showed several of the features mentioned above. His petition also highlighted two of the other phenomena associated with solitary confinement: the intrusive and morbid ruminations, and the dominating fear that he was on the edge of an emotional breakdown ("insanity" was his word). It must be borne in mind that Oscar had always been a highly extroverted personality who was constantly dependent on extraneous stimuli. He was easily bored by his own company and acutely intolerant of loneliness. He told Ross that during his last month at Berneval he was "so lonely that I was on the brink of killing myself".[23]

My own assessment of Wilde's petition, which approaches 2000 words in length, is that it borders on circumlocution. The themes of insanity and sexual perversity are laboured tediously throughout the text. The style is exaggerated and self-pitying (even melodramatic at times), but the language is good and all the sentences are expressed lucidly and coherently. There is therefore no suggestion of illogical or bizarre thinking. The petition evokes sadness and it drives home the fact that Wilde was in a precarious state. There is no evidence of psychosis but there is much else – anxiety, depression, hopelessness, and obsessional ruminations. His blatant confession of "sexual perversities" and the horror he expressed towards them were not primarily a contrived ploy to manipulate the authorities and win his release from prison. Certainly the purpose of the petition was to seek his freedom, but I believe that the emotions he displayed were not manufactured but a genuine barometer of his underlying depressed and morbid frame of mind.

At the time the petition was written, Wilde was exposed to an imminent event that affected him deeply. On 7 July 1896 Trooper Charles Thomas Wooldridge was hanged at Reading Prison for the murder of his wife in a fit of passion. An atmosphere of foreboding and apprehension clouded the prison in the preceding days and, in his already agitated and anguished mood, this placed an additional psychological burden on Wilde that enhanced his insecurity and fear of insanity. The impact of the execution was so profound and haunting that it impelled him to compose *The Ballad of Reading Gaol* merely weeks after his release.

As soon as Wilde's petition was placed before the governor, the latter asked Dr Maurice for a medical report to forward to the Prison Commissioners together with the petition. This was provided on 3 July and read as follows:

The health of the Prisoner Wylde [*sic*] has improved considerably since he came to Reading, and he has gained flesh. I have never been able to see any evidence of insanity or approaching insanity, and while fully recognising the trial it must be to a man of his antecedents to be in the *position* he now is, having carefully read his Petition, it is to my mind, from the way in which he quotes authorities and gives his own ideas of insanity, clear evidence of his present sanity, and I can confirm I see no reason to think that there is any evidence of his mind giving way. It is perfectly true that he has a slight perforation of the drum of the right ear, but there is no evidence of mischief in the left, nor of any defect in his vision.[24]

On receipt of the petition and medical report, Ruggles-Brise decided that he had to take the matter further. Frank Harris had given him his input from Reading just over a fortnight before and had not been complimentary about either the governor or the doctor. Ruggles-Brise needed an independent inquiry, and to this end he called upon the Visiting Committee, which functioned as a statutory inspectorate of prisons, to perform that task.

On 10 July 1896 five members of this body assembled at Reading Prison. They interviewed Wilde, the governor, the medical officer and the chaplain. Their report is contained in the Visiting Committee Book of Reading Prison (now located at Berkshire Record Office, Reading). Isaacson transcribed the report himself and sent his copy to the Prison Commissioners. The conclusions of the Committee are reproduced here:

1. The Committee do not consider from the enquiry that there is danger of the Prisoner becoming insane, but as the Prisoner's petition is based upon the fear of insanity, always a difficult subject, the Committee think that an expert medical enquiry may well be held upon his case, to include an examination of his hearing and eyesight.

2. The Committee consider that the Prisoner has been well treated. He himself states that his treatment has been good and the dietary sufficient. He has been relieved of oakum picking, has been allowed more books, and more exercise than the other prisoners. He has increased eight pounds in weight since he entered the prison. Prison life must of course be more irksome and severe to a prisoner of his education and antecedents than it would be to an ordinary one.

Signed: Cobham, Hay, Hunter, Thursby, Palmer

Once again Ruggles-Brise was in a dilemma. Although the Visiting Committee members had been satisfied with Wilde's general condition, they had still hedged their bets by proposing a further medical inquiry. This left the fate of the petition unsettled. But Ruggles-Brise decided that, under the circumstances and after Harris's representation to him, he could not afford to ignore the recommendation for an expert inquiry. On 15 July 1896 he sent the following verbose communication to the Under-Secretary for the Home Office:

In transcribing the enclosed petition from the prisoner Oscar Wilde, certificate by Medical Officer for Reading Prison, and copy extract from Book of the Visiting Committee, I have the honour to say that, having regard to the fact that the prisoner is evidently in a very morbid state of mind and living under artificial conditions calculated to intensify any tendency to unsoundness and, having regard also to the fact that the Visiting Committee are in favour of an expert medical inquiry, the Commissioners beg to recommend that an independent medical inquiry should be made into the state of the prisoner's mind, and that the gentleman who shall be selected for this duty shall be invited to name a consulting physician of repute to accompany and assist him in the inquiry. The Commissioners have consulted Dr Gover and he concurs with this opinion, and suggests Dr Maudsley might properly be invited to undertake this duty.

The expenses, which would in the first instance be ascertained, could, I think, be met out of the Prison Vote. The instructions of the Secretary of State are requested.[25]

It is ironic that Henry Maudsley (1835–1918) was the selected expert because it was Maudsley who had endorsed the diagnosis of "masturbatory insanity" and had vilified as "degenerates of mankind" those who practised masturbation (see page 30). But Maudsley was the intellectual doyen of late Victorian psychiatry, its foremost academic spokesman and the dominant psychiatric authority of the age. He edited the renowned *Journal of Mental Science* and authored several books, including the landmark *Physiology and Pathology of Mind* (1867), from which Charles Darwin had quoted in *The Descent of Man* (1871) and *The Expression of the Emotions in Man and Animals* (1872). His name has been immortalized in the Maudsley Hospital, London, which he founded and to which he donated a huge sum of money. To this day the Maudsley Hospital has maintained its reputation of being one of the premier psychiatric institutions in the world.

In spite of his brilliant intellect, Maudsley was a strict moralist and vehemently intolerant of views opposed to his own, while he himself was given to some remarkably bigoted attitudes, as exemplified by his stance on masturbation. He was a steadfast opponent of the educational advancement of women and an advocate for the sexual division of labour, where females were destined only for reproduction and child-rearing.[26]

As it happened, although Maudsley was nominated to examine Wilde, he was not eventually appointed. There was an element of resistance within the Home Office to the setting up a medical inquiry, as advised by Ruggles-Brise. One of the senior officers wrote to Sir Kenelm Digby, the Under-Secretary, on

18 July 1896 that neither the medical officer nor the Visiting Committee predicted any danger of insanity and that Wilde had gained weight; this was not consistent with his "dread of madness". He concluded:

> Before any inquiry is decided upon I suggest that it might be well to see Dr Nicolson and possibly Dr Brayn who conducted the former inquiry. Oscar Wilde talked freely to the former about his life, his crime, and his mental and physical condition.[27]

Digby responded:

> I think it would be well to let Dr Nicolson see this remarkable petition which certainly does not contain internal evidence of failure of brain-power and then discuss the matter with me.[27]

The Secretary of State agreed but still supported the Visiting Committee's recommendation for a specialist medical inquiry.[27]

The papers were forwarded to Dr Nicolson, who at that stage had left Broadmoor to take up the position within the Home Office of Lord Chancellor's Visitor in Lunacy. Nicolson's opinion was conveyed to the Secretary of State by Digby on 24 July:

> Dr Nicolson has seen these papers and does not advise any inquiry into Wilde's mental condition. He sees no indication of insanity or approaching insanity in the petitioner. He thinks the reports show that Wilde is better than when he saw him at Wandsworth last December [actually October]. As more than half of his sentence has now elapsed he thinks the burden in his mind will diminish as time goes on and the period of his release approaches. He thinks it would be well to give him increased and exceptional facilities as to books and writing mate-rials. As to his bodily health I think it hardly necessary to call in further medical assistance at present, unless the Medical Officer desires it.[27]

The Secretary of State was reassured and the plan for a medical inquiry led by Maudsley lapsed. Instead the Prison Commissioners were asked to draft a set of instructions for the governor of Reading Prison which embodied Nicolson's recommendations. This document was issued by Ruggles-Brise on 27 July, the full contents of which have been published by Hyde.[28] In summary, Wilde was to be provided with pen, ink and paper under supervision and with certain conditions attached – for example, that this privilege was not to interfere with his ordinary prison occupation or arouse undue comment among other prisoners. He was to be allowed his own choice of books, and the rules restricting their number were to be relaxed, although not to the point of extravagance. Finally, the medical officer had to monitor Wilde's health and he was authorized to call in a second opinion, if he desired it, in respect of the ear trouble and the alleged eyesight problem.

It is surprising to me that Nicolson did not offer to visit Wilde at Reading and make a follow-up clinical assessment. He had examined him thoroughly nine months before at Wandsworth and it would have been a valuable exercise to have had the benefit of his comparative analysis. It is true that the clarity and persuasiveness of Wilde's petition attested to the integrity of his cognitive abilities and belied the existence of a frank psychotic disorder. In the late Victorian era the benchmark of mental illness was the manifestation of psychosis (or "insanity", as it was then termed) such as delusions, hallucinations and incoherent thinking. Wilde showed none of these phenomena and he was therefore adjudged to be free of major mental illness.

Today the perspective has changed, and conditions like anxiety, depression and obsessive-compulsive disorder (especially if present to a severe degree) are recognized as being as serious as the true psychotic conditions. Thus, by modern criteria, Wilde's depressed and agitated state, his obsessional ruminations and his gross fear of impending insanity would have been regarded much more seriously, and might even have led to the contemplation of an early discharge from prison on psychiatric grounds. It is clear that his mental suffering at that particular phase of his imprisonment was intense, and to have minimized or discounted this because it was not formally classifiable as a psychosis was singularly unenlightened.

There are two other factors that weaken the validity of the psychiatric evaluations of Wilde in prison. The first is that the examining doctors did not seek statements from Oscar's close family and friends about his usual behaviour (his "premorbid state", to use the appropriate term). It is a requirement that any complete mental assessment of a patient must embrace such information in order to determine the "before and after" changes. Failure to do so may produce spurious conclusions. I have already emphasized the marked discrepancy between the consistently wretched observations of his friends and the blandly understated pronouncements of the medical personnel. Had Nicolson and colleagues had direct access to descriptions of Oscar's premorbid personality and behaviour, they might have appraised the situation in a different light.

The second factor is an aspect that was raised by certain friends. Ross, in a letter written after he had seen Wilde at the Bankruptcy Court in November 1895, remarked that unfortunately, because of his great courage and pride, Oscar either could not or would not pretend to be ill.[29] More Adey, in a draft petition he was formulating for Oscar's release, incorporated the following sentence.

> For I know from an intimate acquaintance that Oscar Wilde, with the vanity natural to him, would make great efforts to conceal any signs of weakness, whether mental or physical, from medical men sent especially to find signs of either.[30]

But, as a counter-argument, Oscar was prepared to write a petition to the Home Secretary fully declaring his mental and physical afflictions and unequivocally exposing his emotions and vulnerabilities. Perhaps when he did so he had reached the point of desperation and hopelessness that overcame pride and vanity.

It is tempting to speculate on how Henry Maudsley, the most eminent of contemporary psychiatrists, would have evaluated Wilde's clinical state had he been invited to do so. My view is that Oscar received a far better deal from Nicolson, who at least made some constructive recommendations regarding books and writing materials. Maudsley, as depicted above, was a man with an intellectually hidebound and insensitive mindset. Exactly a year before he had delivered a paper on the topic of criminal responsibility at the annual meeting of the Medico-Psychological Association of Great Britain and Ireland. The following excerpt from his talk gives an intimation of how he might have responded to Wilde's case:

> The business of every society is to protect itself, and it has the might, which for it is always the right, to make what laws and inflict what punishment it likes for its own protection . . . but be the enacted law, right or wrong, the individual, in whatever social medium he is placed, must obey it or suffer the penalties of disobedience; for he lives for society, not society for him, and, living for it, he must die for it, even though he be insane, if we think fit.[31]

It is obvious that Maudsley placed the interests of society above those of his hapless patients. I expect that he would have reacted to homosexuality with the same virulent attitude as he harboured towards masturbation. If so, he is likely to have approached Wilde's situation with prejudice and hostility and consequently to have adopted a moralistic and punitive standpoint. It was probably fortunate for Oscar that he was never made an object of Henry Maudsley's austere adjudication.

The critical turning-point during Oscar Wilde's entire period of imprisonment emerged in late July 1896 with the replacement of Lieutenant-Colonel Isaacson by Major James Osmond Nelson (1859–1914) as governor. The former departed from Reading to become governor of Brixton Prison.[2] The timing of the change – at the height of the furore over Wilde's fate – tends to support the belief that the Prison Commissioners engineered the switch in governorship because they recognized that the continuing conflictual relationship between Isaacson and Wilde was a bad omen for the uneventful completion of Oscar Wilde's sentence. In this respect, Frank Harris's direct involvement may well have had an influence.

But whether the advent of Major Nelson was planned or spontaneous, his arrival was a *deus ex machina*. Nelson was the antithesis of Isaacson: where Isaacson had been rigid, rule-bound and unsympathetic, Nelson was flexible, sensitive and compassionate. In a letter Wilde wrote to Nelson shortly after his release, he expressed "*affectionate* gratitude to you for your kindness and gentleness to me in prison, and for the real care that you took of me at the end".[32] In addition to this private accolade, Oscar also paid a public tribute to Nelson in a letter which appeared in the *Daily Chronicle* on 28 May 1897:

[T]he present Governor of Reading is a man of gentle and humane character, greatly liked and respected by all the prisoners. He was appointed in July last, and though he cannot alter the rules of the prison system he has altered the spirit in which they used to be carried out under his predecessor. He is very popular with the prisoners and with the warders. Indeed he has quite altered the whole tone of the prison life.

Nelson had a genuine liking for Oscar and was able to transcend his prisoner status and relate to him as a normal human being. Indeed they became firm friends: "my good and kind friend" was how Oscar described him to More Adey.[33] Buttressed by the newly received instructions regarding Wilde from Ruggles-Brise, Nelson relaxed the rules and granted Oscar privileges to ease his predicament and meet some of his needs. For example, one of his first actions as a governor was to propose to the Commissioners (successfully) that Wilde receive a strong, coarsely bound manuscript book for his use. The possession of writing materials had a definite enhancing effect on Oscar's morale. He wrote to Adey: "[T]he mere handling of pen and ink helps me . . . I cling to my notebook: it helps me: before I had it my brain was going in very evil circles."[34]

Nelson was a model governor who had a natural flair for implementing the true spirit of the Gladstone recommendations. It was under his benign and benevolent administration that Wilde was able to regain a greater degree of equilibrium and confidence. Without it he would probably have been released from prison in a much less integrated state and experienced greater difficulty in his subsequent adjustment. The composition of *De Profundis* during the first quarter of 1897 provided Oscar with the long overdue outlet for unburdening his emotions onto Bosie Douglas. The cathartic effects of this letter assisted him in coming to terms with the immediate past. In it he admitted to Bosie that had he been released a year earlier (May 1896), as he had attempted to be, "I would have left this place loathing it and every official in it with a bitterness of hatred that would have poisoned my life".[35]

The salutary results of Nelson's governance on Wilde's spirit are apparent from More Adey's feedback after successive visits to Oscar at Reading. On 16 July 1896 Adey was granted permission for a special visit to discuss Oscar's domestic situation, and on 30 July he conveyed his impressions to Constance:

> I was very much shocked at the state in which I found him. Though he is not looking so ill in body as when I saw him last November, his mental condition is most distressing. He is in terrible apprehension of permanently losing his reason, and lives in great mental agony on that account. I must say, though I shall pain you, that his manner and expression of his eyes fully justify his fears. I fear that his state also entails considerable physical suffering. [36]

Admittedly Adey's motive in writing to Constance was to entreat her to appeal privately to the Home Secretary for her husband's immediate release for medical treatment abroad. But despite this, his report on Oscar was not deliberately exaggerated; it was in fact remarkably similar to the independent comments of Ross and Sherard.

Adey's next visit to Wilde was on 4 September, and he briefed Constance on 22 September 1896:

> As I was obliged to give you a very bad account of Mr Wilde's health when I visited him in July, I think you will be relieved to hear that I visited him again about ten days or a fortnight ago and found him *wonderfully better* [my italics] in appearance and in his spirits. The Home Secretary could not release him on the ground of health but he gave no answer as to whether his term of imprisonment would be shortened on some other ground. I am still sure that a private appeal from you would yet carry much weight. [37]

Adey was referring to the decision of the Home Secretary that there was no justification for the mitigation of Wilde's sentence. Consequently, Adey, who had spent a great deal of time and effort in drafting a clemency petition and in trying to garner signatures (with very meagre success), eventually abandoned the project.

The signs of improvement in Oscar's condition noted by Adey in early September 1896 had grown dramatically by the time of his next visit on 28 January 1897. After exactly six months of Nelson's governorship, Adey was able to issue a decidedly optimistic bulletin to Adela Schuster:

> I think the last time you heard anything from me was just before I went to see Oscar in January. I had an hour's interview with him, quite alone, on January 28th. It was very satisfactory. He was in excellent spirits, in one of his playful moods. He alluded frequently to the past, perfectly naturally, and in a calm philosophic manner. He said that he had made up his mind to go abroad immediately on his release . . . He said 'I shall have to face the world sometime and I intend to do it immediately' . . . He also talked to me very clearly for some time about his prospects and his business affairs, of his hopes to make a success of his writing again, and how anxious he was to be able to pay off gradually his debts of honour and the creditors under his bankruptcy . . . Since this visit I have received two long letters from and written to him four times. The governor has never yet refused to let him have any letter which I have written to him. [38]

Adey made a further visit on 27 February 1897, in the company of Robert Ross and Ernest Leverson. In the same letter to Miss Schuster as quoted above, he added:

> As I had seen him so often, it was not my turn to talk to him much on this occasion. However, we saw him in the solicitor's room for a whole hour; a warder was present, but he stood some way off, near the door. Oscar was looking better than he was the month before; they had begun to give him meat once a day, and he was sleeping better in consequence. [38]

In May 1897, about ten days before Wilde's release, his friend Charles Ricketts visited him (accompanied by Ross and Adey) and commented that Oscar seemed "radiant with health and humour" and looked "stouter than formerly in his loose-fitting prison clothes". [39] And herein lies the irony: in May 1896 Wilde was virtually destroyed, body and mind, by the rigours and privations of prison life; by May 1897, after a further year of imprisonment, he had been virtually restored, body and mind.

Lady Wilde was reputed to have muttered on her deathbed: "May the prison help him." To the extent that Oscar's pre-prison lifestyle was markedly unhealthy with excessive eating, drinking, smoking and negligible exercise, her wish was fulfilled by the enforced removal of those bad habits during his sentence. But ultimately the influence of Sir Evelyn Ruggles-Brise was paramount in exerting pressure to reclaim Wilde's dignity and humanity. His stroke of brilliance was in the installation of Major James Nelson, who not only played an inspiring role as governor but also acted more particularly as Oscar Wilde's personal mentor and confidant. The Battle of Reading Gaol had finally been won.

5

"PASSING FROM ONE PRISON INTO ANOTHER"

ON the morning of his release from prison, Wednesday 19 May 1897, Oscar Wilde emerged from Pentonville into a waiting cab and, accompanied by More Adey and Stewart Headlam, was driven to Headlam's house. He was a free man and in fine fettle physically. His good friend Ada Leverson ("the Sphinx") was one of the first to see him and she remarked: "He came in with the dignity of a king returning from exile. He came in talking, laughing, smoking a cigarette . . . and he looked markedly better, slighter and younger than he had two years previously." [1] Robert Ross, when he met Oscar in the early hours of the next morning at Dieppe, came to the same conclusion: "His face had lost all its coarseness and he looked as he must have looked at Oxford in the early days before I knew him . . ." [2] Robert Sherard added confirmation: "Degradation had failed to degrade him. His intimates noted how vastly he was improved in physique, nerve and muscle, in energy and courage; how his whole being seemed rejuvenated." [3]

During his very brief stay at Headlam's house, Oscar wrote a letter to the Jesuits at Farm Street asking for a six-month retreat. He sent it by messenger, who returned after some time with the reply that they would not accept him on an impulse: he needed at least a year's deliberation. According to Ada Leverson's memoirs, Oscar was crestfallen at the news and "he broke down and sobbed bitterly". [1] There is some collaboration for this surprising decision of Oscar's to opt for a period of monastic life immediately after two years of solitary cellular confinement. The journalist Chris Healy met Wilde in Paris and had a long conversation with him, during which Oscar is reported to have said:

> I cannot say what I am going to do with my life; I am wondering what my life is going to do with me. I would like to retire to some monastery – to some grey-stoned cell where I could have my books, write verses, and reverently smoke my cigarettes. [4]

On 14 May 1897 a Mr James Adderley, honorary president of St Philips Mission, Plaistow East, had written to the Prison Commissioners requesting an order to visit Wilde because "the prisoner is very anxious to see me before his release", and explaining that he was a friend of Wilde's. Adderley was sent a visiting order on 15 May[5] and he probably came to Reading Prison on Monday 17 May, the day before Oscar's transfer to Pentonville. In a letter Wilde subsequently wrote to the *Daily Chronicle* about prison conditions, he mentioned that he had had an interview with a friend in the reception room on that Monday.[6] I have not been able to establish any more information on James Adderley or St Philips Mission, but it is possible that the purpose of his visit was to discuss a religious retreat with Oscar, whom he may well have advised to apply to the Jesuits at Farm Street on his release.

A commonly held belief is that imprisonment ruined Oscar Wilde. This view is based on the aimless and unproductive life that he led in the three-and-a-half years of his exile. In this chapter I shall examine that hypothesis and attempt to reach some conclusion as to its validity.

In the early part of his post-prison life, Oscar expressed optimism about his ability to write again. "I do hope to do some work in these six weeks, that when you come I shall be able to read you something," he told Ross about ten days after his release.[7] To Alfred Douglas, a few days later, he wrote: "All I want is to have my artistic reappearance, and my own rehabilitation through art, in *Paris*, not in London."[8] He was in a very happy and relaxed mood when he first moved to Berneval (near Dieppe) and he entertained hopes of a pleasant existence, enjoying the natural rural pleasures of the village and contemplating the prospect of creative work.

In fact Wilde wasted little time before he put pen to paper. On 24 May 1897, or shortly thereafter, he began a long and heart-rending letter to the *Daily Chronicle* after having learned of the dismissal of the warder Thomas Martin from Reading Prison for giving a biscuit to a child. This excellent letter[9] must have taken considerable time and stamina; it was written with feeling and sensitivity but at the same time in a factually accurate and well-reasoned way. Apart from this, Oscar was generally very active in correspondence, writing about a hundred letters (some of them lengthy) in the first two months of his freedom. And, during the months of July and August, he worked on, and almost completed, the first draft of his finest poem, *The Ballad of Reading Gaol*. After *The Ballad* he set himself the task of beginning his comedy.[10]

Thus, in the first two to three months after his release, Oscar was remarkably energetic in terms of his output of letters and in the composition of his poem. If these contributions are taken in conjunction with the eighty closely written foolscap pages of *De Profundis*, then he was bordering on being prolific! It seems almost as if Wilde had undergone a spell of post-imprisonment euphoria at the joy of freedom, coupled with the fresh air, the sea and the beautiful surroundings. This state of mind gave him the momentum to write letters to his friends, announcing his renaissance, and to construct *The Ballad of Reading Gaol*, symbolizing his punishment. In addition, in the first few months he had the company of friends who made special visits to welcome him back to a new life.

But, with the passage of time, his friends departed and the novelty of being a free man gradually transformed itself into the ordeal of loneliness and boredom. To complicate matters, Constance would not agree to his contact with the children and this refusal added significantly to Oscar's growing sense of isolation and frustration.

By the end of August 1897 he found life at Berneval "black and dreadful, and quite suicidal".[11] He was becoming increasingly depressed and bored by the solitude of his surroundings and the bleak weather. It was then that he signalled his despair to William Rothenstein: "I am not in the mood to do the work I want, and I fear I shall never be. The intense energy of creation has been kicked out of me."[12] Oscar had had an intuitive feeling that events might turn out this way. Had he not written to Ross from gaol: "Of course from one point of view I know that on the day of my release I shall be merely passing from one prison into another . . . "?[13]

In September 1897 Wilde decided that, if he was ever going to regain his equanimity and creativity, he had to change his lifestyle. To this end he left Berneval and moved to Naples where he met up with Bosie and established a home with him. Their cohabitation lasted for about ten weeks, after which Bosie left for Paris. Oscar remained in Naples until February 1898 and then settled in Paris. He spent most of the remainder of his life there with the exception of three interludes: about five months (December 1898 to May 1899) on the French Riviera, in Switzerland and in Italy; two months (April and May 1900) in Italy (mostly Rome) and Switzerland; and a spell in Switzerland in August 1900.

In terms of his literary accomplishments, he completed *The Ballad of Reading Gaol* during his stay in Naples, and he had a second letter published in the *Daily Chronicle* (24 March 1898) relating to the degrading and repugnant conditions of English prisons that he had personally experienced.[14] This was a convincing yet dispassionate communication which was intended to lend weight to the parliamentary debate on the Prison Bill which had begun on that day. As before, he kept up a regular and abundant correspondence, especially with Ross, Leonard Smithers and Reginald Turner. The only other work done by him was the undemanding task of editing the copy of both *The Importance of Being Earnest* and *An Ideal Husband* for publication.

It is of note that from the beginning of 1898 until his death nearly three years later Oscar wrote nothing of significant literary value. Some Wilde schol-

ars have attributed this dearth of creative work to the psychologically destructive effects of imprisonment. Wilde himself had written to Ross in August 1898:
"I don't think I shall ever really write again. Something is killed in me . . . Of
course my first year in prison destroyed me body and soul. It could not have
been otherwise."[15]

Were Wilde and his biographers correct in blaming imprisonment for the
loss of his motivation and creative capacity? There are numerous studies of what
was termed the "concentration camp syndrome" in which, years after liberation,
survivors of the Nazi camps demonstrated evidence of organic brain disorder,
with chronic depression and anxiety, psychosomatic symptoms and features of
fatigue, apathy, failing memory and impaired concentration.[16] This syndrome
was ascribed to head injuries, torture and severe malnutrition. More recently a
new diagnostic category has been introduced: *post-traumatic stress disorder*
(PTSD). This bears a close similarity to the concentration camp syndrome and
includes symptoms such as intrusive recollections of past traumatic events,
defective concentration, marked loss of interest, reduced emotional responsive-
ness and feelings of detachment and estrangement from others.

A survey of sixty-two former United States prisoners-of-war (Second
World War) showed that half of these men satisfied the criteria for PTSD in the
year following repatriation and that nearly thirty per cent continued to meet the
criteria forty years later. The strongest predictors for the development of PTSD
were gross loss of weight (due to severe malnutrition) and the experience of
physical torture during captivity. The average weight loss of the former prisoners-of-war with a diagnosis of PTSD was of the order of thirty-six per cent of
previous body weight.[17]

As discussed at length in the previous chapters, Wilde's imprisonment was
severe and stressful but it cannot be equated with the concentration camp experience or with the experiences of the former prisoners-of-war with PTSD. It is
true that there was solitary confinement; the diet was coarse and inadequate,
producing diarrhoea and marked weight loss; and sleep was poor from a highly
uncomfortable bed. But there was no torture or physical abuse; nor did Wilde
sustain a brain injury. On the contrary, he was subjected to regular medical
surveillance and was placed under a restorative regimen in the Wandsworth
infirmary for about six weeks. Furthermore, the second year of his imprisonment was decidedly easier than the first, mainly because of the benign and
benevolent governorship of Major Nelson. Compared with the brutal and
inhuman circumstances endured by many thousands of American prisoners-of-
war (and especially those held captive in the Pacific theatre), Wilde's confinement was mild.

I believe that there is no justification for invoking a direct causative link
between Wilde's imprisonment and his subsequent loss of volition and creativ-

ity. Ironically, two of his most significant and enduring literary pieces were created in the last years of his life; these were *De Profundis* and *The Ballad of Reading Gaol*, composed in the final phase of his imprisonment and shortly after his release, respectively. In the context of his post-imprisonment record, Oscar was at his most productive in the first six months and at his least productive from the spring of 1898 until his death. Indeed Wilde accurately predicted to Carlos Blacker in March 1898 that *The Ballad of Reading Gaol* was his *"chant de cygne"* and that "I don't think that I shall ever write again: *la joie de vivre* is gone, and that, with will-power, is the basis of art".[18]

Another argument is that, had Wilde genuinely suffered a post-imprisonment syndrome, he would have shown impairment not only of his creative capabilities but also of his general intellectual abilities and his social and emotional functioning. There is no evidence of any deterioration in the latter domains. The contents of his post-prison correspondence are typical of the Wilde of earlier days: the sparkle, the wit, the descriptive powers are all there. Bosie Douglas commented that after his "bitter ruin" Oscar's talk was just as wonderful: "He talked better, if possible, after his downfall than he did before."[19] Photographs of that period reveal him to be well-dressed, pompous and portly – not the portrait of a degraded, déclassé ex-prisoner (Figure 5). His sexual life showed no signs of abatement during his exile. As chronicled by McKenna,[20] Oscar lost none of his formerly strong libido and was highly active in pursuing good-looking lads on the Parisian boulevards, the Italian piazzas and the various coastal resorts he visited. William Rothenstein, on one of his occasional trips to Paris, entertained Oscar to dinner at an open-air restaurant with a small orchestra. He was greatly annoyed with Wilde and resolved never to see him again (although in fact he did) because he spent the evening trying to flirt with one of the young musicians.[21]

The crux of the matter is that Oscar's erratic post-prison lifestyle was not a consequence of imprisonment *per se* but rather a reflection of his pre-imprisonment life. The personality traits that he had manifested previously were predictably reproduced during his period of exile. To the unsuspecting observer, Wilde's precarious existence after his release and his lack of productivity might have suggested that his adjustment to life had been marred by his prison term. On the contrary, his basic character remained unchanged and undamaged by the two-year sentence.

In terms of his literary output, there were long stretches in his earlier years when he also failed to produce any work of major significance. Take the three-and-a-half year period (exactly equivalent to the duration of his post-prison exile) from May 1883 – when he had returned to London after his American lecture tour and a three-month sojourn in Paris – until the end of 1886. He undertook a fairly strenuous lecturing tour of the British Isles during some of

Figure 5   *Oscar Wilde in Naples about six months after his release from prison. He looks prosperous and self-contented – contrary to what one might have expected after his ordeal of a two-year sentence with solitary confinement.*

(Photograph courtesy of Sotheby's London)

this time (especially 1884–1885) and wrote several dozen reviews (mainly for the *Pall Mall Gazette* and *The Dramatic Review*). But he did not accomplish anything of true or lasting worth. Certainly he was no *less* productive during his years of exile, during which his letters cover 360 pages of *The Complete Letters of Oscar Wilde*;[2] and, if *De Profundis* is also included, these account for nearly forty per cent of his total recorded lifetime correspondence. Obviously Oscar was on the Continent and geographically removed from his friends and acquaintances, thereby making letter writing the only means of communication. But notwithstanding this, the volume of correspondence in his last four years militates against any suggestion that Oscar had lapsed into a state of apathy or inertia.

But in respect of Wilde's strictly literary contributions (as opposed to his casual letters), it must be borne in mind that Oscar had an idle disposition of which he himself had been aware as far back as his Oxford days. He told his friend William Ward in March 1877 that he would not get the annual Ireland scholarship because he had wasted his time and not studied adequately for it: "I look back on weeks and months of extravagance, trivial talk, utter vacancy of employment, *with feelings so bitter that I have lost faith in myself*."[22] Years later he declared publicly in a letter to the *Scots Observer* (13 August 1890): "I must frankly confess that, by nature and by choice, I am extremely indolent. Cultivated idleness seems to me the proper occupation for man." To Wilde "work is the curse of the drinking classes", and the only reason he periodically worked was to earn the money to continue remaining idle. When he edited *The Woman's World* (1887–1889), it was not long before he became bored and inactive. Arthur Fish, who was Wilde's assistant editor, described how Oscar's own editorial input into the magazine fell off so steeply with time that the publishers became exasperated with his lack of diligence. He resigned his position after two years.[23]

From the physical standpoint he was exceedingly lethargic. He once said that the only possible exercise was to talk, not to walk. He would take a hansom cab at every opportunity and for the shortest of distances. Graham Robertson was astounded at Oscar's lack of fitness. He described how after a short stroll in the country Oscar became very uncomfortable and insisted on sitting down. Robertson protested that they would never get home if they sat down, to which Wilde responded: "I shall never get home if we don't."[24]

I have highlighted these examples of Wilde's creative and physical inactivity to corroborate the argument that his post-prison motivational deficit was merely an extension of his pre-prison behaviour; it was not, as Oscar tried to rationalize, a new phenomenon triggered by the mental and physical stress of imprisonment itself.

Wilde led a purposeless and unsettled existence during his exile and was subject to fairly marked mood swings. There was one substantial difference between his pre-prison and post-prison state which exerted a considerable influence on his creative potential during his exile. After the trials he fell into disgrace, his name became a taboo word, and his work was withdrawn from circulation. Although living abroad, he was forced to assume the pseudonym of Sebastian Melmoth to protect himself from harassment and humiliation. Even among the French literati there were some who avoided him, and he was always fearful of meeting English tourists or expatriates lest they snub him. He was in fact cut by his own former friends and acquaintances, including George Alexander.[25] This atmosphere of rejection and hostility was inimical to Wilde's personality. He unquestionably needed to operate within a milieu of public acceptance and acclaim. Living on the Continent as an outcast, he had forfeited one of the greatest impetuses to producing literary work of high quality – the expectancy of an attentive, applauding audience. His fall from grace removed him from an erstwhile sympathetic and admiring public and induced feelings of isolation and alienation that damaged his confidence and destroyed his inspiration to create new work.

An inspection of Wilde's letters after his release reveals a recurrent and dominating theme, namely, his parlous financial situation. His letters are replete with self-pitying and almost obsequious requests for loans, advances or just hand-outs, and these pleas were made frequently, persistently and bluntly. They were directed at any potential source of funding but several of his friends were the principal target. In May 1898 he wrote to Carlos Blacker complaining that he had received no money that month and "if you could let me have fifty francs it would be an inestimable service".[26] To Leonard Smithers he appealed in April 1899: "Do you know anybody in the world who would advance me £100? . . . It is absurd the way I drift on in grotesque penury."[27] And in July 1899 he tried to wheedle money out of Frank Harris: "I am in a great mess over things, and if you have £15 that you would like to throw to the poets, do send me a cheque for it."[28]

Wilde's chronic state of poverty naturally caused him excessive anxiety and insecurity but it was not a new development. He was an inveterate and profligate spendthrift, and even when he was earning several thousand pounds a year from the royalties of his plays, he managed to squander it on his pleasures so that he was soon bereft of funds to pay for household and other basic expenses. This sequence replayed itself during his years on the Continent.

The fact is that Oscar should never have been short of money. When he left prison there was a sum of some several hundred pounds available to him. He also obtained an annual allowance of £150 from his wife, which he continued to receive after her death. Lady Queensberry sent him £200 and George Alexander £100. Many of his friends gave him donations of money on a regular basis or treated him to expensive and extended holidays. Frank Harris and Harold

Mellor were especially generous in the latter respect. Leonard Smithers paid him royalties from the sale of *The Ballad of Reading Gaol*, and Oscar himself acquired an appreciable income from selling the scenario of *Mr and Mrs Daventry* to several different people. During the last year of Oscar's life, Bosie Douglas alone provided him with at least £300 to £400 and as he remarked: "He really got quite enough to have lived comfortably . . . If one gave him a hundred pounds on Monday he had generally spent it all by the following Saturday . . ."[29]

Oscar's inherent inability to curb his wilful expenditure persisted until his death. He seemed unable to learn from his previous painful experiences: the forced sale of the contents of his Tite Street house and the humiliation of his bankruptcy. Robert Ross tried to reassure Adela Schuster after Oscar's death: "There are so many sad and grievous circumstances in his later career, that there is no necessity for those who were interested in him to be harrowed by imaginary pictures of his poverty."[30] Despite these words, Wilde left a substantial debt which Ross had the onerous responsibility of settling. Unhappily, most of what was owing related to the unpaid bills of two persons who had shown Oscar concern and kindness during his last illness: his hotel proprietor (Jean Dupoirier) and his general practitioner (Dr Maurice a'Court Tucker).

Finally, there remains another clinically relevant factor which contributed to the decline in Wilde's creative activity. Towards the end of 1899 Oscar started to complain of lassitude and general malaise, and in the following year the diagnosis of "neurasthenia" was made (see page 111). A very likely cause of this condition was Oscar's heavy drinking towards the end of his life. Dupoirier claimed that Wilde was consuming one litre of brandy a night and this was supplemented during the day by absinthe and other liquors.

Bernard Thornton, treasurer of the Grand Opera House of New York, was first introduced to Wilde in Paris during the last year of Oscar's life, but met him several times after that. On the last occasion he recorded the following impression:

> My own final picture of Wilde is not a pleasant one, but no doubt it was a characteristic one of the poet in the last days of his life. He sought oblivion in the glass. He had no money in his pockets, but at the drinking suggestion of any stranger he would run eagerly and swallow greedily a great glass of absinthe. He forgot me, he forgot everyone in his glass. Absinthe was his one remaining emotion, and for absinthe he would have hobnobbed with a porter. Pride, ambition, self-respect – all these had disappeared.[31]

6

THE VEXATIOUS DOMESTIC SAGA

WHILE Oscar Wilde languished in prison, a confused interplay of legal wrangling was taking place between Mrs Constance Wilde, her solicitor, and the solicitors representing Wilde's interests. The matter under dispute was the fate of the life interest of the marriage settlement between Oscar and Constance. This became a hornets' nest and it extended into issues of divorce, separation and guardianship of the children.

It is important to realize that the middle to late Victorian era was one of momentous change with regard to marriage, children, and women's rights, and before embarking on a consideration of Wilde's domestic situation I shall sketch a brief history of the spectrum of legislative reforms relating to husband and wife that spanned the second half of the nineteenth century in England.[1] This account will set the scene for the matrimonial complications that entangled the Wildes and their children.

During most of the nineteenth century the popular maxim was: "In law husband and wife are one person, and the husband is that person." This meant that under common law a married woman was effectively dispossessed of her personal property (i.e., property other than land), whether this was hers at the time of her marriage or whether she acquired it, or became entitled to it, after marriage. Her husband had absolute control of this property and could use or dispose of it as he deemed fit without reference to his wife. Any will she had made as a single person disposing of her property was revoked by marriage. As the legal owner of her personal property, the husband could bequeath it by will (without her consent) while she, in turn, could only bequeath her own property with her husband's consent, which he could withdraw at any time before the will was proved. This state of affairs was patently unjust because many a woman in that era went out to work, but her wages (often her only personal property) belonged legally to her husband, who had total control and could use or misuse them as he desired.

The law regarding the custody of children was a mirror image of that pertaining to property. The father had the absolute right to custody of his children while the mother had no rights at all. He could remove them from her care against her will without penalty, whereas if she prevented him from contact with them – for reasons such as his bad character – he could legally enforce his right to possession of them.

Under common law the married woman was subject to the exclusive control and protection of her husband. She was essentially deprived of a legal existence and of a citizen's basic rights, and this disability imposed formidable hardships on the conduct of her life. However, from the seventeenth century onwards, rules of equity were devised in direct contrast to common law principles. These aimed to provide a mechanism for sequestering a married woman's property so that is could be used for her (and not her husband's) benefit. Thus, although at law she could not own property, in equity property could be settled upon her, before and after marriage, by her family and friends for her use under the management of a trustee. The latter was responsible to the Court of Chancery for implementing the terms of the trust.[1] In practice then equity protected a woman from her husband during marriage!

A common way of establishing a married woman's separate property was by the drawing up of a *marriage settlement*. This was a contract negotiated between the parties to a marriage, or their families, before the marriage took place. Such a contract was enforceable only in the Courts of Chancery because the common law did not recognize contracts between men and women who later married. The marriage settlement specifically defined the rights of the future wife as to the disposition of her separate property. A married woman with unrestricted rights, for example, could use her property entirely according to her own wishes.

The equity provisions were also applicable to the custody of children. While the common law gave the father the absolute right to custody, equity perceived the welfare of the child as the primary consideration. The court would refuse custody to a father on the basis of his poor character or conduct, or his unwillingness to support the child; it would proceed to appoint a guardian in his place and prevent further interference from him.[1]

Married women with separate property in equity obviously enjoyed a great advantage over their counterparts who fell under the burden of the common law. They acquired an independent identity by virtue of their ability to control property, whereas the others were enslaved by their husbands. But the major criticism of this dualistic system of common law versus equity was that the latter was available only to wealthy women. The fees for a marriage settlement were costly and were justified only if the value of the property was proportionately large. And so, in effect, the system created the unacceptable situation of "one law for the rich and another for the poor".

There was impetus for reform but this was a long and slow process. It began in earnest in the 1860s and was inspired to a large extent by John Stuart Mill, the eminent liberal philosopher of the period, who was deeply committed to women's rights, as exemplified in his book *The Subjection of Women* (1869). Mill's election to Parliament in 1865 and his outspoken support in the House of Commons for the feminist cause did much to spearhead the campaign. But resistance was strong and fears were fuelled that reform would be revolutionary and would precipitate a breakdown in family life. The freedom women would gain by financial independence would erode marital harmony by emasculating the husband.

Eventually in 1870 the Married Women's Property Act was promulgated. It recognized the right of married women without marriage settlements to have certain categories of property free from their husbands' control. But restrictive qualifications remained and, although the Act was a mark of progress, it was in need of substantial revision almost as soon as it appeared. This was to take more than a decade, but ultimately the Married Women's Property Act of 1882 materialized, an Act that appropriately enshrined the principles that married women should have the same rights over property as unmarried women and that husbands and wives should have separate interests in their respective properties. The Act did not nullify existing marriage settlements or remove the power to make such settlements in the future. Women now had complete control of their property, whether it was in their possession at the time of marriage or was acquired or inherited by them after marriage. To many observers 1 January 1883, the day the Act became operative, was hailed as the day of emancipation for married women.

The other legislative watershed of the mid-nineteenth century was the Divorce Act of 1857. The history of divorce laws derives from the fundamental concept that marriage was a matter for the church and not for the secular authorities. Since the Middle Ages the ecclesiastical courts presided over cases of matrimonial failure and allowed two kinds of divorce: a divorce *a vinculo matrimonii* (from the bonds of matrimony) and a divorce *a mensa et thoro* (from bed and board). The first was granted on the ground that the marriage was null and void because of some defect present from the start (e.g., insanity or impotence). The parties could remarry although any children from that marriage were deemed illegitimate. The second, which was awarded on grounds such as adultery, sodomy, or cruelty (physical violence), did not dissolve the marriage (remarriage was prohibited) but merely prevented the partners from cohabitation. It was the equivalent of judicial separation, and couples had to remain sexually inactive during their separation. There were serious criticisms of ecclesiastical divorce: the proceedings were expensive; the grounds for divorce *a mensa et thoro* did not include desertion and, above all, this type of divorce prevented the right of remarriage.

The next phase in England (1670–1857) was the dissolution of individual marriages by private Act of Parliament. Adultery was the sole ground, but to earn the divorce the petitioner had to undergo a three-stage process: first, a successful civil action against the accomplice in adultery; next, the award of a decree of separation (*a mensa et thoro*) by an ecclesiastical court; and finally the dissolution of the marriage with the right to remarry. These parliamentary divorces were therefore cumbersome, lengthy and very expensive (£600–£800 in the 1850s), but there was no other legal route for dissolving marriages.[2]

It is obvious that parliamentary divorce in England was a privilege for the very wealthy. This made it a rare occurrence, and during the period 1670–1857 there were 325 divorces by Act of Parliament (four only granted to women!), an average of between one and two a year. Towards the middle of the nineteenth century there was increasing discontentment and frustration with the long-outdated divorce procedures and the amount of time required by each bill to dissolve a marriage. The divorce bill first needed approval by the Lords; then it passed through the House of Commons before receiving the royal assent. Consequently, in 1850 a Royal Commission was appointed to examine all aspects of divorce law. Its report, published in 1853, proposed a transfer of jurisdiction in matrimonial cases to the civil courts and away from Parliament and the ecclesiastical courts. It allowed for divorce on proof of adultery, but also provided for a less final alternative in the form of a judicial separation, procurable on grounds of adultery, gross cruelty or desertion. Four years after this report, the Divorce Act of 1857 became law.

The legalization of divorce in England in 1857 did not imply that the grounds had been relaxed. Adultery remained the only ground, as it had been for the preceding two centuries. It was not until the Matrimonial Causes Act of 1937 that fresh grounds (cruelty, desertion and insanity) were introduced. Furthermore, the 1857 Act was discriminatory: a man could divorce his wife on the basis of her adultery alone, but for a woman the ground had to be *aggravated* adultery – that is, adultery combined with some other offence such as cruelty, incest or bigamy. (This blatant inequality in the English law was rectified only in 1923 when women seeking divorce had merely to prove simple adultery.) Notwithstanding these limitations, the Divorce Act made divorce more widely available to a broader socioeconomic range of the population, and wives were the main beneficiaries of the new legislation. They accounted for over forty per cent of the nearly 18,000 divorces granted between 1859 and 1909.[2]

It is interesting that, unlike the generally inaccessible English system prior to 1857, Scotland had offered divorce for adultery or desertion since the sixteenth century, and the Scottish divorce laws treated the sexes equally. Hence the escape to Gretna Green by English men and women. But the most striking contrast to England was France between 1792 and 1803. Divorce was intro-

duced during the French Revolution with great publicity and acclaim as a political measure to revive the ancient rights of the French people, which had been
suppressed by the church. Divorce was obtained on very liberal grounds, including mutual consent by the couple. It is estimated that between 1792 and 1803
there were almost 20 000 divorces, most of which originated in cities or towns.
In 1803 a more restrictive divorce law was put in place as part of the Napoleonic
Code, and in 1816, after the restoration of the Bourbon monarchy in France,
the pendulum had swung to the opposite pole with the abolition of divorce *per
se* until it was reinstated in 1880.[2]

Having given a brief history of the legislation relating to women's rights and
divorce, I turn to the domestic legal issues that dominated the lives of
Constance and Oscar Wilde during the period 1895–1898. The intrusive and
recurring theme during Wilde's imprisonment was the question of the life interest in Constance's marriage settlement.

As indicated above, it was common practice among women of means to
execute a marriage settlement before their marriage. This settlement was an
instrument whereby the enjoyment and devolution of a woman's property
were regulated. Its object was the preservation of her property (both land
and personal) in the family, with safeguards to prevent its reckless and
extravagant use and to guarantee that the interests of the children were
protected. The Married Women's Property Act came into operation on 1
January 1883, less than eighteen months before the Wildes' wedding day on
29 May 1884. The Act, radical as it was, did not remove a woman's right to
make a marriage settlement and nor did it interfere with the arrangements
made therein.

The usual situation (and this applied to Constance and Oscar) was for the
wife to enjoy, in her personal capacity during her lifetime, the interest that
accrued from investment of the monies settled on her (the *life interest*). Generally
the husband had a contingent or reversionary life interest in his wife's marriage
settlement – that is, if she predeceased him, her prior life interest would be paid
to him for the duration of his life and then, on his death, it would revert to the
children of the marriage. Not infrequently there was a clause of forfeiture in the
event of the husband becoming bankrupt but, *in the absence* of such a clause, his
reversionary life interest would vest in his trustee in bankruptcy.

Constance Wilde's marriage settlement yielded an income of about £800 a
year, although in 1897 Oscar estimated the figure to be about £1000 a year.[3]
Oscar had the reversionary life interest but unfortunately, as it subsequently
turned out, there was no clause of forfeiture in the event of his bankruptcy.

Such a clause would have ensured that on Constance's death the life interest would have devolved upon their two children. This would have bypassed the legal wrangling and bitterness that ensued during Oscar's imprisonment and that resulted in Constance's animosity towards Oscar and his friends. The absence of the forfeiture clause meant that, with the advent of Oscar's bankruptcy, his life interest in the marriage settlement became a potential asset in his estate and was therefore placed in the hands of the Official Receiver of Bankruptcy.

There was another unresolved aspect to the marriage settlement business. On the deed of covenant, dated 29 May 1884 (the Wildes' wedding day), the sum of £1000 (£100,000 in today's money) was advanced to Oscar Wilde with interest at five per cent per annum. Wilde never made any interim payment to redeem this loan and by August 1895 (when bankruptcy proceedings were instituted) his liability had grown to £1558.[4] Ironically, this made Constance herself Oscar's largest creditor.

Because Wilde's contingent interest in the marriage settlement represented an asset in the bankruptcy, the creditors demanded that it be sold for their benefit. Constance was determined that she had to purchase it for the obvious reason that, on her death, the children would have the life interest for their maintenance, education and welfare. However, Oscar's friends – and particularly More Adey and Robert Ross – also resolved to bid for it, with the intention of resettling the money on Oscar and the two children. The ridiculousness of this situation was that each side would be bidding against the other and thereby inflating the final price.

There were preliminary overtures between the parties in an attempt to reach an amicable agreement. These are outlined by Montgomery Hyde,[5] who had in his possession the original correspondence between Adey, his solicitors and Constance's solicitors. But Constance made an irrevocable decision: she refused to be party to any arrangement that did not confer on her the entire control of the children. This stance effectively brought an end to further negotiations. Wilde's friends would not accept this condition and they also put pressure on Oscar not to do so. They were adamant that such a concession would compromise Oscar's future relationships with his sons. He would be deprived of any influence on their education or development and, to Adey and Ross, this sacrifice would greatly weaken his self-esteem and authority. The Victorian father was the paterfamilias, and for Oscar to leave prison not only a bankrupt but also bereft of his parental rights was hardly a platform for his rehabilitation and reintegration into society. This was an eminently reasonable approach and it was taken up solely for Oscar's well-being; it was not meant to be obstructive. Sadly, though, the good intentions of Adey and Ross turned horribly sour.

Another explanation for the friends' desire to bid for the life interest was that Oscar would be a pauper on his release and wholly dependent on the generosity of others. Ross and Adey were certainly not in a position to support him, and it was uncertain to what extent Constance would make provision for him, either during her lifetime or after her death. There was no clarity at the time whether circumstances would lead the couple to reconciliation and togetherness or to estrangement and divorce. The possession of the life interest (or a portion of it) would at least give Oscar some financial security should Constance predecease him. And, on this matter, there was serious concern about the state of Constance's health. She had sustained an injury to the neck on slipping down the stairs at Tite Street. Since that accident she had developed a partial paralysis of her right arm and leg which had progressively debilitated her. Ross was fully aware of her ill health and he later admitted that "Mrs Wilde was in a very precarious state of health and that it was quite possible that she would die before her husband".[6]

The above reasons were convincing, and the Oscar Wilde camp stood their ground. But Constance had an equally strong case. Her primary and single-minded concern was for the welfare of her two boys. The family had suffered deeply from the scandal. She and the children were innocent victims and she was resolute in her determination to retrieve for them a modicum of future stability, security and dignity. If Oscar secured the life interest on her death, she knew that he could never be trusted to use the money responsibly for the children's needs. He would squander it recklessly on his own pleasures and passions. He had not supported her adequately during the marriage, and in the years of prosperity before the trials he had neglected her and kept her short of funds.[7] She required unfettered control of the children, with the freedom to make her own decisions on their education and upbringing without reference to Oscar. Moreover, she was deeply concerned at the effects on her sons of the recent upheaval in their lives, coupled with the secrecy surrounding their father's fate, and she wanted the sole discretion to decide on future contact between them and Oscar.

It is noteworthy that, when Constance visited Reading to bring Oscar news of his mother's death (19 February 1896), she took advantage of her stay in England to consult her solicitors on her will, which was signed on 29 February 1896. She appointed Adrian Hope, her cousin, as her executor and bequeathed the whole of her personal estate to him in trust for the benefit of Cyril and Vyvyan Wilde. Furthermore, she declared it her earnest wish that after her death Adrian Hope would endeavour to secure the guardianship and sole control of her sons independently of their father – if necessary, by an application to Court, the costs of which were to be borne from her estate.[8]

Figure 6 *Constance Wilde. At the time of this photograph (1892), Oscar was already immersed in extramarital homosexual affairs of which Constance was completely unaware. It was only at the time of the Queensberry libel trial, in the spring of 1895, that she was confronted with the stark reality.*
(Photograph courtesy of Sotheby's London)

Although it was the stated goal of Adey and Ross to bid for the life interest and then to settle a substantial amount of the income on Cyril and Vyvyan, Constance refused to acquiesce in this. In a letter to Ross she indicated that this was a short-sighted policy and she would not accept such a gift to her sons.[9] This was an understandable reaction on her part. After all it was *her* money and she was entitled to it *tout court*. Robert Ross had been a good friend of hers and she had previously delighted in his company. But the recent turn of events had made her question even his sincerity. In this mood of ambivalence she was certainly not prepared to trust Oscar's friends to underwrite her children's interests once she was dead. She was also puzzled by, but did not believe, a rumour Ross had conveyed to her, namely, that the Marquess of Queensberry was planning to buy the life interest.[9]

And so, by the end of 1895, the scene was set for a contest. Constance wanted to purchase the life interest at the lowest possible price but Oscar's friends were intent on bidding against her. Hargrove, her solicitor, made an offer of £25 to the Official Receiver to which Martin Holman, the solicitor engaged by More Adey, responded with a bid of £30. The outcome was that Hargrove informed Wilde that if he (or his friends) withdrew opposition to her purchase of the whole life interest, Constance would settle on him one-third of the income from the settlement in the event of her death, and that during her lifetime she would pay him £200 a year, but again with the proviso that she had full control of the children.[5]

Wilde, from his prison cell in Reading, reacted favourably to these terms and on 10 March 1896 he requested Ross to communicate at once with Hargrove, accepting the deal and confirming the withdrawal of his opposition to the life interest purchase. He wrote that Constance had been gentle and good to him (she had visited him at Reading three weeks before) and "I feel that I have brought such unhappiness on her and such ruin on my children that I have no right to go against her wishes".[10]

This was Oscar's unequivocal decision; to him it was a just and balanced proposition in that it satisfied both Constance's moral right to bid for the life interest unimpeded and his own need for a secure and reasonable allowance for the rest of his life. In addition, it would have been interpreted as a generous gesture and as a token of atonement which would have consolidated the healing process that was beginning to develop between them. In retrospect, Ross and Adey should have heeded Oscar's instructions. Instead they disregarded them, principally it appears because of Constance's condition that he had to renounce his legal rights over the children. They also had no faith in Oscar's capacity to make a valid judgement in view of his poor state of health and adverse environmental circumstances. What is surprising was that they and their solicitor did not anticipate the possibility that Constance already had sufficient legal grounds to deprive Oscar of the children – an action that she was eventually forced into taking.

Oscar's friends proceeded to acquire the life interest. They offered the Official Receiver £50 for a half-share in the expectation that Constance would buy the other half for the benefit of the children. After a lengthy delay, during which Wilde's creditors were consulted, the Official Receiver announced that he was going to accept this offer. This led Hargrove to write directly to Wilde at Reading in December 1896, threatening that if this bid was not withdrawn Constance's offer of an allowance (by this time reduced to £150) would also be withdrawn.[5] Oscar was stunned by this "cruel and heartless" approach of Constance's and in a fit of disillusionment he immediately wrote to Adey expressing full confidence in the course he and others were following in the matter.[11]

It is pertinent to mention that Constance believed that Oscar would not emerge from prison penniless. According to Hargrove, Arthur Clifton had informed him that two or three thousand pounds had been raised by Wilde's friends for his use. Constance told Ross that with proper investment this sum should generate a fair income which (at that time) she had intended augmenting with her annual allowance of £150.[9] This information from Hargrove was not correct, and the money mentioned (actually only about £1000) was collected in order to avert Wilde's bankruptcy. Because of fresh claims made by creditors at the eleventh hour, the venture failed and the bulk of the subscribed funds was returned to the donors.[12] There was only a relatively small amount (several hundred pounds) available to Oscar on his release.

Buoyed by Oscar's sudden letter of support and encouragement, Adey wrote to Holman, his solicitor, as follows on 6 January 1897:

> If time permits, would you first make the following offer to Messrs Hargrove:
>
> 1) A annuity of £200 during Mrs Wilde's life, to be secured *now* to Mr Oscar Wilde, subject to his debt to Mr Lloyd which may be paid off at Mr Oscar Wilde's pleasure; and
> 2) one-third of the life interest on Mrs Wilde's death to be secured to him *now*;
> 3) no condition whatever concerning Mr and Mrs Oscar Wilde's domestic arrangements is admissible.
>
> If this has already been done, or if Messrs Hargrove refuse, then please offer the Official Receiver:
> First, £50 for one-half of the life interest, at once, with the option of buying the second half: and second, if he will not agree to this, £75 for the whole.
> If absolutely necessary go up to £100 for the whole.[13]

The debt to Otho Holland Lloyd, Constance's brother, arose when Oscar borrowed £500 from him at five per cent interest on the security of a £1000 life insurance policy issued to Wilde in 1885.

The first option specified the monetary conditions under which Oscar's friends would have withdrawn their opposition to Constance's bid for the life interest, but again subject to Oscar's retention of his legal rights over the children. As this was rejected by Hargrove, the second option came into force. The outcome was that the offer of £75 for the whole life interest was accepted by the Official Receiver. Oscar's friends thereby achieved their objective of gaining the life interest but, far from the issue being finalized in Oscar's favour, this development served only to trigger a series of consequences detrimental to Wilde's situation.

Miss Adela Schuster now comes into the picture. She was the daughter of Leo Schuster, a wealthy Frankfurt banker and chairman of the London and Brighton railway. Wilde called her "the Lady of Wimbledon" because she lived in a large mansion (named "Cannizaro") at Wimbledon. She was a person with great affection and admiration for Oscar and, when he fell on hard times during the trials, she made a magnanimous donation of £1000 for his and his mother's use. Just before he was sentenced, Oscar handed this money to Ernest Leverson to hold in trust for him. Schuster's compassion for Wilde during his imprisonment was laudable and she played an active role in striving for his release. At the same time she showed a considerable sympathy for Constance's position and was a strong advocate for the restoration of the life interest to Constance. Her opinion in this respect, and the tenacity with which she held it, are evident from her remarkable and voluminous correspondence with More Adey, which is lodged at the William Andrews Clark Memorial Library, University of California, Los Angeles.

When the subject of the life interest first came to the fore, Miss Schuster was eager to obtain it for Wilde. "I would not hesitate to promise my modest sum if I could feel quite certain that I were doing no injustice to Mrs Wilde," she wrote to Adey.[14] But when she was shown Oscar's letter to Ross of 10 March 1896, in which he directed that Constance should not be opposed in her bid, she became indignant and urged Adey to comply with Oscar's request:

[S]he [Constance] is in the main a good and tenderhearted woman, and I am absolutely convinced that she will, if not opposed now by his friends, keep her promise to him and settle one-third of the life interest on him . . . she has suffered tortures for years – all the more because she adored him . . . she feels that she has been cruelly treated all along, and that now Oscar's friends are adding to the injustice by trying to get the money which is really hers (or the ultimate disposal of it) out of her hands. I do beg of you to trust her – to give way to her – not for her sake but first because it is just and right and secondly for Oscar's sake. They will not persecute him if she is pacified by your withdrawal from opposition now. And she will be ready to do more for him in every way if not opposed.[15]

Adey in turn gave his reasons for opposing Constance but Schuster was not persuaded:

> Let me assure you that I neither think you 'obstinate and unfeeling' nor do I suspect you of allowing any personal dislike you may have of Mrs Wilde to influence you in this matter.
>
> But I am still convinced that Oscar's interests would be best consulted by *not* opposing Mrs Wilde; and that justice demands that Mrs Wilde should be allowed to have her own way (she being the injured person) even if his interests suffer by it.[16]

Adela Schuster repeatedly tried to convince Adey to take the morally just and correct course of action by permitting Constance to purchase the life interest unopposed. But it was in vain.

Schuster and Adey were also working to get Wilde an early release from prison. This plan took place at the time when Oscar's mental and physical health at Reading had reached a low point (first half of 1896). Since the end of 1895 Adey had been drafting a clemency petition, but he struggled to find a sufficient number of people to sign it. Eventually the project was abandoned at the beginning of 1897.

The other option pursued by Schuster, Adey and others was to get Oscar discharged on medical grounds. This was difficult in Wilde's case because the Prison Commissioners had been diligent in seeking regular reports on his health and had even summoned mental specialists to examine him. It was therefore virtually impossible for outsiders to be able to override these medical opinions. It will be recalled that the reason Wilde was transferred from Pentonville to Wandsworth was because of the insinuation by the authorities that Oscar's friends were "tampering with prison officials" (see page 26). This is intriguing because Adela Schuster's letters to More Adey lend credence to this suspicion. The following excerpt is a reference to clandestine interference with the prison chaplains:

> You told me (in confidence) about the chaplain of Wandsworth having been unwise in befriending Oscar too openly. I, of course, have not repeated and will not repeat this to anyone without your permission. But I know the person who made friends with the chaplain and induced him to be specially kind to Oscar. This person has probably no idea that he was partly the cause for Oscar's removal. He may begin again with the Reading chaplain. May I warn him to be careful – even if I may not tell him the reason why? I am afraid of his defeating his own object, if he does more without knowing what happened at

Wandsworth. If you should object, of course I will be silent – have no fear of my repeating without your permission.[17]

In the following letter we have the first intimation of an "infiltration" into the ranks of the doctors:

It is depressing to know that there is so little hope of getting Oscar out before his time. I fear petitions are useless, yet one hopes to be doing something instead of acquiescing idly in his terrible fate. I believe with you that the doctors are the only hope now; unfortunately I know nothing of the Reading doctors, and I don't even know any one of the big London doctors who might be persuaded to *influence* a humbler confrère. The last friend I had amongst the great doctors is dead now; he might have done something. Directly Frank Harris returns I will beg him to try again to 'get at' the doctors. I can think of no other plan. It would be as well if someone could ascertain who the Reading doctor is, and if he has any get-atable relations; or *any special ambition*.[18]

The next communication to Adey is even more direct:

I cannot think that there would be any question of 'buying' the doctors till we have tried all other means, but *if money is necessary* [my italics] I will certainly try to subscribe. I fear however that this might be a false step. We are in the right – our case is good – do not let us put ourselves in the wrong if we can help it. I believe myself that the forcible and eloquently expressed opinion of a clever man may move even the doctor. I mean that every man is influenced by the opinions of his fellow man.[19]

Of course the "forcible, eloquently expressed and clever man" was Frank Harris, who visited Wilde at Reading on 16 June 1896 (see page 54). He was obviously briefed by Schuster to speak to the doctor at Reading and to coax him into releasing Oscar on medical grounds – and, as a last resort, even to bribe him! Nothing would have come as a greater disappointment to Schuster, Adey and the others than Harris's impression that Dr Oliver Maurice, the medical officer at Reading, was not only unsympathetic but almost inhuman (see Chapter 4).

By the second half of 1896 Wilde's circle of friends were desperate. Nothing was proceeding according to plan and Oscar was likely to have to endure imprisonment until the bitter end. There was a last resort, as explained to Adey by Schuster on 11 June 1896:

I am told on good authority that nothing would have so much weight with the Home Secretary as an appeal from Mrs Wilde. If she would write either to him or to any third person who could show the letter, speaking of her distress for him [Wilde], and begging for his release it would be of more use than all the rest we can do. Of course I would continue my efforts all the same. I don't know whether you would think it possible to go to Heidelberg yourself, take her by surprise, and speak to her on the subject.[20]

More Adey had visited Wilde at Reading in July 1896, finding him to be in a very poor mental condition. Oscar had requested Adey to pass on several messages to his wife, and this provided Adey with the opportunity to write to Constance, whose address in Heidelberg had been secretly obtained for him by Schuster.

Adey opened his letter to Constance (dated 30 July 1896) by describing the miserable state in which he found Oscar during his visit (see page 64), but then went on:

He [Oscar] told me to communicate with you and to ask you to write a private letter to the Home Secretary on his behalf. He desires you to entreat the Home Secretary to release him in order that he may imme-diately place himself under competent medical direction out of England, until he is cured. He also begs you to write to Mr Arthur Balfour to ask for his help and influence on his behalf and favour . . . a private letter from you to the Home Secretary *is likely, especially at this particular time*, to have great weight with him . . . I told Oscar that I supposed he would not interfere in any way with your children, after his release, but would leave their education entirely to you and would also leave to you your money in your control to bring them up as you thought best. He answered quite impatiently, 'Oh, of course, of course – I have no right to have the care of my children. It would be impossi-ble for them to live with me; it would not be fair to them; people would always be finding out who I was. Of course my wife must have complete control over her money. Whatever she wishes should be done. It was because I wished her wishes carried out that I sent direc-tions last March that those people who proposed to buy my life inter-est for me should be requested not to do so.' He also said that he could not even ask you to receive him to live with you at present as he was not in a fit mental condition to be with you until he was cured.[21]

Adey's letter made a point of emphasizing that Oscar himself had repudi-ated the attempt by his friends to oppose Constance's bid for the life interest, thereby absolving him of any responsibility for this unfortunate action against her. There is repeated reassurance that Constance would have complete control of her money. As discussed above, the Married Women's Property Act of 1882 had already given married women that right, and it is remarkable that thirteen years later this fundamental change in the law had seemingly not been grasped by Adey or Wilde.

Constance was swift in her reply to Adey. On 3 August 1896 she wrote from Heidelberg, expressing shock at Oscar's condition and promising to write both to the Home Secretary and to Balfour. But she firmly laid down the condition that she had to be free to raise the children on her own and that Oscar's friends had to submit a written statement to her lawyer that they would be withdrawing their offer to the Official Receiver for the life interest of the marriage settlement.[22]

There was an interesting sidelight to this letter of Constance's. She had erroneously addressed it to "Mr Rady", but more glaring was that the handwriting was so uncharacteristic of Constance's usual script that Adey and Ross actually doubted that she had written it. Adela Schuster, however, compared this letter with one that Constance had written to her a few weeks before. Her verdict was that the letter was definitely in the hand of Mrs Wilde, but she added that it had "evidently been written either under the stress of some emotion or very slowly – with pauses for thought, which has somewhat checked the flow of the writing".[23]

The truth was that Adey and Ross had been correct in observing an alteration in Constance's handwriting. As mentioned above, Constance had developed progressive lameness in her right arm (and right leg) as a result of an injury to her cervical spine after her fall down the stairs in Tite Street in the winter of 1895. Because of this disability she experienced increasing difficulty and fatigue in writing, with deterioration in the shape and form of her letters and words. Towards the end of her life her handwriting became a scrawl scarcely recognizable as hers. To compensate for the problem she eventually resorted to a typewriter.[24]

Adey responded to the conditions that Constance had set before she would act on Oscar's release. He made the legitimate point that "any appeal from you to the Home Secretary must – in order to have any weight with him whatever – be perfectly spontaneous in tone: anything suggestive of its being written in compliance with some agreement would deprive it of its value".[25]

Inspired by Constance's letter to Adey, Adela Schuster became more strident in her attempt to convince Adey and friends to withdraw from the life interest contest and thereby allow Constance to plead with the Home Secretary as she had promised. Such a plea, if successful, would spare Oscar nine months of imprisonment.

Do you suppose that if he [Oscar] had the choice and there were only *one choice in ten* that his wife's letter would bring him freedom, he would not jump at it, even at the risk of losing some material advantage in future? You know he would. Have you the right to deprive him of this choice?[26]

Schuster had also enlisted the support of Ernest Flower (later Sir Ernest), a philanthropist and Conservative Member of Parliament, who was prepared to reinforce an appeal from Constance Wilde with his own forceful recommendation to the Home Secretary, with whom he had some influence.[27] But by the beginning of October 1896 news had reached Flower that there was no chance of Wilde's release before the expiration of his sentence.[28] Indeed, by then too More Adey had received the same message personally from the Home Office.[29]

Adey, Ross and Oscar's other friends turned a deaf ear to Schuster's persistent and passionate calls for them to renounce their bid on the life interest in favour of Mrs Wilde. Whatever substance they found in her arguments was outweighed by their conviction that possession of the life interest was irrefutably for Oscar's long-term material good. Their success in achieving this goal in January 1897 was short-lived, and in the final analysis their rejection of the intuitive wisdom and sound pragmatism of Adela Schuster plunged Oscar into a legal morass from which he never recovered.

Within a fortnight of Oscar's arrest on 5 April 1895 Mrs Constance Wilde was pondering on her and her children's grim future. On 19 April she wrote to the fortune-teller Mrs. Robinson asking her to pronounce on the fate of her husband and on the outcome of her life – "cut to pieces as my hand is by its lines", as she put it.[30] But Constance was definite on one point: that after the trial she had to obtain a judicial separation, or if possible a divorce, in order to get the guardianship of her two sons.[30] This attitude was confirmed in a letter to a friend in June 1895 in which she explained that she had to sue for divorce to free the children; she had discovered that she was not eligible for a judicial separation.[31]

Constance's overriding concern throughout the entire sordid aftermath of the trials was the welfare of Cyril and Vyvyan. They had suffered greatly from the psychological turmoil and the geographical dislocations in their lives; from the veil of shame and secrecy around their father's calamity; from the change in their surnames; and much else. Constance was determined to protect them from further stress and insecurity. She realized immediately, as the scandal broke, that Oscar was totally incapable of fatherhood. She had long endured his irresponsibility and recklessness with money, and in the years before the trials he had been an absent husband and father and had effectively deserted them, sometimes without leaving any indication of his whereabouts. He could never again be trusted to fulfil his family obligations, and Constance knew that after her death she could never consign the children to the mercy of his self-indulgent and financially disastrous lifestyle. For her peace of mind the guardianship of her sons became a crucial issue.

As Oscar underwent the first phase of his imprisonment, Constance had the opportunity to reflect and re-evaluate her outlook. There was talk of reconciliation and forgiveness, and Robert Sherard was particularly active in promoting this. In September 1895 she received an exceptionally moving and contrite letter from Oscar, which even touched Hargrove, her solicitor, with its sincerity. On the strength of it, Constance decided not to proceed with the divorce, and Hargrove pointed out that if the family reunited it would have to be on the other side of the world and under a new name.[32]

Oscar's fervent desire for a restoration of the marriage motivated Constance to apply to the Prison Commissioners for a special visit to discuss their intimate family affairs and future plans. This occurred at Wandsworth on 21 September 1895, and just prior to the visit (18 September 1895) the governor reported as follows:

> I have no suggestion to make regarding his [Wilde's] treatment. I have reason to think that a more helpful prospect about his family arrangements and future, which has recently been opened to him, has relieved his mind of one great cause of despondency, and will probably enable him to bear his imprisonment better.[33]

The visit was a positive one for both parties, and Constance relayed her feelings to her friend Emily Thursfield three weeks later. She did not wish to divorce; Oscar had been very repentant for all the misery he had brought on her and the boys and, on a note of optimism, she remarked that "by sticking to him now, I may save him from even worse and I believe that he cares now for no-one but myself and the children".[34] She admitted to the high risk involved but maintained that she could always leave him if he became impossible. In the same vein a few days later, she told another friend that she was withdrawing from divorce proceedings and that Oscar was "weak rather than wicked ... and I cannot refuse to him the forgiveness that he has asked".[35]

Constance next visited Oscar at Reading on 19 February 1896 to break the news of his mother's death (see page 52). Her meeting with him kindled mutual warmth and sympathy, and not long afterwards Constance made the reasonably generous financial offer described above, which Oscar explicitly instructed

Robert Ross to accept in his letter of 10 March 1896. Had Ross and the others complied, it is likely that the developing goodwill and reconciliation between Oscar and Constance would have strengthened. Instead, the pursuit by the friends of the life interest bid vitiated the hard-won progress already made towards marital harmony and wrecked any future prospects. By the end of 1896 Constance was at daggers drawn with Oscar and poised to proceed with issues of guardianship and divorce.

As discussed above, the common law of England entrenched the right of the father to the custody of the children unless he did something to forfeit it. Under the Guardianship of Infants Act of 1886, if sufficient grounds existed the mother was able to apply to the court for an order removing the control and custody of her child from the father and securing her own rights and powers. The grounds for interference by the court were gross misconduct and profligacy on the part of the father, who by his behaviour had shown that he was utterly unfit for the upbringing of his children. Moreover, if the court was satisfied that the father of young children had been guilty of an unnatural crime (even though not convicted of it), it would be its duty to remove them from him. But mere poverty or insolvency by themselves did not constitute grounds for interference.[36]

There was no doubt that indisputable legal grounds existed for Wilde to be deprived of the guardianship of his sons. Hargrove accordingly advised Mrs Wilde to serve an originating summons on Wilde under the Guardianship of Infants Act. This was done on 21 January 1897, and at about the same time Oscar was visited by Hansell, his newly appointed solicitor, for instructions. He was told that he would have no case whatever in opposing the action and he therefore (unhappily) acquiesced in the proposed removal of his guardianship. For months before, Oscar's friends had been exhorting him not to give up his legal rights over the children. "My rights! I had none," Wilde later wrote angrily to Ross. "A claim that a formal application to a Judge in Chambers can quash in ten minutes is not a right."[37]

The case was heard in chambers in the Court of Chancery before Mr Justice Kekewick on 1 March 1897. The children, Cyril and Vyvyan, were placed under the jurisdiction of the Court and had to return to it immediately and whenever ordered to do so by the Court. Constance Wilde and Adrian Hope were appointed to act as their guardians. The order continued as follows:

And it is ordered that the applicant do have the charge and superintendence of the education of the said infants . . . undertaking that they will duly and properly provide for the care, maintenance and education of the said infants. And it is ordered that the said infants be at liberty to remain at school abroad until further order. And it is ordered that the said guardians do report to the Court twice a year as to the welfare of the said infants and any of the parties are to be at liberty to apply as they may be advised.[38]

With the guardianship of the children having been ceded to her and Adrian Hope, Constance's next move was to institute divorce proceedings. This had been her intention at the time of the trials two years before but she had subsequently changed her mind during the interlude of apparent reconciliation. She had also considered judicial separation, which was less final, but she did not have the grounds – namely, adultery or cruelty, or desertion without cause for two years or more.[36]

Constance's main motivation for a divorce was because the Divorce Court had the power to vary and alter marriage settlements on the dissolution of the marriage, particularly for the benefit of the children.[36] On this basis it was highly likely that if Constance were to obtain a divorce, the provisions of her marriage settlement would be amended by the Court so that the controversial life interest reverted directly to the children on her death. This was now the only avenue open to her for regaining control of the life interest.

The singularly distasteful component of her proposed divorce suit was that the sole ground on which she was eligible was proof of sodomy.[36] During his trials Wilde was never charged with sodomy and nor was any evidence of it adduced against him. Constance and her legal team would have had to ferret out witnesses to testify to the commission of the act with Wilde. The whole scenario resurrected the spectre of the Old Bailey trials with their vile publicity and malicious gossip. For the sensitive and dignified Constance it would have created a most detestable situation and, even if she had succeeded, it would have amounted to a Pyrrhic victory for her and her family. Oscar, too, was highly apprehensive of a divorce hearing, and in his gloomier moments in his cell at Reading he envisaged being divorced for sodomy, re-arrested, retried and sent back to prison!

During the last six weeks of his incarceration, Wilde became extraordinarily angry at the way in which his friends – and especially More Adey – had flouted his original wishes over the life interest bid and thereby bungled his affairs. In his letters he rebuked them for their outright incompetence and ignorance of the law. While he admitted Adey's fine qualities of kindness, gentleness and patience, he was vitriolic about his business sense: "*stupid*", "*extremely dense*", "the most solemn donkey that ever stepped", and "incapable of managing the domestic affairs of a tom-tit in a hedge for a single afternoon".[39] It was a grossly unfair attack on one who had dedicated so much of his time and energy to promoting Oscar's welfare and alleviating his plight. But Oscar was furious at the way the tide had turned against him and, as he poignantly declared, he no

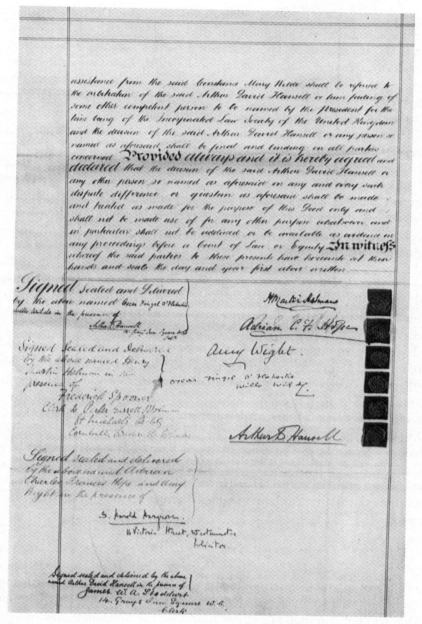

Figure 7 *The deed of separation between Oscar and Constance Wilde. It was signed by Oscar, with his full names, at Reading Gaol in the presence of Arthur Hansell, his solicitor, on the eve of his release from prison.*

(Photograph courtesy of Sotheby's London)

longer had "(1) any wife, (2) any children, (3) any income, (4) any possibility of ever coming to London to produce a play".[39]

And so, because of the potential sordidness of divorce proceedings, the parties resolved to find a more discreet way forward. There were three routes of putting an end to, or suspending, the relation of husband and wife: divorce, judicial separation, and mutual separation. The first two involved a court action whilst the third was effected by mutual and voluntary arrangement between the parties and their friends in a domestic rather than judicial forum. To avoid recriminations and unpleasant, even scandalous, exposures in open court and more effectively to provide for their altered circumstances, the parties executed deeds of arrangement which were called "separation deeds".[36] An agreement for separation became valid and enforceable only once the actual separation had occurred, and it was no less binding because it had been made voluntarily. However, a separation deed did not preclude the possibility of a future reconciliation and return to cohabitation.

In late March 1897 Hansell visited Wilde at Reading Prison to discuss Constance's threatened divorce plans and to take instructions on possible settlement proposals in lieu of divorce. On 10 April Hansell sent the terms of an arrangement that had been formulated between himself and Hargrove, and which Wilde, with alacrity and great relief, accepted.[40]

Eventually the final version of the deed of separation was adopted by the various parties and their respective solicitors (Hargrove, Hansell and Holman) together with Adrian Hope as guardian of Cyril and Vyvyan Wilde (Figure 7). The embattled issue of the life interest of the marriage settlement finally came to a resolution. Oscar's friends Adey and Ross, who had purchased it for Oscar for £75, assigned it to Constance under the deed. In return for its surrender, Wilde was to receive an allowance of £150 a year from his wife, with the assurance that this would continue to be paid after her death. But the deed, as set down below, stipulated that Hansell, in his discretion, had the authority to discontinue the allowance should Wilde behave immorally or keep disreputable company:

[T]he said Oscar Fingal O'Flahertie Wills Wilde shall lead a respectable life and shall not annoy or molest the said Constance Mary Wilde or in any manner compel or attempt to compel her to cohabit with him or live or attempt to live in the same house with her without her consent and shall not at any time after the nineteenth day of May One thousand eight hundred and ninety seven do any act or thing which would entitle the said Constance Mary Wilde to a divorce or a decree for a judicial separation or be guilty of any moral misconduct or notoriously consort with evil or disreputable companions or by his

mode of living forfeit [the yearly allowance] in the opinion of the said
Arthur David Hansell or any person named in his place . . . [41]

These conditions bothered Adey who, in a letter to Holman dated 14 May
1897, maintained that the words "moral misconduct" were superfluous and
might be used too liberally to allow petty interference in Wilde's *private* moral
conduct (whether in a natural or unnatural direction) in contradistinction to the
right to interfere in his *public* moral conduct.[42] In the same letter Adey queried
whether Constance Wilde's letter of condonation, as offered by Hargrove, had
arrived because "that is an essential part of the agreement as far as we are
concerned, and I have already urged Mr Wilde on no account to sign the deed
until he had received it".[42] Wilde wanted a letter of condonation from his wife
that forgave him all his past homosexual liaisons. Such a document would
provide him with a safeguard against any contemplated divorce action in the
future.

There was another matter that needed clarification. Wilde was personally
informed by Hansell at Reading that the continuation of his relationship with
Lord Alfred Douglas after his release would be deemed by him, qua arbiter of
the separation agreement, as "disreputable" and would therefore lead to the
cessation of his annuity from Constance. Wilde accepted this warning from
Hansell at the time but, when he resumed his affair with Douglas by living with
him in Naples towards the end of 1897, he became incensed when Hansell did
in fact terminate the allowance. Constance reinstated it some time after Oscar
and Douglas had parted and shortly before her death in April 1898. On 4 March
she wrote to Carlos Blacker: "He [Oscar] has, as you know, behaved exceedingly
badly both to myself and my children and all possibility of our living together
has come to an end . . ."[43]

The deed of separation was signed by Oscar Wilde at Reading Prison on
Monday 17 May 1897, just about thirty-six hours before his release. Two years
before he had lost his physical freedom but still had his rights: two years later
he had regained his freedom but had lost his rights.

7

THE GREAT SYPHILIS DEBATE

ONE of the recurring questions over the past seventy-five years has been whether Oscar Wilde suffered from, and possibly died of, syphilis. In the late nineteenth century syphilis was one of the great scourges, analogous to HIV/AIDS in the present day. It is estimated that about ten per cent of the Victorian and Edwardian population were infected with it, and a century ago the commonest cause of cardiovascular and neuropsychiatric disorders was syphilis.

Syphilis has also been termed "the great imitator" in that it was able to manifest itself in multifarious ways so that, according to the dictum of that eminent physician Sir William Osler, "Know syphilis and you know medicine".

It is also of interest that during Wilde's lifetime the causative organism of syphilis, *Treponema pallidum*, had not yet been discovered. This happened only in 1905, and two years later the first diagnostic blood test for syphilis came into being. Thus the diagnosis of a syphilitic illness in the late nineteenth century was based exclusively on the patient's history, the clinical examination and the presenting pattern of signs and symptoms.

The history and clinical features of syphilis have been lucidly described by Deborah Hayden in her intriguing book,[1] where she highlighted, by way of individual case studies, the profound impact of the disease on the lives, careers and personalities of a number of famous musical, literary and artistic figures, e.g., Beethoven, Schumann, Baudelaire, Flaubert and Van Gogh. She also included Oscar Wilde in this gallery – a highly contentious choice but one for which she has provided a comprehensive and closely reasoned analysis.

It was in the late fifteenth century that an epidemic of syphilis spread across Europe. The current hypothesis is that it was imported from the New World into Spain by Columbus on his return from expeditions in the Americas. It reached France and by 1494, after the French invasion of Naples, almost all of Italy was affected.[2] Owing to the huge toll exacted by the disease, cures were actively sought. It was in the sixteenth century that mercury was first introduced as a treatment. Despite its toxicity and adverse effects, mercury became the established, albeit controversial, therapy for syphilis until the twentieth century when it was replaced by bismuth and thereafter by the more effective arsenicals (salvarsan and neosalvarsan) for which Paul Ehrlich won the Nobel Prize in 1908. But it was only in the 1940s, when the antibiotic penicillin became generally available to the public, that a truly successful and safe drug against syphilis emerged. To this day penicillin has been the mainstay in the treatment of the infection.[2]

During Wilde's time mercurial administration was accepted as the therapy for syphilis although its use attracted a great deal of criticism, not only because of its highly unpleasant and hazardous side-effects but because there was considerable scepticism as to its efficacy. English physicians of the nineteenth century advised their patients to abstain from sexual intercourse for two years to prevent transmission during this potentially infectious phase and to take mercury daily throughout that period: "two minutes with venus, two years with mercury"![2]

Syphilis is a sexually transmitted disease acquired predominantly by sexual intercourse (including oro-genital and ano-rectal) and sometimes by kissing or close bodily contact. The disease is divided into the three stages of primary, secondary and tertiary.

Primary syphilis usually occurs about three to six weeks after the infection and is characterized by the so-called "chancre", which is a painless sore or ulcer on the genitals or on the lips, mouth or tongue. This heals completely within four to eight weeks.

Secondary syphilis appears within six to twelve weeks of the infection, usually in the form of a *non-itchy* reddish skin rash (resembling measles) which may extend to involve the whole body. There are often accompanying features such as fever, malaise, fatigue and enlarged lymph nodes. A very small number (one to two per cent) of patients may develop acute syphilitic meningitis, which is generally benign and tends to resolve spontaneously, even without treatment. The patient is very infectious during this stage, which lasts from a few weeks to several months, although during the course of the first year about twenty per cent of patients will relapse.

Tertiary syphilis follows on an exceptionally long latent interval, which ranges from five to thirty years after the infection. Usually it involves two major organs: the heart and the central nervous system (neurosyphilis). Syphilitic heart disease specifically attacks the aorta (the major arterial trunk arising directly from the heart) while tertiary neurosyphilis presents as three principal syndromes: tabes dorsalis (the most common in the pre-antibiotic era) with degeneration of the spinal cord and the spinal nerve roots; general paresis (also termed "general paralysis of the insane") with destruction of the brain tissue itself; and meningovascular syphilis (which tends to occur about ten to fifteen years earlier than the first two) with damage to the cerebral arteries.

Tabes dorsalis causes marked disturbances of gait (locomotor ataxia), bladder problems, lightning pains in the limbs, abnormal eye reflexes, and paroxysms of acute abdominal pain. General paresis is associated with progressive intellectual decline, memory impairment, personality deterioration, emotional lability, behavioural disturbances, and psychotic features (delusions and hallucinations). In a minority of patients the two syndromes are combined (tabo-paresis). Meningovascular syphilis produces a clinical picture resembling stroke: speech difficulties, paralysis of the limbs, and seizures.

Although the heart and the central nervous system are the classical sites of pathology in tertiary syphilis, there may be extensive involvement of other organs (including skin, bone and joints) by a characteristic tumour-like, destructive lesion called a "gumma". Moreover, it needs to be understood that not all of those who acquired a syphilitic infection advanced to the late stage of the disease: in fact, the commonly accepted figure (regarded by some as an underestimate) is that only one-third of untreated patients developed a clinical form of tertiary syphilis, with about six per cent progressing to tertiary neurosyphilis.

In order to determine whether Oscar Wilde had syphilis it is necessary to sketch his medical history and, in particular, to examine carefully the nature of his terminal illness. At the outset it must be emphasized that this is a difficult undertaking because of the lack of adequate documentation. The medical records pertaining to Wilde's illnesses are scanty, except during the period of his imprisonment when his health was monitored on a fairly regular basis. But in the last year of his life there is a dearth of material, and one is dependent on Oscar's own comments (as reflected in his letters)[3] together with the reports of friends who observed him at the time. These sources are not entirely satisfactory from the medical standpoint since they represent the attitudes and opinions of laymen which, if relied on exclusively, may incline one to a misleading or distorted view. However, the task of retrospective diagnosis was greatly facilitated by the appearance in 1982 of a medical certificate issued several days before Wilde's death by two reputable practitioners in Paris. This report has been the key to dispelling many of the uncertainties and speculations about his terminal illness.

The most conspicuous malady which affected Wilde in the years before his death was his ear disease. He had several other sporadic illnesses during the course of his life. One of these occurred in April 1878 when he was at Magdalen College, Oxford, but it abated fairly quickly and was probably an influenza-like episode. In July 1892 Oscar visited Bad-Homburg (with Bosie Douglas) to take the waters and to recuperate, describing himself to Will Rothenstein at the time as "very ill".4 But this indisposition soon passed and he returned to England invigorated and geared to start writing *A Woman of No Importance*. In late October 1894 Oscar wrote to George Alexander that he had been in bed a long time with "a sort of malarial fever".5 This was an attack of influenza caught from Bosie during their stay in Brighton. Later, in *De Profundis*, Wilde censured Douglas for his shameful neglect of him during the course of that illness.6 In May 1898 Oscar underwent a throat operation for quinsy (peritonsillar abscess) under the local anaesthetic cocaine.7

In February 1900 Wilde had an acute infectious illness, with a very painful throat and high fever, for which he spent ten days in a private hospital.8 He described it as "a sort of blood-poisoning" and as "some disease with a hybrid-Greek name: it attacks the throat and the soul".9 The most obvious diagnosis was septicaemia from a streptococcal sore throat. Although he recovered fully from this episode, his general health was poor – and continued to be so – until his death on 30 November 1900.

It is not possible to trace the beginning of the ear disease that was to bedevil Wilde from 1896. Frank Harris's account[10] was that in October 1895 Oscar fell on his ear in the chapel at Wandsworth Prison, injuring the drum and causing it to bleed. This has been taken as the *locus classicus* by virtually all subsequent biographers up until the present. However, there is no evidence whatever that Wilde's ear complaints originated during that alleged event. There is certainly no mention of a bleeding or injured ear, or burst eardrum, in the prison medical reports. On the contrary, the detailed examination carried out by the visiting specialists, Drs Nicolson and Brayn, while Wilde was in the Wandsworth infirmary noted that "his present bodily condition is satisfactory, and he complains of no bodily illnesses".[11] I have no doubt that had there been trauma to the ear (with bleeding and pain), that would have been recorded, especially as Wilde was then under heightened surveillance.

The only hint that we have about the onset of Oscar's ear complaint is contained in his petition to the Home Secretary from Reading Prison (dated 2 July 1896). He referred to a consultation he had had with Sir William Dalby (some time before his imprisonment) and to the latter's prognosis that "with proper care there was no reason at all why he should lose his hearing".[12] Dalby (1840–1918) became consulting aural surgeon to St George's Hospital, London, in 1872, the first appointment of its kind in the country. He had an enormous practice in London and was highly regarded throughout England for his valuable opinions. He wrote numerous articles on ear diseases and was an authority on the education of the deaf and the dumb by lip-reading. He was knighted in 1886 and was elected the first president of the Otological Society.[13]

Dalby would have felt privileged to have as his patient the son of one of the pioneers of his own speciality, namely, Sir William Wilde. And, to add to the honour, Dalby was well read in English literature; he was a keen and regular theatre-goer and the friend of many leading actors. He would therefore have been very familiar with Wilde's works.

Oscar must have been particularly troubled by his ear condition to have sought the advice of the top British specialist in the field. It is not clear when this visit occurred except that it antedated his trials and imprisonment. Presumably he had then begun to show signs and symptoms of middle ear disease, and the statement in his petition implies that there was already some impairment of hearing. However, Dalby's reassurance that with proper care to the ear Wilde should not lose his hearing indicates that, at the time of his examination, he regarded the condition as more benign than it ultimately turned out to be.

Oscar's hearing difficulty was detected by Bosie Douglas, who commented on his visit to Wilde in Holloway Prison in April 1895: "Poor Oscar was rather deaf. He could hardly hear what I said in the babel." [14] Frank Harris noticed Oscar's deafness at his interview with him in Reading Prison in June 1896; and then some years later in Paris he was forced to change places with Oscar at the theatre in order to be able to talk to him. [15] And Wilde himself complained, in his petition to the Home Secretary on 2 July 1896, that since his imprisonment he had almost entirely lost the hearing in his right ear because of an abscess that had perforated the drum. "But," he wrote, "though the abscess has been running now for the entire time of his imprisonment, and the hearing getting worse every week, nothing has been done in the way of an attempted cure." [16]

Wilde was exaggerating when he dated the aural discharge to "the entire time of his imprisonment": he made no mention of it to the doctors at Pentonville and Wandsworth Prisons. The ear problem probably arose during the first half of 1896 at Reading. As discussed in Chapter 4, this was the period when both his physical and mental health were at their lowest point. His mother had died in February, and this huge personal loss, coupled with the harsh prison environment and solitary confinement, had induced a state of depression and anxiety. It is not surprising therefore that under these circumstances his immune system was significantly compromised, rendering him unusually vulnerable to infections.

Oscar was also bitterly unhappy at the unsympathetic treatment meted out to him by the governor and medical officer. The latter, Dr Oliver Maurice, appears to have been remarkably inattentive to Wilde's ear infection, and Oscar was justified in petitioning the Home Secretary to alleviate his predicament. Wilde noted that the ear had been syringed thrice with plain water for examination purposes but that was all. According to him, Maurice had thrown in the towel and declared that the hearing was irretrievable. [16]

One cannot but wonder whether Dr Maurice was simply incompetent or whether he bore animosity towards Oscar – or, of course, both. It is extraordinary how neglectful he was in his attitude to Wilde's illness. Furthermore, Wilde was a high profile prisoner whose health and welfare were being closely overseen by the Prison Commissioners. The petition was an explicit assault on Maurice's management of the case. Yet when he was instructed by the governor to react, he responded on 3 July 1896 with this inappropriately terse report, in which he added insult to injury by misspelling Wilde's name as "Wylde".

It is perfectly true that he has a slight perforation of the drum of the right ear, but there is no evidence of mischief in the left, nor of any defect of vision.[17]

This was a wholly unsatisfactory, almost contemptuous, description of Wilde's ear disease and it made no attempt to address the grievances expressed in the petition. It is remarkable that Maurice had the temerity to furnish such a report to the Home Secretary. There were no comments about the duration, nature, frequency and severity of the discharge, the hearing loss or the attempted treatment and its result. To seek refuge in the fact that the left ear was intact was absurd. It was well recognized in the late nineteenth century that a discharging ear was not an ailment to be trivialized but a potentially life-threatening condition.

The chairman of the Prison Commission, Evelyn Ruggles-Brise, was insightful enough to ignore Maurice's opinion. Instead he requested the Visiting Committee to interview Wilde and make proposals. This was duly done on 10 July 1896 (see page 58). Among the suggestions was one which recommended referral to an *outside* practitioner for a second opinion on the ear problem.

A month after Oscar had penned his petition, his right ear remained unimproved and continued to discharge pus. Maurice had no option but to summon a colleague for advice.

On 2 August 1896 Dr J.A. Price, a local doctor from Reading, visited Wilde and made the following pithy assessment:

General health bodily and mental good.
Eyesight Vision of both eyes normal. No evidence of any disease whatsoever.
Ears Perforation of left [sic] tympanic membrane – some foul discharge which may be improved by daily syringing of the ear with dilute carbolic lotion.[18]

This again was not a particularly informative report: it failed to give any indication of the past history of the problem or of the deafness, but it was at least more constructive than Maurice's because it did specify a treatment plan. There was also a touch of carelessness in that Price mentioned the wrong (left) ear!

The daily aural toilet was instituted and gradually the infection was brought under control. This was corroborated by Wilde in a further petition to the Home Secretary on 10 November 1896 in which he stated that "his ear, that was in danger of total deafness, is now attended to daily".[19] This petition (which was subsequently rejected) begged for Wilde's release after serving eighteen months of his sentence. Dr Maurice was again required to comment on the petition. He did so on 16 November, enclosing Dr Price's above report and noting: "His ear which was a serious case is better, and need cause no anxiety."[18] At long last – and with the worst behind him – Maurice was prepared to concede that Oscar's suffering had been serious. This belated admission attests to his prior professional dishonesty and denial. I suspect, too, that under the humane regime of the new governor, Major Nelson, Maurice had found it politic to be more solicitous and sensitive towards his patient.

Oscar Wilde was scathing in his remarks about the prison doctors of his day.[20] But it is disturbing to reflect that even in the twenty-first century the health needs of British prisoners are relatively ignored and the quality of care in prisons falls below acceptable standards. A 2001 report issued by the British Medical Association entitled *Prison Medicine: A Crisis Waiting to Break* spells out the urgent problems within the prison medical services. These include underfunding, insufficient support for prison doctors (with over-interference by administrators in their clinical autonomy), and the disturbingly high prevalence of mental disorder in the prison population with inadequate resources to deal with it.[21]

Once Wilde's ear infection had settled towards the end of 1896 he had no setbacks for nearly four years, except for progressive deafness in the right ear. But during September 1900, when Oscar was resident at the Hôtel d'Alsace in Paris, he fell ill and was confined to bed under the care of Dr Maurice a'Court Tucker, the British Embassy doctor who acted as Wilde's general practitioner. Tucker (whose bill for FF1360 still survives) visited him sixty-eight times until Oscar's death on 30 November 1900 (Figure 8). Wilde had experienced an acute flare-up of his chronic ear disease but, worse still, the infection had extended from the middle ear into the mastoid, with severe accompanying bone pain and the danger of further extension into the brain.

Tucker attempted conservative treatment but without success. He then consulted with a specialist otologist (whose identity has never been established) and it was decided that an immediate operation was required in order to arrest the spread of the disease to the brain. As Oscar put it in his last recorded letter:

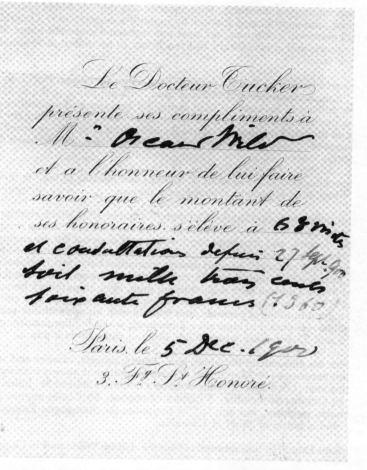

Figure 8 *The account for 1360 francs submitted by Dr Tucker, who had visited Oscar Wilde 68 times between 27 September 1900 and 30 November 1900. It was dated 5 December 1900, five days after Wilde's death, and it was eventually settled by Robert Ross.*

(Photograph courtesy of Sotheby's London)

"[T]he surgeon felt it his duty to inform me that unless I was operated on immediately it would be too late, and that the consequences of the delay would probably be fatal."[22]

On 10 October 1900 surgery was performed under chloroform in Wilde's hotel bedroom. "The operation I have had to undergo was a most terrible one," wrote Oscar shortly afterwards.[23] The surgery was extensive and costly (about £4000 in today's currency), and it required intensive and prolonged post-oper-

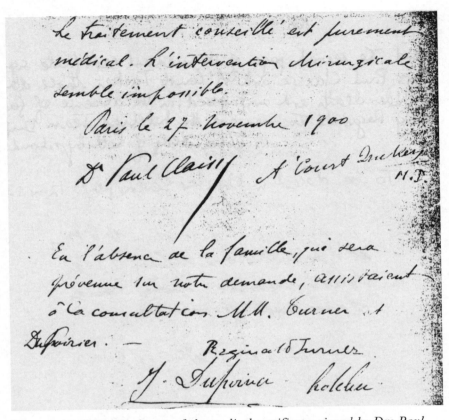

Figure 9 *The second page of the medical certificate, signed by Drs Paul Claisse and A'Court Tucker three days before Wilde's death and witnessed, in the absence of family members, by Reginald Turner and the hotelier Jean Dupoirier.*

(Photograph courtesy of Sotheby's London)

ative nursing and management. This involved cavity packing of the open wounds, frequent dressings, and energetic pain relief with morphine injections, oral opium and chloral.

Towards the end of October Oscar had improved sufficiently to be able to venture on walks and brief outings into the city and, apart from some unsteadiness of gait and giddiness, he appeared to be on the road to recovery. Unfortunately, in the second week of November, there was a relapse of the infection, which gradually progressed to involve the brain – the much dreaded complication of chronic suppurative (pus-producing) middle ear disease.

On 25 November Oscar's condition became more critical and he was unable to rise from bed. Thereafter he lapsed rapidly into a delirium, with restlessness and fluctuating consciousness, and then into a deep coma from which he died in the early afternoon of Friday 30 November 1900.

As mentioned earlier, our knowledge of Wilde's terminal illness was greatly enhanced by the advent, at a Sotheby's auction in London in 1982, of the medical certificate that was written on 27 November 1900 and signed by both Dr Paul Claisse and Dr Tucker. In late November Tucker became concerned at Oscar's deteriorating clinical state and he called on the expert advice of Claisse, who was considered one of the most accomplished physicians in Paris, having had a brilliant academic record with publications on a range of medical subjects. Claisse first examined Oscar on 25 November when his condition had worsened. Two days later he was in no doubt about the diagnosis and, together with Tucker, he issued the crucial certificate (Figure 9). The original, in French, is reproduced by Ellmann[24] and the following is a translation:

> The undersigned doctors, having examined Mr Oscar Wilde, called Melmoth, on Sunday 25th November, have found serious cerebral disturbances resulting from a long-standing suppuration of the right ear which has been undergoing treatment for several years. On the 27th the symptoms became much worse. The diagnosis of meningoencephalitis must be made without doubt. In the absence of any localizing signs one cannot contemplate trepanation. The recommended treatment is purely medical. Surgical intervention seems not to be possible.
>
> Paris 27 November 1900
>
> (signed) Dr Paul Claisse   A' Court Tucker M.D.
>
> In the absence of the family, who are to be notified at our request, Messrs Turner and Dupoirier were present at the consultation.
>
> (signed) Reginald Turner
> J. Dupoirier hotelier

This certificate established the diagnosis indisputably – meningoencephalitis as a result of the chronic suppurative ear infection. On the basis of this decisive assessment, Professor Sean Sellars (an otologist from the University of Cape Town Medical School) and I were able to make a retrospective formulation of Wilde's ear disease. We published this in *The Lancet* on 25 November 2000, almost exactly a century after his death.

The most obvious aspect of Wilde's illness is that it was a chronic condition which had begun at least six years (and possibly much longer) before his death.

He consulted Sir William Dalby prior to the trials with the complaint of deafness, which was likely to have been present for some time beforehand. There were two serious recurrences: one was the prolonged episode at Reading Prison and the other a severe, more extensive attack in Paris four years later with complications that ended his life. During the intervening period the deafness in the right ear intensified.

In short, the signs that presented themselves were: relapsing middle ear infection, perforation of the right eardrum, a persistent and offensive purulent (pus-producing) discharge, progressive right-sided deafness and ear pain. These features are characteristic of chronic suppurative otitis media (middle ear disease). Moreover, we suggested that these signs, together with the acute-on-chronic and deteriorating course of the illness, were consistent with the more destructive variant termed *cholesteatoma*.

Cholesteatoma actually means the presence of a pocket of foreign, skin-like tissue within the middle ear cleft. This focus expands and, in doing so, erodes neighbouring bony structures such as the ossicles, which are responsible for the conduction of sound. One of the most frequent complications during acute exacerbations of chronic suppurative otitis media – and especially the form of it associated with cholesteatoma – is the spread of the disease to the brain. The middle ear and mastoid are separated from the brain and its coverings (the meninges) by only a thin plate of bone, and once this barrier is destroyed by the infective disease process meningitis and encephalitis rapidly ensue.

In Wilde's case, by late September and early October 1900, the disease had extended to the mastoid during the quiescent stage following the Reading Prison illness. He was then seriously ill with an acute-on-chronic otitis media *and* mastoiditis, the latter producing intense bone pain. It was clear to the attending doctors that the scene was set for penetration into the brain with resultant meningitis which, in the pre-antibiotic era, was invariably fatal. The sole measure to prevent this complication was immediate surgery.

Although several medical authors have endeavoured to resolve the question of Wilde's final illness and cause of death,[26-29] none has been able to identify the nature of the operation performed on him. Suggestions have been mooted that it might have been a paracentesis of the eardrum (puncture with aspiration of pus), or removal of polyps, or even the incision for mastoid infection ("Wilde's incision") introduced decades before by Oscar's eminent father, the otologist Sir William Wilde. But all of these were minor and relatively simple procedures whereas, as outlined above, the operation undergone by Oscar was extensive, expensive and required protracted post-operative care and nursing.

Professor Sean Sellars had made a special study of the history of mastoid surgery,[30] and it was from this review that he and I were able to draw a reasonably accurate inference as to the type of surgery performed on Wilde in October 1900. Prior to the 1870s there were no acceptable or successful surgical approaches to the management of mastoiditis. The "Wilde's incision" brought immediate symptomatic relief in cases of acute mastoiditis, but it failed to cure the underlying pathology or control the original mastoid infection. It is interesting that leeches were then liberally employed in the initial management of acute mastoiditis, and they were even applied to Oscar Wilde's head in his dying days.

In 1873 a German otologist, Hermann Schwartze, published details of a simple mastoidectomy, an operation designed to improve the results in the acute, acute-on-chronic and chronic infections of the mastoid. The principle of this procedure was primarily to open the affected mastoid cavity and evacuate the diseased tissue. But with the passage of time and after considerable clinical experience, the limitations and dangers of Schwartze's operation were recognized. One of its principal drawbacks was that, while suitable for acute mastoiditis, it had a high failure rate in the type of acute-on-chronic mastoid infection (for example, cholesteatoma) that affected Oscar Wilde. In order to rectify this shortcoming, Küster in 1889 formulated a more complicated operation, the radical mastoidectomy; and in the early 1890s other otologists in Germany (notably Zaufal and Stacke) published their own version of radical mastoid surgery. This operation became fairly widely practised by the turn of the century, especially in Germany and France: in fact, by then it had won acceptance as the desired treatment for the potentially lethal forms of chronic suppurative otitis media. The aim of the radical operation was to eradicate all the diseased tissue and to exteriorize the middle ear and mastoid cavity, which are the sites of disease recurrence.

Thus it was that the ear surgeon consulted by Dr Tucker recognized at once that Oscar's clinical state was ominous and brain involvement imminent. He therefore performed an urgent radical mastoidectomy as a last resort to avert this. In this respect he was acting precisely in accordance with the best practice of the day, and the lack of success of the operation was certainly not due to any professional incompetence on his part. On the contrary, there was an initial improvement in the weeks following surgery. But there was a significant relapse rate with radical mastoidectomy, exacerbated in Wilde's case by the non-availability of antibiotics.

There was another factor which undoubtedly aggravated Wilde's illness and impeded his recuperation – his heavy alcohol consumption, which has been briefly mentioned previously. Towards the end of his life he was reputed to be imbibing one litre of brandy a night in addition to large quantities of absinthe and other liquors. The absinthe then sold in France contained a potent ingredient known as thujone, which was a neurotoxic agent with well-established psychotic effects. Artists in nineteenth and early twentieth century France were

Figure 10 *Oscar Wilde on his deathbed. This photograph was taken the day after his demise. The wreath has been carefully positioned to conceal his right ear and the adjacent site of the operation performed seven weeks before.*

(Courtesy of Jeremy Mason)

attracted to absinthe for its enhancing actions on mood, perception and creativity. (Edouard Manet's *The Absinthe Drinker* and Degas's *L'Absinthe* portray this fashion.) Contrary to expectations, though, the drink ultimately turned out to be destructive of their lives. In 1915 *La Fee Verte* ("The Green Fairy"), as the French dubbed it, was banned in France.

Oscar's drinking had begun long before his imprisonment. Max Beerbohm remarked in April 1893: "I am sorry to say that Oscar drinks far more than he ought: indeed the first time I saw him . . . he was in a hopeless state of intoxication."[31] George Bernard Shaw put it bluntly: "[T]hough he was to the end an incomparable talker he drank himself into complete impotence as a writer . . . "[32] And, if more confirmation is needed, Robert Ross admitted that Oscar was inclined to take "a great deal too much" alcohol at times but without showing outward signs of it.[33] In fact, after the operation Ross was informed by both Dr Tucker and the male nurse Hennion that Oscar could not live long unless he stopped drinking.[34]

There was a definite pattern of drinking in the Wilde family. Sir William Wilde lapsed into chronic depression and heavy drinking towards the end of his life. Oscar's brother, Willie, became a chronic alcoholic and died at the age of forty-six from the effects thereof. Willie's daughter, Dolly, had an alcohol and drug problem and died at forty-five under circumstances which suggested a drug overdose (although this was never conclusively established).[35]

Oscar's excessive alcohol intake in the period before his death would have impaired his general health and lowered his resistance to illness and infection. It probably contributed to his septicaemic illness in late February 1900; to the sudden onset of his terminal ear disease in September; and to his post-operative relapse in November. Certainly his doctor and nurse, as Ross noted, were deeply concerned about his alcoholic habits.

But throughout 1900 Wilde also complained of symptoms of lethargy and inactivity. "I simply cannot write . . . It is a mode of paralysis," he told Ross in April of that year.[36] He had earlier disclosed that his doctor had declared him to be *neurasthenic*: "I have all the symptoms. It is comforting to have them *all*, it makes one a perfect type."[37] "Neurasthenia" was a term much used (and abused) by doctors and the laity in the late nineteenth century. Originating in America and later imported into England, it referred to a deficiency in nervous energy, or nervous exhaustion. Neurasthenia became a popular attribution for all kinds of neurotic conditions deemed to emanate from mental weakness and nervous over-sensitivity, and it offered a more fashionable diagnostic label that the somewhat pejorative term "nervous weakness". In Oscar's case it was appropriately applied (for its time) to describe his overwhelming mental fatigue and inertia. I believe that to a large extent this state was the result of his prolonged overindulgence in alcohol. Alcohol is a potent depressant of the central nervous system, and the consumption of large quantities over extended periods will lead to a blunting of motivation, drive and creativity.

The other troublesome ailment that plagued Wilde during 1900 was a skin rash. There are such scant details available on the appearance and characteristics of this rash that it is not possible to attempt any kind of diagnosis: indeed, it would be most imprudent to do so. According to Oscar's one-sentence description[37] and Frank Harris's remarks,[38] it was an irritating ("very painful") and itchy rash with red blotches ("like a leopard" in Oscar's words and due to "poisoning by mussels"), covering a large area of the body (arms, chest and back). It apparently disappeared dramatically after some months,[39] only to recur several months later.[38,40]

One of the most intriguing explanations suggested for the rash was that it was due to a skin sensitivity to hair dye.[41] Both Ross and Harris (independently) had noticed during their respective visits to Oscar at Reading Prison that his hair was streaked with grey, and it was assumed that he subsequently used dye to conceal these changes. The dyes available in those days contained a chemical substance (phenylenediamine) that had a tendency to provoke allergic reactions. Thus, if during the application of the hair dye Oscar had spilled droplets onto his body, he would have become sensitized and then developed the widespread reddish skin reaction after subsequent applications. This hypothesis gains some support (not cited in the original paper) from a letter by Boucicault to Wilde in 1894 in which he wrote: "I am very grey, but I think it is rather becoming – so I shall not dye my hair as you suggest."[42] And Oscar himself had opined: "In old days people had a great respect for grey hairs. Now they have a great respect for dyed hair. That shows a distinct advance."[43]

As stated above, it is just not realistic to reach any kind of diagnosis of Wilde's skin rash on the skimpy information at hand. However, it is improbable that syphilis would have produced such a rash. The rash of secondary syphilis characteristically does *not* itch, while the skin eruptions of tertiary syphilis are localized (not generalized as they were with Oscar) and unlikely to disappear as rapidly as they had done in his case.

At this stage, it is appropriate to inquire how the notion that Wilde had syphilis had crept into his medical history. In the first edition (1912) of *Oscar Wilde: A Critical Study* Arthur Ransome, under the guidance of Ross, wrote:

> His death was hurried by his inability to give up the drinking to which he had become accustomed. It was directly due to meningitis, the legacy of an attack of tertiary syphilis. For some months he had increasingly painful head-aches. On October 10 he was operated upon.[44]

Interestingly, in the second edition of the book (1913), Ransome made certain changes to the text: in particular, he deleted the derogatory passages about Alfred Douglas; but he also omitted the reference to Wilde's death from syphilis. For this action Robert Sherard commented as follows in *The Real Oscar Wilde*:

> Ransome attributed to him a certain disease, and added that it was the final cause of his death. I see that, in his new edition, Mr Ransome omits this indiscretion. I can only say that, during the seventeen years, I never saw in Wilde the slightest sign of a malady which has a very distinct way of announcing its existence, a disease which certainly does

THE GREAT SYPHILIS DEBATE

not hide its fatal light under any bushel whatsoever. The fact is, the man had a wonderful constitution, just as he had a wonderful brain.[45]

It is extraordinary that, having committed himself to this standpoint, Sherard then underwent a complete reversal of attitude some twenty years later. In the mid-1930s he suddenly unleashed a series of startling allegations about Oscar Wilde: that as an Oxford undergraduate he had acquired syphilis from the local prostitute; that he had been subjected to mercurial treatment which had "cleared" him for marriage; that he subsequently suffered a relapse which terminated conjugal relations and supposedly switched him to homosexuality.

It was at this time that Reginald Turner had written to Sherard:

The ear trouble, which I believe began in prison, was only shortly before his death diagnosed as a tertiary symptom of an infection he had contracted when he was twenty. He had a rash in the spring of 1900 which he thought was due to eating shellfish in Italy but which was supposed to be another symptom.[46]

It is probable that this recollection of Turner's was the stimulus for Sherard's extravagant outpourings. Merlin Holland, having examined the background to the syphilis accusations, has discredited their source and denounced their substance as unfounded and even fabricated.[47,48] On the other hand, Deborah Hayden has argued the pro-syphilis position in detail, giving credence to the fact that Wilde's close friends (Ross, Turner, Sherard and Harris) independently corroborated, at some stage, that he had syphilis.[49] Her opinion is that there is a repository of evidence here which, taken collectively, just cannot simply be ignored or dismissed. She emphasizes the disgrace of syphilis and the secrecy in which it was cloaked at that time; hence the failure of Drs Claisse and Tucker to mention it explicitly in their medical certificate. I am puzzled though that Bosie Douglas was one intimate friend who did not align himself with the others on this matter. He wrote: "Sherard makes statements about a malady which he declares Wilde had contracted, but I fail to find that he gives any proof or evidence of this. I am in no position to disprove what he says, but frankly I do not believe it."[50]

I have discovered that the story that Wilde had been infected with syphilis in his youth and recovered from it before his marriage did not originate with Sherard in the 1930s. It was in fact recorded in the *page proofs* of Ransome's first edition (1912) of *Oscar Wilde*[51] but was deleted before publication.

It is difficult for any serious scholar to evaluate the various affirmations about Wilde's alleged syphilis and to decide whether these represent the truth or whether they are more consistent with rumour, speculation and distortion. There is really no reliable basis on which to make a meaningful or objective assessment. The task is further complicated because several generations of reputable biographers, from Basil Brasol to Hesketh Pearson to Montgomery Hyde and finally to Richard Ellmann, have clouded the issue by stamping authority on the syphilitic theory. The example *par excellence* is Ellmann, who in his masterly biography dogmatically pronounced that Wilde had syphilis and died of it.[52]

A diagnosis of syphilis is not based on hearsay or anecdote; it is determined solely on the patient's clinical presentation and on the previous medical history. Even if Oscar's circle of friends had genuinely believed that he had syphilis, that is hardly proof of the diagnosis. Some of the friends only revealed this information decades after Wilde's death, not only casting doubt on the reliability of their recall but also, in certain instances, questioning the integrity of their motives. Myth, plausibility and reality are so intertwined that it is impossible to separate them.

Wilde's health was regularly monitored during his two-year term of imprisonment. I have estimated that he was examined by at least seven doctors, including two specialists. There is no reference to syphilis in any of the medical reports in the Home Office (Prison Commission) files. Prison doctors in Wilde's day were particularly familiar with syphilis and its clinical features on account of its high prevalence among the inmates. It was one of the statutory duties of the prison medical officer to make an examination of every prisoner on reception and to document specifically his past illnesses. Thus Wilde would have been interrogated about his previous health. Had he contracted syphilis as an undergraduate and then been prescribed a prolonged course of mercurial treatment (as per rumour), he might have divulged this when initially questioned about his medical history. It is possible of course that the stigma of having suffered from syphilis might have deterred him at first from disclosure, especially within the unfamiliar and threatening prison milieu. But, subsequently, when he became seriously ill with florid signs of ear disease, he would surely not have concealed that fact, realizing that to do so would mislead the doctors, contribute to inappropriate treatment and ultimately jeopardize his prospects of recovery.

Did Wilde die of syphilis? No; he died of meningoencephalitis due to an extension of his chronic suppurative otitis media (with mastoiditis) into the brain. Syphilis did not enter into the equation. It is true that syphilis itself may cause meningitis: either as an uncommon manifestation of secondary syphilis that is usually benign and self-resolving, or as meningovascular (tertiary) syphilis, where the signs of meningitis are accompanied by features of a stroke. Neither of these was applicable to Wilde's terminal illness, in which the meningoencephalitis was an undisputed sequel to antecedent middle ear disease of long duration.

Was the antecedent chronic ear disease itself syphilitic in origin? Again the answer is negative. The pattern and course of Oscar's ear disease, as described earlier, was wholly compatible with a diagnosis of chronic suppurative otitis media (probably associated with cholesteatoma). Syphilis is "the great imitator" in that it can mimic many other diseases, but ironically the type of chronic middle ear disease exemplified in Wilde's case was not part of its repertoire. There are isolated references in the older medical literature to an association between syphilis and chronic ear disease but, rather than establishing a causal link between the two, this probably reflected the coincidental existence of two conditions that were relatively common in that era. Syphilitic tumours (gummas) of the middle ear and mastoid did occur very rarely but they would not have followed the prolonged and fluctuating course characteristic of Wilde's illness. However, it needs to be mentioned that there is a distinct and uncommon form of tertiary neurosyphilis that attacks the *inner ear* sensory structures and the auditory nerve with resultant *sensorineural* deafness. This is an entirely separate condition from the middle ear disease that Wilde suffered, and, although he complained of marked deafness in the right ear, this was of a different type, namely, *conductive*.

There is a final issue to be settled. Did Wilde show any evidence of either of the two major forms of tertiary neurosyphilis – general paresis and tabes dorsalis? Once more the answer is unequivocally negative. Tertiary neurosyphilis would have resulted in progressive intellectual deterioration, personality changes, behavioural abnormalities, psychotic features and impairment of neurological functions such as gait and bladder disturbances. Wilde showed no evidence of any of these signs. As explained above, although he did complain of debilitating loss of energy and initiative ("neurasthenia"), his mental abilities remained unimpaired up until the final week of his life. The letters that he wrote in his last year betray no defects whatever in cognitive, semantic or logical processes.

While I have argued that Oscar Wilde's illnesses were not due to syphilis, there is a corollary that has to be entertained: one cannot state with certainty that he was *free* of syphilis. As the saying goes, "Absence of evidence is not evidence of absence". And in this context it is pertinent to consider an aspect that has hitherto been overlooked by biographers. The suspicion has been that Oscar contracted the infection from a female prostitute whereas, in fact, homosexually acquired syphilis is as important a means of transmission as heterosexual contact. West[53] has provided useful statistics, based on a number of surveys, on the prevalence of venereal disease in the male homosexual population of Great Britain. It is important to note that these studies were conducted before the HIV/AIDS epidemic in the 1980s because, since then, the sexual activities of homosexual men have altered towards safer practices with a resultant decrease in the proportion of early syphilis cases.

West has shown that during the period of publication of these surveys (1964–1973) male homosexuals ran a particularly high risk of acquired sexually transmitted diseases. In the year 1971, data from 176 British venereal disease clinics demonstrated that 45 per cent of 830 cases of recent syphilis in men were homosexually acquired. Previous research at various London clinics yielded even higher proportions of early syphilis in active homosexuals – from 68 per cent to 83 per cent. As West has pointed out, these proportions may have been underestimates because some homosexual patients, for fear of stigma, would have falsely admitted to heterosexual contact. The higher London figures highlighted the tendency for homosexuals to be drawn to the metropolis. A more recent investigation (1980) found that 58 per cent of male syphilitic cases in the United Kingdom occurred in homosexuals.[54] The situation in the United States between 1977 and 1982 was similar, with homosexual and bisexual men accounting for approximately half of all patients with early syphilis.[55] The current outbreak of syphilis in large cities on the West Coast has involved men who practise homosexual sex, a high proportion of whom are also infected with HIV.[55]

There are of course no such surveys for the London of the 1890s, except that it is generally acknowledged that about ten per cent of Victorian men were infected with syphilis. It is reasonable to assume that a significant proportion of these affected men had acquired it through homosexual practices.

Oscar Wilde was a physically active homosexual and practised his sex with rent-boys and male prostitutes. Although he denied participation in sodomy, he engaged in other forms – especially oro-genital sex – that would have put him at high risk of infection. It might well have been that he contracted syphilis, developed the primary and secondary stages, and then entered the long latent period that was devoid of clinical signs and could last for up to thirty years, if indeed it ever manifested.

It has always been perplexing to me that Wilde was deemed to be syphilitic on the grounds of flimsy and probably apocryphal evidence of contact with a female prostitute, but with virtually total oversight of the fact that he was far more likely to have succumbed to the disease through his vigorous and promiscuous lifestyle of the 1890s.

8

THE PRECIPITOUS ROAD
TO HOMOSEXUAL LAW REFORM

I F Oscar Wilde had lived at the time of the Ancient Greeks he might well have been hailed as an exemplary citizen. His marriage with two children would have satisfied the society's procreative needs while his love of, and passion for, adolescent boys and young men were consistent with Greek culture. To the Greeks the spiritual and sensual love of an older man for a handsome youth (*paiderastia*) was pure and noble. As Plato expressed it, through Phaedrus, in the *Symposium*: "I know not any greater blessing to a young man beginning life than a virtuous lover, or to the lover than a beloved youth."

But Wilde happened to live at a time when the prevailing ethos was the antithesis of that in Greece two millennia earlier; and, in his eloquent speech from the dock of the Old Bailey on the "love that dare not speak its name", he drew the court's attention to the noble notion of Greek love.

The laws in force against so-called "unnatural offences" derived from the emperor Justinian (538 AD), and thereafter such actions were regarded with abhorrence and hostility by western Christianity. The word *sodomy* had its origin in the Genesis story of the destruction of the city of Sodom by fire and brim-stone because of the unnatural practices of its inhabitants. It was dubbed *crimen tantum horribile non inter Christianos nominandum* ("the crime so horrible as not to be mentioned among Christians") and the penalty under ecclesiastical law was death at the stake, although this was virtually never enforced. In 1533 Henry VIII introduced hanging for "the detestable and abominable Vice of Buggery", but again this sentence was hardly ever imposed during the sixteenth and seventeenth centuries and only very infrequently during the eighteenth. It was only in the first thirty-five years of the nineteenth century that executions for sodomy became more established, with 55 having been carried out between 1805 and 1835 out of a total of 1930 executions (of which only 406 were for murder).[1] These statistics showed the remarkably high percentage of hangings for relatively minor crimes (e.g., theft). There were strong moves by leading statesmen such as Sir Robert Peel and Lord John Russell to remove the death penalty for sodomy, but this was achieved only in 1861 (1889 in Scotland) with the passage of the Offences Against the Persons Act. However, although convicted sodomites were sentenced to death up until 1861, the last execution for sodomy took place in 1835. The new Act replaced capital punishment for sodomy with sentences of between ten years and life. It is of interest that in 1873 the Pre-Raphaelite artist Simeon Solomon (several of whose paintings were owned by Oscar Wilde) was arrested in a public urinal in London and charged with indecent exposure and attempted sodomy. He escaped a sentence of imprisonment but was fined £100 and released under police supervision.

Sodomy, in its legal sense, had the specific connotation of anal intercourse and it applied as much to homosexual as to heterosexual sex. Indeed, it is currently estimated that about a third of heterosexual couples in Britain use anal sex occasionally, with about ten per cent employing it as the preferred or regular method. Roughly a half to two-thirds of gay men practise anal sex. Thus the surprising conclusion emerges that, in absolute numbers, there are more heterosexuals than gay men participating in anal sex.[2]

In England prior to 1886 there was no legislation against homosexual acts (excluding sodomy) conducted between consenting adults in private. This legal tolerance did not signify that non-penetrative forms of homosexual behaviour were socially acceptable. They were considered to be almost as repugnant as sodomy itself, but it had been generally believed that it was inappropriate and invidious for the law to intervene in the private lives of its citizens. In this respect it is pertinent to reflect that in modern France the *Code Napoléon* did not distinguish between heterosexual and homosexual orientations. Adults were permitted to indulge in whatever form of sex they desired; the law was invoked only to protect against violence, public indecency and exploitation of minors. Belgium, Holland and Spain had followed the same example (and in 1889 Italy came into line), whereas in 1871 and 1885 the German Reich and Britain, respectively, moved distinctly in the opposite direction.

What is especially interesting is that it was only in the latter half of the nineteenth century that the concept of same-sex love began to emerge. The word *homosexual* ("Homosexualität") was coined by the Hungarian writer Kertbeny (Karl Maria Benkert) in 1869 but it was incorporated into common usage only in the 1890s. (It appears that Oscar Wilde himself never used the word.) Previous terms had included "Uranian love", "sexual inversion" and "unisexuality".

During the 1860s the German jurist Karl Henrich Ulrichs, a self-confessed homosexual, was one of the pioneers in campaigning against the prejudice and stigma towards same-sex love, to which he had applied the term "Uranian love" (from the Greek "Uranos" (Heaven)). He attempted to explain the phenomenon along pseudo-scientific lines by postulating that there were three sexes: a normal man *(Dioning)*, a normal woman *(Dioningin)* and a third sex called *Urning* (including *Uringin*). The Urning is predominantly congenital and arises from a failure of differentiation in the foetal developmental process. The result of this anomaly is *anima muliebris virili corpore inclusa* ("a female soul incorporated in a male body"). Although the Urning's mind is feminine, he is masculine in physique and therefore unfitted for sexual intercourse with men, although attracted towards them by natural instinct. Ulrichs even advocated marriage between people of the same sex, an extraordinary proposal for the mid-nineteenth century. Ulrichs was not medically qualified but he laid the foundations on which subsequent medical hypotheses were predicated. He introduced a paradigmatic shift, namely, that homosexuality was not a sin or a crime to be punished but rather an inborn constitutional state which was highly unlikely to yield to change.

During the late nineteenth century the medical model was formulated and elaborated by a series of German and French doctors. For its time this was construed positively because it induced the medical profession to perceive homosexual patients not as criminals or insane but as people with disturbed sexual histories and life experiences. The value of the individual case study was appreciated and generally a less judgemental and more clinically oriented approach was utilized. This new focus was epitomized by Richard von Krafft-Ebing, a German psychiatrist, in his celebrated work *Psychopathia sexualis* (1886) where, in the English translation of 1892, the words "homosexual" and "heterosexual" màde their first definitive appearances.[3] In this book he presented detailed clinical descriptions of forty-five homosexual cases, largely based on the patients' own personal accounts of their sexual behaviour. With succeeding editions the number of cases increased so that the twelfth edition (1903) contained 238 individual reports. Krafft-Ebing's work was a landmark in delivering the first truly clinical psychiatric survey of homosexuality. It also had the beneficial effect of fostering a widespread public awareness of same-sex relationships and of liberating otherwise suppressed homosexuals from secrecy, fear and ignorance.[4] But the most enlightened and rational exposition of homosexuality emanated from Albert Moll, a young German doctor, whose *Die conträre Sexualempfindung* (1891) demythologized the whole subject. In his remarkably progressive analysis he proposed that homosexuality was not a disease; it was a naturally occurring variety of human sexuality and as such the idea of a "cure" was not applicable.[5]

Unfortunately for Oscar Wilde the major initiative in the medicalization of homosexuality occurred on the Continent. Britain remained benighted and firmly anchored in the traditional mindset that homosexuals were abhorrent, morally depraved and unfit for normal society. In fact some doctors were unwilling to treat homosexual patients, especially if their symptoms related to the sexual organs or functions. In response to this, one angry medical commentator argued that "if a pathological state such as congenital sex perversion is too disgusting to be recognized, then a pathological state producing syphilitic sores of the genitals ought by parity of reasoning to be too filthy to be treated".[6] This punitive and reactionary attitude to homosexuality was evident in this extract from the psychiatric report on Oscar Wilde, issued during his imprisonment at Wandsworth in October 1895 (see pages 41–45):

> [Wilde] practised the most disgusting and odious criminal offences with others of his own sex and that too not with one or two individuals of a better station in life, but apparently with the most casual acquaintances of comparatively low social position.[7]

Such an unedifying standpoint by the country's most reputable forensic psychiatrists in 1895 is an indictment, and it highlights the isolation of British medicine from the relatively enlightened academic influences in Europe at the turn of the twentieth century. Wilde himself was cognizant of this backwardness because in his petition to the Home Secretary (2 July 1896) he requested to be freed and allowed to be taken abroad for care and treatment by physicians who understood the medical basis of what he termed "erotomania".[8]

Few voices were raised in England at the time against the legal position of homosexuals. John Addington Symonds in his *A Problem in Modern Ethics* (1891) discussed Karl Ulrichs's theories of the Urning, the iniquity of the law against homosexuals, and proposals for legal and educational reform. Edward Carpenter articulated similar sentiments in his description of "homogenic love"[9] that he later expanded into a book, *The Intermediate Sex* (1908). George Cecil Ives founded a small-scale and secret homosexual reform movement known as the "Order of Chaeronea".

But the most striking event involved the English doctor and sexologist Havelock Ellis, who collaborated with J.A. Symonds to produce a book entitled *Sexual Inversion*. This was the first volume in the series *Studies in the Psychology of Sex*, and it detailed the case histories of homosexual subjects to illustrate that they were the product not of acquired vice or insane tendencies but of an innate constitutional predisposition. Ellis and Symonds declared that homosexuals must be free to live according to their natural instincts and unfettered by legal sanctions or social ostracism. In the face of resistance to any open debate on homosexuality and certainly to any plea for tolerance, Ellis had difficulty in finding an English publisher. In 1896 the book was actually translated into German and published under the title *Das Konträre Geschlechtsgefühl*. It was hailed as a seminal work in German scientific circles. An English version of *Sexual Inversion* eventually appeared in 1897,[10] but with

Symonds's name removed after pressure from the family following his death in 1893.

The Legitimation League, founded in 1897, initially campaigned for the legal recognition of children born out of wedlock but it expanded its remit to espouse the principles of free love (and even free trade in prostitution) through its monthly journal, *The Adult*. Radicals like Edward Carpenter and Havelock Ellis supported the League, and the League in turn welcomed the stance taken by these two men in the promotion of free homosexual love. Ellis's book *Sexual Inversion* was warmly received by the League and it was displayed in its offices, which also served as an informal bookshop. The premises happened to be the home of George Bedborough, who was secretary of the League and editor of *The Adult*. Scotland Yard kept the League under surveillance as it suspected that it was being used as a front for anarchists. Detective Inspector John Sweeney actually infiltrated the League as an undercover agent and, when the moment for action arrived, he purchased a copy of *Sexual Inversion* from Bedborough. A warrant of arrest was obtained and Bedborough was apprehended in May 1898 and charged at Bow Street with attempting to "vitiate and corrupt the morals of the liege subjects of our said Lady the Queen" by selling "a certain lewd, wicked, bawdy, scandalous and obscene libel" in the form of *Sexual Inversion*. Ten further charges were added by the prosecution. The case came before the Recorder at the Old Bailey in October 1898. Under the strong influence of Sweeney, Bedborough agreed to a plea bargain where he pleaded guilty to three charges while the remaining eight were dropped. He was bound over in £100 to come up for judgement if called upon. Bedborough disbanded the Legitimation League and *The Adult* was discontinued.[11] Havelock Ellis was not prosecuted, but his *Sexual Inversion* was effectively banned in Britain without any evidence being led on its merits and without acknowledgement that the book was not an obscene work but a scientific publication.[12] The British Museum received its copy of *Sexual Inversion* but concealed it from readers by omitting it from the catalogue. The Oscar Wilde trials of 1895 had cast a long and lingering shadow.

Prior to 1886 non-penetrative homosexual acts between consenting adults in private did not constitute an offence under English law. But then one of the most nefarious pieces of legislation on the statute book came into being; a piece of legislation that for eighty years was to have profoundly destructive effects on the lives and reputations of otherwise law-abiding citizens. This was the Criminal Law Amendment Act, which became operative on 1 January 1886.

The bill that came before the Houses of Parliament was entitled "A Bill to make further provision for the protection of women and girls, the suppression of brothels, and other purposes". Essentially the bill's other purposes were to prevent both the procuring of girls for prostitution and the selling of young British women and girls into sexual slavery abroad (the "white slave traffic"). An additional objective was to raise the age of consent from thirteen to sixteen.

The background to the bill was that during July 1885 W.T. Stead, editor of the *Pall Mall Gazette*, published a series of provocative articles ("The Maiden Tribute of Modern Babylon") in which he described the methods used to coax and capture young girls and then their appalling treatment in unfamiliar and foreign surroundings.

In a flush of investigative journalism, Stead himself (with the aid of some female assistants) procured for £5 – and with little difficulty – a girl of thirteen and then had her sent to Paris. He erred by not obtaining her father's permission and was accused of removing her fraudulently from her parents' possession. As a result he was sentenced to three months' imprisonment. But the impact of his campaign, backed by feminists and social purity organizations (such as the National Vigilance Association), aroused moral outrage and virtually forced the Salisbury government to present the bill.

As is well known, it was Henry Labouchère, Liberal Member of Parliament for Northampton and editor of *Truth*, who sabotaged the generally laudable aims of the original bill by moving his notorious amendment (popularly dubbed "the Labouchère Amendment"). The bill, as initially drafted, was introduced and passed in the House of Lords. After the second reading in the House of Commons without comment, it was referred to a committee of the whole House. There, late at night on 6 August 1885 and with a sparse attendance, Labouchère rose to propose an amendment by way of a new clause which came to be numbered as Clause Eleven. The bizarre circumstance was that this clause had nothing whatever to do with the overall tenor of the bill: instead it created a new class of offence – acts of gross indecency between male persons in public or *in private*. This had dire implications because it attacked the basis of the private homosexual lifestyle. With the stroke of the royal assent, the active homosexual population of the country was converted into a potentially criminal class with the omnipresent risk of blackmail. Moreover, whereas previously the law had specifically punished the act of sodomy *per se*, it was now encompassing the entire spectrum of homosexual activity. Labouchère had succeeded in demarcating, in legal terms, homosexual people as a qualitatively distinct and morally offensive subgroup of humankind.

What is exceptional is that such a momentous social and legislative measure should have been dealt with by Parliament with short shrift and indifference. From the time that Henry Labouchère sat down after proposing the amendment, I have estimated that the ensuing debate on the subject did not exceed two minutes! Only one Member was attentive enough to raise the highly relevant point of order as to whether it was appropriate at that stage to introduce a clause dealing with a totally different class of offence from that specified by the bill. The Speaker, presumably weary and not prepared to extend the lateness of the hour, ruled that anything could be introduced by leave of the House. The only other speaker was Sir Henry James, who had been Attorney General until June 1885, when Gladstone was defeated. The amendment as set out by Labouchère restricted the punishment of the offence to one year's imprisonment, with or without hard labour. James moved to amend the clause by substituting *two* years' imprisonment. Labouchère had no objection to this and the clause, as amended, was agreed to and added to the bill.[13] On the following night, 7 August 1885, the bill was rushed through its third reading and passed.

Thus came into force the Criminal Law Amendment Act of 1885 with its infamous Clause Eleven (subsequently to become Section Eleven). J.A. Symonds referred to it as "a disgrace to legislation by its vagueness of diction and the obvious incitement to false accusation".[14]

There is a question that has repeatedly intrigued historians and biographers. What was Labouchère's reason for proposing his incongruous amendment, and for doing so without prior warning or consultation? There is an undercurrent of speculation about this, especially as Labouchère was not known to have any particular concern with male homosexuality. Smith[15] has argued that Labouchère was disenchanted with the shoddy way in which the bill had been drawn up. There had been horse-trading among the political parties over age of consent and other issues, and the resultant patchwork of amendments did little to improve the bill's structural integrity. In reality, though, Labouchère had been opposed to the bill right from the start; he had been contemptuous of the scandal arising from Stead's exaggerated coverage of the white slave traffic and of what he perceived as the hypocritical cant of the social purity campaigners. There may also have been some degree of rivalry between him and Stead as fellow editors, aggravated by the latter's scoop with the "Maiden Tribute" articles. All of these factors led Smith to conclude that, in tabling his loosely worded and damaging amendment, Labouchère was being mischievous and obstructive and that his basic intention was to scupper the bill and compel the government to refer it to a select committee, as should have been done in the first place.

If Smith is correct in his view that Henry Labouchère manufactured the notion of "gross indecency" and its criminalization merely as a ploy to embarrass the government, then the advent of Section Eleven becomes even more tragically preposterous.

It is interesting that the inclusion of Labouchère's clause went unnoticed at first. *The Lancet*, a day after the bill was approved, reported on its contents in detail and declared that the new legislation would have the support of the medical profession. "On the whole, the Criminal Law Amendment Act in its present form promises to be one of the most useful pieces of legislation passed this session."[16] Not a word was mentioned about the new offence of gross indecency between males. Similarly, Section Eleven was not taken up with any enthusiasm by the police: indeed, there was a definite reluctance to apply it. The subject of homosexuality was taboo in late Victorian Britain and it was feared that prosecution would incite morbid curiosity and possibly invite imitation. It was therefore more important to suppress publicity, and there were even suggestions that such cases should be heard *in camera*.[17]

Notwithstanding this, the Criminal Law Amendment Act of 1885 certainly had an effect in raising the conviction rate for sexual offences in England and Wales, especially during the 1890s; but the increase was of the order of forty per cent and thus far from dramatic.[1] It was only in the twentieth century – and, in particular, the middle decades – that the authorities began to seek out homosexual offenders with vigour. In 1938, for example, 320 prosecutions occurred for gross indecency: in 1955 there were 2322 cases. In the period between 1930 and 1955 homosexual offences known to the police increased by 850 per cent compared with 223 per cent for all indictable offences.[18] This meant that, in 1955, one in every 125 homosexual men in England and Wales became a criminal statistic.[19] Some of the notable casualties in the early 1950s were Sir John Gielgud (for homosexual soliciting), Rupert Croft-Cooke, Lord Montagu of Beaulieu, Michael Pitt-Rivers, Peter Wildeblood and Alan Turing (all of these under Section Eleven). Turing was the pioneer of computer theory and one of the most profound and original mathematical minds of the generation. Convicted in 1952, he was not gaoled but ordered to undergo a year's course of hormonal (oestrogen) therapy. He committed suicide by cyanide poisoning two years after his trial.

The most brutal assault in history on homosexual men was witnessed during the Nazi era in Germany. In 1871 Paragraph 175 of the German Imperial Code made "unnatural vice committed by two persons of the male sex" an imprisonable offence. Although lists of homosexuals were compiled by the pederasty division of the German police, these were rarely used during the nineteenth century. The then head of the division was an enlightened man who worked closely with Dr Albert Moll (see above) and was thoroughly persuaded that homosexuality was not a vice.[19]

But in 1935 Hitler ordered a revision of Paragraph 175 so that "criminally indecent activities" between men, such as homosexual kissing and embracing, became prohibited. The Nazis regarded homosexuals as degenerate; Heinrich Himmler proposed their eradication to preserve Aryan purity. Not only were tens of thousands convicted and imprisoned, but up to 15,000 were sent to concentration camps where they were distinguished by a pink triangle affixed onto their uniforms. Many were subjected to castration, and half of all homosexuals in the camps perished under atrocious conditions.[20] To add to the horror, when the camps were liberated in 1945 many of the surviving homosexual inmates were transferred to prisons since the post-war government still regarded them as guilty of a punishable crime. Hitler's anti-homosexual laws continued in East and West Germany until the late 1960s.

Judged against the situation in the twentieth century, homosexual men in late Victorian Britain were left relatively unscathed by the police. As stated by Graham Ross: "Nineteenth-century homosexuals lived under a cloud, but it seldom rained." [19] It is arguable whether Oscar Wilde would ever have been arrested and convicted had it not been through the agency of the Marquess of Queensberry.

There was, however, one event that rocked London during Wilde's era. This was the Cleveland Street brothel scandal in 1889–1890, which has been the subject of at least two full-length books.[21,22] This sensational affair centred around a male brothel at 19 Cleveland Street, London, which was serviced by Post Office telegraph boys and frequented by men of superior social standing. Lord Arthur Somerset was the most conspicuous of the clientele but suspicion also fell on Prince Albert Victor ("Prince Eddy"), the eldest son of the Prince of Wales, Queen Victoria's grandson and heir presumptive to the British throne. For the first time since the appearance of Section Eleven, the government directly experienced the backlash of the Labouchère Amendment. On the one hand, considerable pressure was exerted on them from several quarters to prosecute Lord Arthur while, on the other, there was strong resistance from those who feared the potential harm that would result to several aristocratic reputations and to the royal family. Various machinations ensued between top government officers, including Lord Salisbury, and eventually a warrant for the arrest of Somerset was issued, but not before he had escaped abroad. This procrastination led to the allegation of a top-level conspiracy to prevent Somerset's prosecution. Instead two unknown individuals were convicted and gaoled (for four months and nine months, respectively) for their part in the Cleveland Street scandal, but they were really only scapegoats for Lord Arthur Somerset.

Another remarkable but much less publicized case that fell foul of the law in the early 1890s was that of Edward Samuel de Cobain, a Conservative Member of Parliament who sat for Belfast East from 1885 to 1892. A warrant for his arrest was obtained in 1891, charging him with having committed acts of gross indecency but, like Somerset, he had fled to the Continent.

The problem was that De Cobain was a sitting Member of Parliament who had fled the country to evade arrest. This forced the House of Commons to take action, and on 23 July 1891 and 23 February 1892 he was ordered to attend the House. He failed to do so on both occasions, and on 26 February 1982 Mr A.J.

Balfour, Leader of the House, moved the motion that De Cobain be expelled from the House because "we ought not to allow one to remain among our number who, with such a charge hanging over him, refuses to submit himself to the tribunals of this country, to have his name cleared, if so be he is innocent".[23] The motion was approved and Edward de Cobain was expelled.

When De Cobain eventually returned to Belfast he was arrested, appeared before the Resident Magistrate on 22 February 1893 and was committed for trial. On 21 March 1893 he was convicted under the Criminal Law Amendment Act (1885) on ten counts of gross indecency (involving five persons), all of which had occurred several years before. He was sentenced to a year's imprisonment with hard labour and confined to Mountjoy Prison, Dublin. He was released on 7 March 1894 and died in 1908.[24]

There is a precedent from the De Cobain case that has a specific bearing on Oscar Wilde. Wilde was strongly encouraged to leave England: first, when he withdrew from the Queensberry trial, and later when he was out on bail before his second criminal trial. Had he taken such advice, he would have been arrested if he ever re-entered the country, thus forcing him to remain a permanent fugitive from justice in order to retain his freedom. But even this had its hazards. In a letter to *The Times* (2 May 1891), in which De Cobain denounced the allegations against him, he disclosed that the law of extradition had been used to hunt him down; and it appears that he moved from country to country. This was an indication that, in the long term, escaping from the forces of British law was not quite so simple a proposition as Wilde's friends had envisaged.

The prosecution of Oscar Wilde had a disturbing impact on British homosexual society. Prior to that, the Labouchère Amendment was, if anything, honoured more in the breach than in the observance. But the Wilde saga, which from the arrest of Queensberry to the sentencing of Wilde extended over a period of nearly three months, evoked a massive press reaction and a huge public outcry of horror and disgust. Whereas previously the population, embedded in the mores of Victorianism, was generally unaware of the specifics of homosexuality (a matter only for those dealing with criminals or the insane), it was now exposed to more information than ever before. Notwithstanding this, the newspapers were highly cautious in the manner in which they conveyed some of the more prurient aspects of the case. In the Central Criminal Court Sessions Papers, all three of the Oscar Wilde trials were recorded but without any description whatever of the actual proceedings. There was merely a statement on the outcome or verdict.[25] In the criminal libel case against Queensberry it was noted that "the details of the case are unfit for publication".

Newspaper reports of the trials were similarly discreet, either avoiding any mention of the words in Queensberry's alleged libel or leaving a blank for the word "sodomite". It must be noted that it was a misdemeanour at common law to publish indecent matter just as it was to publish blasphemous material.

As a result of the sensational aura surrounding the Wilde trials there was a more determined attempt to curb such publicity in the future. Lord Halsbury, the Lord Chancellor, introduced the Publication of Indecent Evidence Bill in 1896. Essentially this empowered a judge of the High Court to prohibit the publication of any evidence that he believed was of an indecent character and prejudicial to public morality. This, of course, placed a heavy responsibility on the judge and on his capacity to draw the line between publishable and non-publishable testimony. The debate that took place in the House of Lords produced a wide divergence of views, with the Marquess of Salisbury supporting and Lord Rosebery and the Lord Chief Justice opposing the measure.[26] The medical profession was in favour of shielding the public but argued that medical journals should be exempt from such censorship in the interests of science and scholarship.[27] There was vehement pressure against the proposals from newspaper groups lest press freedom and judicial transparency be jeopardized. In the end the bill was abandoned.

The Criminal Law Amendment Act had another airing in Parliament in 1921, when the Commons faced a new amendment to that Act, namely, to extend Labouchère's Section Eleven in exactly the same terms to women. The House voted in its favour by 148 to 53. Although male homosexuality had been an offence for thirty-five years, lesbianism was overlooked by the criminal statutes. The change in thinking was motivated partly by the criminal libel prosecution brought by the dancer Maud Allan against the eccentric Member of Parliament Noel Pemberton Billing in early 1918 and at which Lord Alfred Douglas testified for the defence. (It was then that Douglas made his astounding assertion that "I think he [Oscar Wilde] is the greatest force for evil that has appeared in Europe during the last 350 years".) Maud Allan was playing the title role in Wilde's *Salome* and, according to Billing, the stage presentation of the play (the "Cult of the Clitoris", as he called it) would attract many people whose names allegedly appeared in a "Black Book", a list of 47,000 British citizens, both male and female, whose perverse sexual activities were known to the German Secret Service for the purpose of blackmail. Billing was acquitted, somewhat unfairly, but probably because of the prevailing anti-German war frenzy.

But the trial, with its overtones of "sexual vices" in women as well as men, contributed to the perception by the Commons that lesbianism needed to be outlawed. However, the House of Lords took an entirely different view. The Earl of Desart (who, as Hamilton Cuffe, had been Director of Public

Prosecutions at the time of Wilde's trials) was emphatic. He referred to "the sort of romantic, almost hysterical, friendships that are made between young women at certain periods of their lives" and how these could lead to false accusations and blackmail. He vigorously protested against creating the idea of an offence of which the enormous majority of women had never heard, never thought and never dreamed. "I think that is a very great mischief," he declaimed.[28]

In the face of such dismay – and defiance – from Lord Desart, who was supported by several other influential peers, the proposed amendment perished in the House of Lords and was never again presented to Parliament. But the reason for its rejection, namely, to prevent the female population from being alerted to the concept of homosexuality among women, was undermined in 1928 when Radclyffe Hall's novel of lesbian love, *The Well of Loneliness*, was banned and the publishers prosecuted. This event was probably the single most crucial factor in raising the awareness of lesbianism as a sexual entity and in imbuing it with a name and an image.[29]

As discussed earlier, prosecutions for offences in England and Wales reached a peak in 1955. The trials and prison sentences of Croft-Cooke and of Wildeblood (with Montagu and Pitt-Rivers) in 1953 and 1954, respectively, had demoralized the public, especially as their convictions were based (as with Oscar Wilde) on the questionable and contaminated evidence of accomplices. But there were important individuals like Earl Winterton who were deeply concerned at the magnitude of homosexual crime in Britain. Winterton, during a House of Lords debate in May 1954, inveighed against "the filthy, disgusting and unnatural vice of homosexuality" which he was convinced "lowers the pres-tige, weakens the moral fibre, and injures the physique of a nation".[30]

Despite these sentiments there was a growing feeling that the law against male homosexuality was unjust, fomented blackmail and was being enforced with a zeal disproportionate to the nature of the offence. Moreover, it was an invasion of the privacy of the individuals' lives, individuals who were often talented, professional and law-abiding men. In October 1953 Sir John Gielgud was arrested for homosexual soliciting in a public lavatory in Chelsea. He was convicted and fined £10 but not without dramatic newspaper reportage, especially as he had been knighted only a few months before. But when he returned to the theatre days after his conviction he was greeted with an uproarious standing ovation by the audience. The theatre-going public sent out a vociferous signal that what John Gielgud, their idol, had done in his private time would detract not a whit from the love and admiration that they had for him.[31]

In 1954 the Conservative Home Secretary (in Churchill's cabinet) was forced to respond to the mounting pressure for reform and decriminalization and he (reluctantly) established a Departmental Committee to review the law and practice relating to both homosexual offences and prostitution. The chairman was John Wolfenden, Vice-Chancellor of Reading University, and in 1957 the Committee produced its report, which has since become known as the "Wolfenden Report". This Report made a strong case on both moral and practical grounds for decriminalization, and it found no basis to accept that homosexual behaviour between men was any more destructive of family life than adultery, fornication and lesbianism. The Report was favourably received in some quarters but negatively in others, including the government. The homophobic attitude of the latter hampered efforts to change the law in spite of continuing public debate and activism. There were several abortive attempts in both Houses to introduce motions to implement the Wolfenden proposals and it was only in 1967, a decade after the Report was presented, that the Sexual Offences Act was promulgated.

The new Act was by no means revolutionary, but it did decriminalize homosexual acts (including sodomy) between two consenting males, provided the behaviour occurred in private (with no more than two persons present) and that both parties were over the age of twenty-one. These provisions did not apply to members of the armed forces. But there was another side to the coin: where a man of twenty-one or over committed an act of gross indecency with another man who was under the age of twenty-one but over sixteen he was liable to a maximum prison sentence of *five* years (not two, as previously), and, if the other person was under sixteen, to ten years' imprisonment. Where sodomy was committed with a person under sixteen (male or female) the maximum penalty was life imprisonment.

The reason for the increased sentences, where acts were committed with individuals below the age of twenty-one, was the belief that homosexual practices with younger persons would interfere with their normal heterosexual development and convert them into homosexuality. More recent surveys of young adult and adolescent male prostitutes have in fact shown that about seventy per cent of them were inherently homosexual or bisexual. There was little evidence that the prostitution practices *per se* changed their natural sexual inclinations.[32]

There is an irony in the Sexual Offences Act of 1967 that pertains to Oscar Wilde. Had Wilde been tried in 1895 under the 1967 Act, Mr Justice Wills would almost certainly have meted out the maximum term of five years' imprisonment. One of the consistent themes during Wilde's trials was the youthfulness of his sexual partners, almost all of whom were *under* the age of twenty-one and some around sixteen or seventeen. Recall those memorable and chilling words of the judge: "I shall, under the circumstances, be expected to pass the *severest sentence that the law allows* [my italics]. In my judgment it is totally inadequate for such a case as this." He then pronounced the maximum sentence of two years with hard labour, but he would surely have been greatly pleased with the (supposedly "adequate") maximum of five years accorded to his colleagues under the 1967 legislation.

As discussed above, Ulrichs had written in the 1860s that homosexuals (or Urnings) represented a "third sex". For him homosexuality was an inborn constitutional anomaly due to faulty biological processes in the foetus. His theories contributed to the medical (as opposed to the criminal) model of homosexuality. It is interesting that during the 1990s two remarkable research findings were announced that attracted keen publicity.[33] The first (1991) was that, in the brains of homosexual men, a certain nucleus (group of nerve cells) in the hypothalamus was two to three times smaller than in the brains of heterosexual men. This discovery was followed in 1993 by the disclosure that a gene (or genes) for homosexuality had been identified on the X chromosome (inherited from the mother). These demonstrations of a structural (neuroanatomical) and genetic basis for homosexuality corroborated Ulrichs's ideas of 130 years earlier that his so-called "Urnings" were congenital. These research leads were criticized both on methodological grounds and because of a lack of replication by independent studies.[34]

A fairly recent and comprehensive review article critically examines the present state of biological research on human sexual orientation.[35] It concludes that the latter is influenced by biological factors to some degree (e.g., prenatal exposure to hormones, neuroanatomical and genetic determinants) but how and when these factors act and interact – and to what extent – in shaping sexual orientation in men and women remain puzzling and outstanding questions. Indeed, the latest findings from the Swedish twin study of same-sex behaviour (the largest of its kind) refuted the notion of a specific gene or environmental agent for homosexuality; rather they showed that male and female homosexuality is a composite of genetic and non-genetic factors, with the former (surprisingly) having a weaker influence than the latter. [36]

There are serious ethical considerations associated with this kind of research. The results must not be translated by society into a perception that homosexuality constitutes a biologically different entity. Such an outcome would be harmful and divisive and at risk of re-creating new forms of discriminatory attitudes and practices under the guise of medical science – for example, genetic counselling, selective abortion and gene therapy.

Towards the end of the nineteenth century in Europe, the interpretation of male homosexuality changed from a criminal to a pathological and medical model. Thus, homosexuals were deemed not to require punishment but treatment. At first this switch in approach was well received because it fostered a better rapport between homosexual men and their medical practitioners. It enabled the patient to talk openly to the doctor about his condition, and to be heard. To Oscar Wilde in Reading Prison the prospect of medical care and treatment abroad was far preferable to the *status quo*.

But there was another and darker side to the medical model. Homosexuals were seen to be deviating from the heterosexual norms of society, and this aberration legitimized treatments to convert them into heterosexuals. In Britain, therapies to effect this change of orientation reached a peak in the 1960s and early 1970s and have been reviewed in a recent publication.[37] The treatments, which were mainly administered in National Health Service hospitals throughout Britain, involved aversion therapy either with electric shock or (less frequently) by the induction of nausea; oestrogen administration (as was ordered by the court for Alan Turing); various forms of behavioural therapy and psychotherapy; religious counselling; hypnosis; and occasionally electroconvulsive therapy. Most people sought these treatments not out of their own volition but because they were driven to do so by a hostile family, by social pressures or by the courts. The outcome of these various therapeutic manoeuvres was negative; participants did not benefit from them and instead many felt a marked sense of social isolation and shame from their involvement.[37]

The message from the above survey is that the medicalization of homosexuality was a fundamental error. Indeed, the primary focus of the treatment endeavours was not to assist patients with their own personal concerns and problems but to alter their homosexual behaviour because it conflicted with the sociopolitical, moral and religious ethos of society.

In the United States, the Stonewall riots of June 1969 in New York (precipitated by a police raid on a gay pub of that name in Greenwich Village) marked the start of militant gay activism. The resultant struggle for gay liberation in the early 1970s encompassed a challenge to the dominant standards of sexuality. One of their targets was the American Psychiatric Association, whose classification of psychiatric disorders incorporated homosexuality as a specific category. Whereas in the past the attribution of "sick" rather than "criminal" had been welcome, times had changed. The label of psychiatric illness was distressing to homosexual men and women and it had to be expunged. Picket lines and protests were organized by gay activists at lectures and conventions hosted by the orthodox psychiatric associations, and on occasions meetings were physically disrupted. The demand to erase homosexuality from the diagnostic classification caused turmoil within the American Psychiatric Association but, as the pressure escalated, an increasing number of psychiatrists began to rethink the issue.[38] In December 1973 the Nomenclature Committee of the Association voted to delete homosexuality from the *Diagnostic Manual* and to replace it with the term "sexual orientation disturbance", which was aimed at individuals who, although they manifested same-sex interests, were distressed at these or wished to change their sexual orientation.

This proposed nomenclature change evoked a sharp response from the not inconsiderable faction who insisted on retaining the *status quo*. In the end the Association agreed to hold a referendum of all its members, and this duly took place in April 1974. There was clear (but not overwhelming) support for the change, just under sixty per cent voting in favour. Homosexuality *per se* thus ceased to be recognized as a psychiatric disorder by the American psychiatric establishment.[38] The World Health Organization dragged its heels for another twenty years before it ultimately abolished homosexuality from its diagnostic classification of diseases.

Oscar Wilde had written to George Ives in March 1898: "Yes: I have no doubt we shall win, but the road is long, and red with monstrous martyrdoms. Nothing but the repeal of the Criminal Law Amendment Act would do any good."[39]

It is a sad reflection on British society that the eminently rational sentiments and standpoints so courageously articulated by Symonds, Carpenter and Havelock Ellis in the 1890s should have been fully embodied in the law only a century later. Since the Sexual Offences Act of 1967, which set the age of consent for consensual homosexual activity in private at twenty-one, there have been two further reductions: to eighteen in 1994 and then to sixteen in 2000, thereby conferring parity with heterosexual relationships. But the real turning-point was reached in 2004, when the British Parliament passed the Civil Partnership Act. This recognized and legitimized same-sex relationships and created provisions analogous to those pertaining to marriage. However, unlike countries such as the Netherlands and Spain, the Act stopped short of redefining the legal concept of marriage to incorporate homosexual unions, thereby depriving gay couples of the opportunity to proceed to the full and formal status of "marriage"*.[40] Nevertheless, society has at last abandoned its erstwhile prejudices and punitiveness and come to accept that commitment to a homosexual lifestyle is as positive and constructive as to its heterosexual counterpart.

---

* The British government has introduced plans to legalize same-sex marriage by 2015.

9

GAY SUPERSTAR BUT NOT MARTYR

NTIL recently there was a belief that Oscar Wilde did not become an established homosexual until he was initiated into it by Robert Ross in 1886 or 1887, two to three years after his marriage to Constance Lloyd. Ross, then a seventeen-year-old youth, was already an uninhibited and fairly experienced homosexual, and his meeting with Oscar evolved into a devoted and lifelong relationship. Ross was the grandson of the first Prime Minister of Upper Canada and the son of the Attorney General. His father died when he was one, and the family moved to London when he was nearly three. Ross was a sensitive, intelligent and caring person who unfailingly ministered to Oscar's emotional and financial needs and who also became a firm friend of Constance's. After Wilde's death he assumed the executorship of his literary estate and carried out that task meticulously, giving special attention to the welfare of the two sons, Cyril and Vyvyan.

According to Ellmann,[1] both Wilde and Ross independently informed friends that their homosexual encounter had been Oscar's first. Ross told Christopher Millard (Wilde's bibliographer) that he felt responsible for Wilde's children because he had introduced him to homosexuality. Oscar confided to Reginald Turner that it was "little Robbie" who had seduced him.[1]

The impression is thereby created that, at the time of his marriage, Wilde was essentially heterosexual and that his conversion to homosexuality was a subsequent development due to Ross. Rupert Croft-Cooke was one of the first to debunk this notion,[2] but the definitive refutation comes from Neil McKenna, who, in his *Secret Life of Oscar Wilde*, has systematically chronicled Wilde's sexual history (some of it clearly conjectural) from his undergraduate period at Oxford to virtually the end of his life.[3] There is no reliable information available on this subject either during Wilde's schooldays at Portora Royal School or at Trinity College Dublin.

Wilde's earliest meaningful homosexual liaison seems to have been with Frank Miles, an artist whom he met at Oxford in 1876. At that stage Miles, who lived in London, was enjoying the friendship and patronage of Lord Ronald Gower, a sculptor and art critic and a promiscuous homosexual, and both these men had an influence over Oscar. Wilde apparently later admitted to Bosie Douglas on a return visit to Oxford in 1892 that he had been in love and had sex with Miles while a student there.[4,5] When he went down from Oxford, Oscar shared rooms with Frank Miles in London from 1879 until 1881.

Another association that Wilde formed during his spell at Oxford was with a young artist, Arthur May. He wrote to his friend Reginald Harding: "I have taken a great fancy to May, he is quite charming in every way and a beautiful artist."[6] And, about a fortnight later, he commented to William Ward: "I saw a great deal of Arthur May; he is quite charming in every way and we have rushed into friendship."[7]

There was then the interlude with Rennell Rodd, a good-looking Oxford undergraduate at Balliol College who had won the Newdigate Prize for poetry in 1880, two years after Wilde. Wilde and Rodd went on a walking tour in France down the River Loire and had an exhilarating holiday. It is generally supposed that there was a love affair between these two aspiring poets, and some confirmation of this arose in 1882 when, during his American tour, Wilde managed to secure the American publication of a collection of Rodd's poems under a new title of his own choice, *Rose Leaf and Apple Leaf*. Without seeking Rodd's consent he arranged that the book should be dedicated to himself as follows: "To Oscar Wilde – 'Heart's Brother' – These Few Songs and Many Songs to Come"; and in his introduction he wrote that none indeed but Rodd "is dearer to myself". Rodd was embarrassed at this effusiveness and tried to get the dedication removed, but it was too late. (It is alleged that Rodd was so ashamed of the book that he bought up copies of it whenever they came on sale and destroyed them.) Rennell Rodd (later Lord Rennell of Rodd) was appointed British Ambassador to Rome in 1908. His son Peter was sent down from Balliol, Oxford, before taking his degree, on the charge of entertaining women in his rooms after hours! Peter Rodd went on to marry Nancy Mitford but, through his reckless womanizing, the marriage ended in divorce in 1957.[8]

There is a photograph of Oscar Wilde (not part of the Napoleon Sarony series) sent by Oscar to Kenyon Fortescue with the inscription: "To Kenyon Fortescue with his love Oscar Wilde Feb 1882" (Figure 11). This is the only reference I have seen to a Kenyon Fortescue, although in *Oscar Wilde Discovers America* there is a single mention of a "Mrs Marion Fortesque", whose home in New York Oscar had visited shortly after his arrival there in January 1882.[9] There is a listing of both Marian [*sic*] Fortescue (widow of Robert F. Fortescue) and Kenyon at the same street address in the 1885–1886 city directory for New York.[10] It thus seems likely that Kenyon was Marian's son, and that Oscar had

Figure 11 *Photograph of Oscar Wilde with affectionate greeting card to Kenyon Fortescue, a young American friend whose relationship with Wilde has hitherto escaped the attention of biographers. Although dated February 1882, the photograph was not part of the Napoleon Sarony series but was taken in London by Elliott and Fry before Wilde departed on his American lecture tour.*

(Private collection)

probably met him at his mother's house, taken a liking to him and subsequently sent him his photograph with affectionate greetings. Whether there was a continuing relationship between the two of them is unknown.

The cumulative evidence of Wilde's relationships with Miles, May, Rodd and undoubtedly others is indicative of homosexual involvements in the period before his marriage. There were also the impressions of observers that he was "epicene" and "effeminate", based predominantly on Oscar's advocacy of aestheticism and Hellenism, his dress, his demeanour and some of his suggestive poetic contributions in the late 1870s and 1880s. The subtext of Gilbert and Sullivan's *Patience* (1881) clearly linked the aesthete Bunthorne (the "ultra-poetical, super-aesthetical, out-of the-way young man") to what would in later times be caricatured as the "mincing, lisping queen". In 1883 *Punch* called Wilde a "Mary-Ann", a common word for a homosexual prostitute.[11] During his American tour there was considerable denouncement of Wilde by the press in precisely these terms.[12]

Although these observations were relatively benign and even amusing, they may well have had more sinister undertones. It is interesting that at Oxford University itself there was significant institutional resistance to the emergence of an aesthetic movement. This was apparent in the competition for the post of professor of poetry, once occupied by Matthew Arnold (1857–1867). The successful candidate had to be elected by the Congregation, which was essentially the resident academic members of the University, and this turned the contest into a widely debated public campaign. In early 1877 Walter Pater and John Addington Symonds (see page 120) were among the declared candidates; but both of these men encountered strong criticism (and even hostility) from certain quarters of the Oxford community – not on intellectual grounds but because of their shared ideologies. They had admired the Greeks for their idealization of the grace and athleticism of youth and for their recognition of the virtues of homoerotic love. The ensuing opposition to their candidacies eventually led Pater and Symonds to withdraw their names, albeit with justified resentment.[13] The professorship was awarded to the dull Scots cleric John Campbell Shairp, who stifled the rising aesthetic initiative and tried to revive earlier Victorian attitudes. It was probably with reluctance that Shairp was forced, as an *ex officio* judge of the Newdigate Prize, to award it to Oscar Wilde in 1878.[14]

This saga had a sequel in that Shairp, who himself had won the Newdigate in 1842, proposed textual improvements to Oscar's poem *Ravenna* before it was published. Oscar simply ignored the suggestions and had the poem printed as it was.[15] The following year (1879) Wilde entered for the Chancellor's English Essay Prize on the subject of "Historical Criticism among the Ancients". Shairp was once again one of the judges but this time no award was made – only the second time that this had happened since the inception of the Prize in 1768! Thirty years later Ross, who was about to publish Oscar's essay, sent the proofs for correction to the then professor of poetry at Oxford (and a judge for the Chancellor's Prize). The latter found the work to be of an acceptable level and was puzzled that the prize was not awarded at the time.[16] There is a lingering suspicion that Oscar was the rightful winner but that personal bias against him and his unconventional attitudes robbed him of the honour.

Wilde also failed both to gain a fellowship at Oxford and to obtain the archaeological studentship for which he had applied. For one who had done so brilliantly at the University, with one of the best double Firsts in "Greats" as well as the coveted Newdigate Prize, it is surprising that he should not have been offered an academic position within Oxford. Again one questions whether Wilde was excluded because his views and behaviour were not considered consonant with the tenor of the establishment. And was the Oxford Union's rejection of Wilde's *Poems* in 1881 (after the library itself had requested a copy from him) another example of the same prejudice? The following remarks appeared about Wilde in the *Oxford and Cambridge Undergraduate's Journal* (17 November 1882) after a motion to purchase *Poems*, proposed by the Librarian a year later, had been defeated:

> If a man leads an evil life in the University, even though he may not suffer for his acts at the time, yet his character will not have escaped the notice of his colleagues, who afterwards will always have it in their power to call his remembrance to the past.[17]

It is of interest that in 1874 Benjamin Jowett, Master of Balliol, intervened to block Walter Pater's automatic election to the remunerative post of university proctor because of his romantic affair with a nineteen-year-old undergraduate, William Money Hardinge.[18]

In parallel with Wilde's homosexual relationships went a number of dalliances with women, which some biographers have interpreted as a sign of his heterosexual (or bisexual) nature at that time. I do not believe that these associations reflected any serious sexual intent on his part. Like many homosexual men, Oscar had very good rapport with women. In addition to being a scintillating conversationalist, he was charming, kind and gentle and his delicate manners and flattery were very attractive to the opposite sex. They sought his company and he was admired by many. Among the famous women that he knew were Lillie Langtry, Sarah Bernhardt and Ellen Terry, and each one of these had a special affection for him.

The best documented of Wilde's early flirtations was that with Florence Balcombe, whom he met in Dublin in August 1876. In a letter to Reginald Harding he described her as "an exquisitely pretty girl" with "the most perfectly beautiful face I ever saw and not a sixpence of money".[19] He did a drawing of her, presented her with an inscribed watercolour painting, and at Christmas gave her a small gold cross. It appears as though (initially) he was infatuated with her beauty, but the relationship was superficial and there was no real passion or commitment. An examination of Oscar's correspondence during the two-year period of their friendship (most of which Oscar spent in Oxford) reveals scant reference to her existence. There is a letter to Harding in May 1877 from Dublin with the comment "Florrie more lovely than ever";[20] and then in April of the following year a somewhat cool letter to her from Bournemouth (where he was recuperating from an illness) in which he greatly regretted not having been able to come over to Dublin.[21] The next series of three letters[22] relates to her impending marriage to Bram Stoker two months later (in December 1878), about which she did not even have the courtesy to inform Oscar. He was clearly hurt by the rejection, as is evident from his self-pitying tone and the request for the return of the gold cross to serve "as a memory of two sweet years – the sweetest of all the years of my youth".

In 1879 Wilde met Violet Hunt, daughter of the artist Alfred William Hunt and the novelist Margaret Hunt. This encounter (with "the sweetest Violet in England") sparked a mutual admiration between the two and there was even talk of a marriage proposal. But, although Oscar kept up the acquaintance with the Hunt family for some time, nothing materialized.

Leonard Montefiore had been a friend of Oscar's at Oxford. He died unexpectedly in America in September 1879 at the age of twenty-six. Oscar condoled with Leonard's sister Charlotte on her bereavement and endeavoured to establish closer ties with her.[23] He is reputed to have proposed marriage to Charlotte Montefiore in about 1880, but she refused. That evening Wilde sent her a note: "Charlotte, I am so sorry about your decision. With your money and my brain we could have gone far."[23]

Charlotte Montefiore was an impulsive, effusive and enthusiastic person with a very amusing conversational style. Most of the young men who came to her home were devoted admirers. In 1884, a year after her father's death, she married Sir Lewis McIver. The Montefiores were an orthodox Jewish family and Charlotte's proposed marriage to a gentile came as an appalling, almost unbelievable, blow to the mother. Claude Montefiore, Charlotte's brother, was a biblical and Judaic scholar who had studied under Jowett at Balliol in Oxford and was known to Oscar. Claude, despite his strong religious beliefs and his disapproval of mixed marriages, boldly supported his sister when he realized that opposition to her plans was futile. He took her to Germany, where there was a rabbi who was willing to perform a marriage between a Jew and a Christian. Charlotte continued to practise her own religion and she desired that her children should be brought up in it. Her mother later accepted the marriage.[24] (It was Harry Phillips, son-in-law of Charlotte McIver, who in a letter to Sir Rupert Hart-Davis (14 September 1960) gave the information about Oscar's marriage proposal to Charlotte.)[25]

The significance of the above events in Charlotte's life is that in 1880, when Oscar apparently proposed marriage to her, she probably never even contemplated it because she realized it would have been totally tabooed by her religious father (then still alive), whose wrath she would not have dared to risk. After his death and being several years older, she then felt able to assert her will against the family.

In assessing Wilde's heterosexual career during the period between his entry into Oxford and his engagement to Constance Lloyd (a span of nine years

(1874–1883) within a sexually active age range of twenty to twenty-nine), one is struck by the paucity of romantic attachments to women and, where there were such relationships, by their fragmentary and fleeting character. There is no evidence that Wilde prior to his marriage enjoyed any substantial love affairs with women, and certainly not with the same passion and affectionate delight that he demonstrated towards his male lovers. His flirtation with Florence Balcombe perhaps comes the closest but, as indicated above, apart from the initial flush of enthusiasm and pride at squiring a girl of such beauty – and Oscar *did* appreciate beauty – there were no signs of a deeper and more enduring intimacy. On the contrary, Florence felt so frustrated (and possibly neglected) that she abandoned Oscar for Bram Stoker without even apprising him of her intentions.

My conclusion is that Oscar Wilde, a man of high libido, was really devoid of intrinsic heterosexual instincts. He was able to dissemble successfully when necessary, and his capacity for this was a pronounced and well-developed aspect of his personality. I maintain that his true sexual orientation was exclusively homosexual. Why then did he marry? W.H. Auden accepted that Oscar knew himself to be homosexual and characterized his marriage as "certainly the most immoral and perhaps the only really heartless act of Wilde's life".[26]

There was a side of Wilde that was conformist and materialistic. He recognized that he needed the approval of society and that an open declaration of his homosexuality would not promote his advancement and success as a literary figure. Furthermore, his mother, Lady Jane Wilde, had been exerting subtle pressure on him to get married. One of her reasons was that, if the bride was well endowed financially, marriage would solve Oscar's money problems. Oscar himself was fully aware of this overwhelming advantage in terms of a leisured and comfortable existence for the future. He had already referred to money in two of his previous relationships: he described Florence Balcombe as having "not a sixpence of money";[19] and to Charlotte Montefiore he had predicted a prosperous union "with your money and my brain".[23]

By the 1880s and without any gainful employment, Oscar had no illusions about economic security, especially if his purpose in life was to "live up to his blue china". At Oxford he had twice been summoned before the Vice-Chancellor's Court for non-payment of tradesmen's bills. He had been disheartened at the relatively meagre legacies he had received from his father and his half-brother (Henry Wilson) respectively. From the former he had inherited the houses in Bray, but these had a £1000 mortgage on them and, when they were put onto the market, they were sold by two different agents to two different purchasers. This unfortunate situation had to be settled by a court case, and although Wilde won he was still liable for the untaxed costs (see page 216).

From Henry Wilson, who died in June 1877, Oscar received the paltry sum of £100 on condition that he remained a Protestant.

Thus the imperative to marry was strong. As Ellmann succinctly put it: "A wife would save him from the moralists, and a rich one from the moneylenders."[27] Ultimately it was this pursuit of a rich wife that brought Oscar to propose marriage to Miss Constance Lloyd in 1883.

Constance Lloyd's father had died in 1874 at the age of forty-six. She had a small income of her own but was expected to inherit from her paternal grandfather, John Horatio Lloyd, with whom she lived in London. He was a very wealthy man who had been responsible for introducing "Lloyd's Bonds" to provide the financial backing for the development of the British railways. Writing from his prison cell in April 1897, Oscar remarked that Mr Hargrove, who was Constance's family solicitor, had owed his own very considerable wealth to John Horatio Lloyd.[28]

At the time of Wilde's engagement to Constance, John Lloyd (aged eighty-four) was in a precarious state of health and Oscar anticipated that Constance would come in for a large bequest on his death. He probably overestimated the size of the legacy that she would actually receive. However, the realization that marriage to Constance would contribute to his financial security was a powerful incentive.

Oscar first met Constance in May 1881 through his mother, who, as Joy Melville has highlighted, played a significant part in orchestrating (or manipulating) the subsequent turn of events by fostering the relationship between the two and affording a regular meeting place for them at her London salons.[29] Lady Wilde developed a great liking for Constance and she wrote to Oscar in 1882 intimating that she wanted her as a daughter-in-law. Oscar himself appeared to be captivated by Constance. Her brother, Otho Holland Lloyd, reported to his fiancée on an afternoon gathering at his family's home when Oscar had been present: "Wherever she [Constance] went, there followed he, and when he could not approach her then with his eyes he followed her." Otho added, with a healthy dose of scepticism: "If the man were anyone else but Oscar Wilde, one might conclude that he was in love."[30]

Oscar's American tour of 1882 and his sojourn in Paris for several months in 1883 interrupted their meetings until the summer of 1883; their engagement followed in late November that year. They were married on 29 May 1884, Oscar being twenty-nine and Constance twenty-six (Figure 12).

There is no doubt that Constance was very much in love with Oscar and, as she wrote to her brother the day after the engagement: "I am engaged to Oscar Wilde and perfectly and insanely happy."[31] She wrote to Oscar before their marriage: "I love you most passionately with all the strength of my heart and mind . . . I will hold you fast with chains of love and devotion so that you

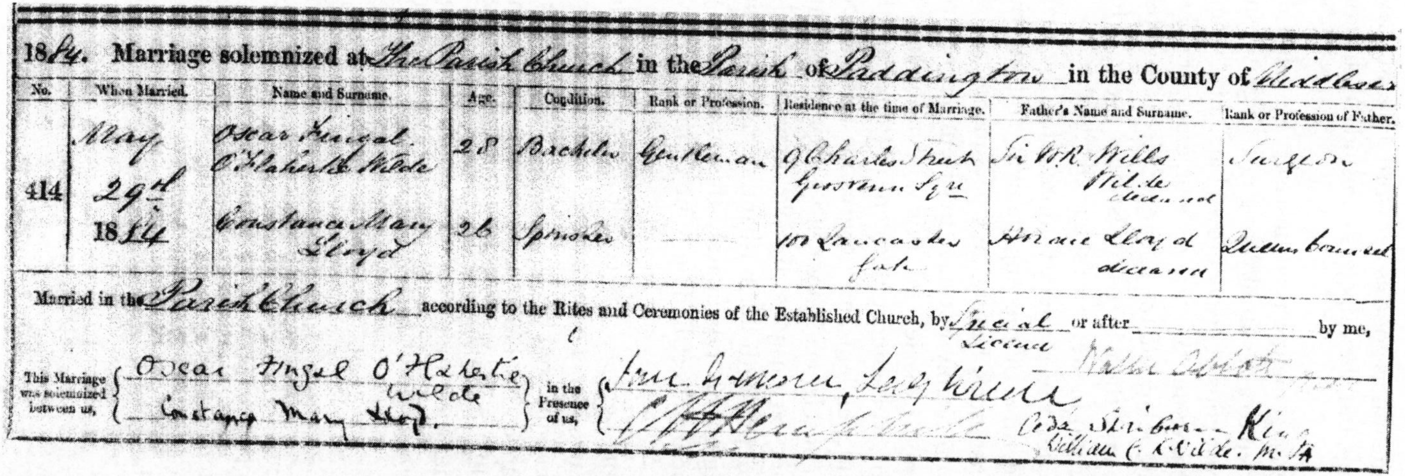

1884. Marriage solemnized at The Parish Church in the Parish of Paddington in the County of Middlesex

No.	When Married.	Name and Surname.	Age.	Condition.	Rank or Profession.	Residence at the time of Marriage.	Father's Name and Surname.	Rank or Profession of Father.
414	May 29th 1884	Oscar Fingal O'Flahertie Wilde	28	Bachelor	Gentleman	9 Charles Street Grosvenor Sqre	Sir W.R. Wills Wilde deceased	Surgeon
		Constance Mary Lloyd	26	Spinster	—	100 Lancaster Gate	Horace Lloyd deceased	Queen's Counsel

Married in the Parish Church according to the Rites and Ceremonies of the Established Church, by Special Licence or after ______ by me,

This Marriage was solemnized between us, { Oscar Fingal O'Flahertie Wilde, Constance Mary Lloyd } in the Presence of us, { Jane Francesca Lady Wilde, Ada Swinburne King, William C. K. Wilde }

Figure 12 *The entry in the marriage register for Oscar and Constance at St James's Church, Sussex Gardens, Paddington. It was witnessed by Lady Wilde, William Wilde, Ada King (Constance's mother) and Charles Hemphill. Note that, while Constance gave her age correctly as 26, Oscar declared his as 28 when in fact he was closer to 30.*

(From the records of St James's Church, Paddington, held at the Greater London Record Office, with courtesy of the Church)

shall never leave me . . ." [32] She was as good as her word; love and devotion were there throughout the marriage but she hopelessly misjudged the consequences of that love and devotion.

Oscar's reaction to the engagement was enthusiastic. He told Lillie Langtry that he was going to be married to a beautiful young girl, "a grave, slight, violet-eyed little Artemis" with "great coils of heavy brown hair" and "wonderful ivory hands".[33] To Waldo Story he wrote: "We are of course desperately in love . . . we telegraph each other twice a day, and the telegraph clerks have become quite romantic in consequence"; and then in true Oscarian style: "However, she knows I am the greatest poet, so in literature she is all right . . ."[33]

Although there was a definite monetary motive for the marriage, it is beyond dispute that at the time of the engagement and marriage he was genuinely attracted to Constance's beauty and personality and had a deep fondness for her. He would probably not have married her, regardless of her material worth, had he not experienced this affection and admiration. Constance was an intelligent, well-educated (fluent in Italian and French) and talented woman with an independent and progressive outlook on life and a strong social and political conscience. Those of Oscar's friends and acquaintances who had depicted her variously as shy, sweet, sentimental and simple but completely out of her depth with her husband's genius and brilliant gifts made a gross error of judgement. Fortunately this injudicious portrayal of Constance has been convincingly rectified by Anne Clark Amor[34,35] and Joyce Bentley.[36]

There was good rapport between the couple in the early phase of their married life. However, Oscar was in a quandary: he knew that he was decidedly homosexual and yet he had committed himself to marriage. Whatever love and affinity he felt for Constance, his basic sexual drive was inconsistent with marriage and he was not able to develop a fulfilling physical relationship with her. With the efflux of time, their fundamental sexual incompatibilities led to discord and disharmony. Bosie Douglas captured the state of the Wildes' relationship in the 1890s:

> Honesty compels me to say that Oscar during the time I knew him was not very kind to his wife . . . [H]e was still fond of her, but he was often impatient with her, and sometimes snubbed her, and he resented, and showed that he resented, the attitude of slight disapproval which she often adopted towards him. Towards the end of the time before the catastrophe . . . the relations between them were distinctly strained.[37]

There are several historical precedents for the marriage of homosexuals. Peter Illich Tchaikovsky was a committed homosexual who became increasingly self-conscious and sensitive about the negative publicity he aroused. In order to stifle this, he entered into a marriage with a mentally unstable music student in 1877, but found himself unable to perform sexually and they separated after a few weeks.[38] As he wrote following his marriage: "All that is left is to pretend. But to pretend to the end of one's life is the highest torment."

John Addington Symonds sought matrimony in an attempt to reverse his homosexuality by channeling those impulses into a heterosexual outlet. He sired four daughters in what was a passionless and duplicitous marriage, but he remained unchanged in his sexual orientation: in fact in later life he became promiscuously homosexual.[39]

After André Gide had been advised by his doctor that marriage would restore him to sexual normality, he married his first cousin Madeleine Rondeaux in 1895. Their marriage was never consummated, and Gide pursued his homosexual lifestyle with abandon while Madeleine's feelings and sensitivities were ruthlessly dismissed in favour of his own love affairs and sexual exploits.[40,41]

In more recent times Peter Wildeblood was prosecuted, convicted and gaoled for homosexual offences. In his book *Against the Law* he discussed the dilemma of becoming married, a prospect which he successfully resisted.

> I fiercely wanted to fall in love, marry and have children, as all my friends did; but this was only an abstract idea . . . There were many women whom I liked, but I could not imagine spending the next fifty years alone with them.[42]

Sir Antony Sher, the actor and author, became aware of his homosexual inclinations in adolescence and had his first gay experience at about eighteen. Nevertheless, years later, he decided to marry, and asked: "Was this my last attempt to be straight, to have that 'normal' life which everything in my upbringing pointed to?" He was confused and, not surprisingly, the marriage ended shortly afterwards.[43]

Karl Ulrichs argued that conversion of inborn homosexuals ("Urnings") into heterosexuals was usually impossible and that where marriage had ensued in these cases it had generally ended in misery for both parties.[44] Krafft-Ebing had noted from his case studies that some innately homosexual men did marry, despite their aversion to intercourse with the female. They did so from either ethical or social considerations; and while in many of these marriages there was a real friendship and regard between the couple, the man continued to experience distaste and even actual physical distress after sexual intercourse. Moreover, Krafft-Ebing observed that marriage did not curb the husband's quest for same-sex partners.[45] The marriage between Oscar and Constance, especially in the first few years, appears to have conformed to this pattern.

It is also interesting that, well over a century ago, Krafft-Ebing observed that a high proportion of his homosexual subjects had demonstrated their first awareness of homosexual urges and desires in childhood, sometimes as early as six or seven years of age.[45] While the onset of homosexual experiences may be in childhood, the recognition of homosexual orientation usually occurs by early adolescence (thirteen or fourteen) and the advent of overt sexual practices by the age of twenty.[46,47] It is unusual for such inclinations to emerge *de novo* after the age of twenty-one. It was found that gay males were more likely than heterosexual males to become sexually active at a younger age – approximately thirteen years versus sixteen.[47] Oscar Wilde was twenty-nine at the time of his engagement, and he was not only fully cognizant of his homosexual disposition but he had probably already engaged in same-sex activities. Certainly the suggestion that it was Robert Ross who first seduced him into homosexual behaviour (when Wilde was thirty-two) is highly unlikely.

A valuable psychological analysis on the married homosexual man was published by Michael Ross.[48] It was based on questionnaire data collected in Australia, New Zealand and Scandinavia in 1975 and 1978. Many of the conclusions reached are applicable to Wilde's situation; and, although this study was conducted many decades later, homosexuality still suffered significant stigmatization during the 1970s. I shall allude very briefly below to some of the more relevant findings from this monograph.

It was estimated then that ten to twenty per cent of homosexual men in Western societies entered into conventional marriages, and that the great majority knew that they were homosexual before marriage. Two-thirds of the wives did not know of their husbands' true sexual orientation at the time of the marriage and, of these, half remained in ignorance throughout. The average age at which homosexual men married was about twenty-five.

Considerable attention was focused on the motives driving the homosexual man to marry.[48] Three main categories were identified (not necessarily ranked in order): first, social pressure from external sources such as family and friends (and particularly in societies that are strongly anti-homosexual); second, as an explicit attempt to remove or de-emphasize his homosexuality (sometimes on medical advice); and, third, because he was genuinely in love with his partner, wanted to live with her and possibly sought the comfort and security of a married home life with children. There was no consistency as to which of these three factors was preponderant, but a survey conducted in the late 1970s found that the third category was commonly cited.[49] In this same study only five per cent of the married respondents reported that they had become *less* homosexual, while a quarter claimed that marriage had intensified their homosexuality. This outcome confirms the long-held belief that marriage, despite its positive social benefits, fails to modify homosexual preference. Indeed, the literature has consistently shown that sexual relations between husband and wife decreased markedly with time and often ceased, with separation or divorce following in the great majority of cases.

As discussed above, Oscar's marriage to Constance appears to have been motivated by two of the categories mentioned. There was pressure from his mother, whom he greatly loved and admired. Then there was his need for financial security as well as the desire, as a celebrity in the making, to project himself to the public as a happily married family man rather than the outlandish aesthetic figure that had previously typified him. Oscar married also because he felt himself to be in love with Constance, and there is certainly evidence that he was initially enamoured of her and her graceful and delicate qualities. Robert Sherard saw the couple on their honeymoon in Paris, and he wrote: "He [Oscar] seemed then very much in love, and said that marriage was a wonderful thing. He seemed radiantly happy . . ."[50]

As mentioned, the great majority of the wives of homosexual men were unaware of their husbands' sexual orientation at marriage, and some never learned of it. One study has examined the reactions of a sample of wives on being confronted with their husbands' homosexuality.[51] In the case where the wife was given a "positive disclosure" – that is, one made sensitively and honestly in the context of a good marriage – then, although she was mildly shaken, her reactions were empathetic and constructive. However, where there was a "negative disclosure" – that is, one made with abuse of trust, lack of concern and in the context of a poor marriage – then she was acutely shocked and became angry and hurt with a strong sense of confusion as to her identity and integrity as a woman.

Constance Wilde was kept in ignorance until virtually the start of the trials in 1895, when all was revealed to her at one fell swoop. It was the characteristically "negative disclosure" of the study just quoted. She was horrified, and in a letter to Mrs Robinson, the fortune-teller, on 19 April 1895 she wrote: "What is to become of my husband who has so betrayed and deceived me and ruined the lives of my darling boys?"[52] Furthermore, she was subsequently exposed to the full force of isolation, ostracism, and stigma to the extent that she was forced to change her name. I have discussed in Chapter 6 how Oscar's declarations of remorse and repentance in prison revived her faith in herself and enabled her to forgive him and even to contemplate a restoration of their marriage, until the saga of the life interest destroyed these intentions.

Predictably, Wilde became increasingly averse to heterosexual intercourse, and conjugal relations ceased in due course. Frank Harris quotes Oscar's alleged description of his repugnance to Constance's pregnancies:

'When I married, my wife was a beautiful girl . . . In a year or so the flower-like grace had all vanished; she became heavy, shapeless, deformed . . . with drawn blotched face and hideous body . . . It was dreadful . . . she was sick always, and – oh! I cannot recall it, it is all loathsome . . . Oh, nature is disgusting; it takes beauty and defiles it . . .'[53]

This particular account has been accepted by Wilde scholars and incorporated into many of the standard biographical works. I do not believe that Oscar ever made these imputations; they were part of Frank Harris's characteristic inventiveness. The alleged conversation between Wilde and Harris on this matter took place in Naples in the winter of 1898/1899, about nine months after Constance's death. I doubt that Oscar would ever have confided this intimate information at such a time, and especially not to Harris whom he regarded as insensitive.[54] Wilde was loyal to the memory of his late wife, and the pregnancies that he had apparently detested brought him the two sons of whom he was very fond. Ironically, Constance's two pregnancies, in quick succession, gave Oscar a welcome respite from sexual intercourse, as husbands in those days desisted during most of the pregnancy and certainly for an extended period after delivery.

The arrival of the Wildes' eldest son, Cyril, on 5 June 1885 was greeted with great delight by Oscar. Writing to his sister-in-law on the day, Oscar expressed warmth for Constance and relief that she had undergone the confinement easily and relatively painlessly (under chloroform).[55] Shortly after that he told his friend Norman Forbes Robertson: "Constance is doing capitally and is in excellent spirits . . . You must get married *at once*!"[56]

Oscar's quest for young male companionship began during the first eighteen months of his marriage. In December 1884 he communicated with nineteen-year-old Philip Griffiths, sending him a photograph of himself and requesting one of Griffiths in return "as a memory of a charming meeting and golden hours passed together".[57] In November 1885 he launched into a fairly passionate correspondence with Harry Marillier (aged twenty) and arranged a number of assignations with him.[58] That affair was intense and short-lived and it was succeeded by a friendship with the then seventeen-year-old Robert Baldwin Ross, which was to last, literally, until Oscar's last breath.

I have rejected the idea that is was Ross who seduced Wilde and converted him to homosexuality. But it may have been that, at the time of their meeting, Oscar himself had finally accepted that he was unequivocally homosexual, having experienced the non-fulfilment and distastefulness of marital sex. With that insight he was perhaps willing to partake of physical love-making with Ross in a more uninhibited way. Despite his youth, Ross had the reputation of being sexually experienced and it is possible that he introduced Wilde to novel and more ambitious forms of homosexual sex. He lived with Oscar and Constance as a paying guest in their Tite Street house for two months in 1887 whilst his mother went abroad, and this would have provided ample opportunity for intimacy and sexual experimentation. Once Ross left there was a parting of the ways and the two saw very little of each other in the ensuing years. The friendship resumed seriously only around the time of the Queensberry débâcle.

After Ross there were many other encounters, flirtations and associations with young men – some fleeting and others longer lasting – all of which have been reviewed in detail by Neil McKenna.[3] The roll-call includes Graham Robertson, Harry Melvill, Frederick Althaus, Clyde Fitch and John Gray. But the love affair *par excellence* – indeed the love affair of the era – was that between Oscar Wilde and Alfred (Bosie) Douglas. They met in June 1891 when Oscar was thirty-six and Bosie twenty, and for the first time in his life Oscar fell headlong and helplessly into a frenzy of love and passion. I shall not discuss the dynamics of this relationship, with its peaks, troughs and vicissitudes, as the subject has been thoroughly explored elsewhere.[59–61]

Wilde's love letters to Douglas – two of which achieved notoriety when they were read out at the Queensberry trial – surpassed anything he had written before in their intensity. The following are examples of some of his outpourings:

> [I]t is a marvel that those red rose-leaf lips of your should have been made no less for music than for the madness of kisses.[62]

> Oh! wait for me! wait for me! I am now, as ever since the day we met, yours devotedly and with immortal love.[63]

> My sweet rose, my delicate flower, my lily of lilies, it is perhaps in prison that I am going to test the power of love. I am going to see if I cannot make the bitter waters sweet by the intensity of the love I bear you.[64]

In later years and long after Oscar's death, Douglas maintained that it was Wilde who first made advances to him which he initially resisted. It was at least six months afterwards when he succumbed and did with Oscar "just what was done among boys at Winchester and Oxford". Sodomy never occurred between them; nor was it ever contemplated but Wilde did practise fellatio ("he sucked me"), something Douglas had not experienced before. Douglas stated that it went against his instincts ("for youth and beauty and softness") to have sex with an older man and that Wilde realized this and eventually stopped.[65]

There was no restriction for either party on sexual escapades outside the relationship. Both Oscar and Bosie pursued a rampant sex life, each in the full knowledge and with the cooperation of the other. Through Alfred Taylor, Wilde was brought into contact with a number of rent-boys and male prostitutes and, during the period when he and Bosie were at the height of their affair, Oscar was enmeshed in a web of sexual liaisons that ultimately led to his downfall.

It was a source of great puzzlement to Carson at the Queensberry trial that Wilde should have consorted with young men far below his social class (valets, grooms, newspaper boys). He dwelt *ad nauseum* on this matter throughout his cross-examination. The psychiatrists who examined Wilde at Wandsworth Prison similarly remarked on the fact that his "most disgusting and odious criminal offences were conducted with the most casual acquaintances of comparatively low social position" (see page 42). At the trial of Lord Montagu, Pitt-Rivers and Wildeblood sixty years later, the same preoccupation with social position emerged. "The real crime of Lord Montagu," wrote Wildeblood, ". . . was that he became acquainted – on no matter what basis – with a man who (to quote the prosecuting counsel) was 'infinitely his social inferior'."[66]

It was a well-known phenomenon in Victorian times that the homosexual subculture was dominated by promiscuity and prostitution that predominantly involved either working class youths in their teens or Guardsmen ("scarlet fever", as one client put it). The Cleveland Street scandal of 1889–1890 (see page 125) illustrated the quest by aristocratic and upper class men for Post Office messenger boys. Many homosexuals did not want to have sex with their friends or members of their own social class but craved a relationship across class barriers. The search for "rough trade" was influenced by the need to escape the moralistic framework of respectable society into what they perceived as the more natural, spontaneous and "animalistic" milieu of working-class prostitution.[67] Even in the modern day, European studies have concluded that most clients of male prostitutes are middle-aged men (often fathers of families) in socially advantaged positions. These individuals maintain their reputations while also satisfying their psychosexual desires by using rent-boys.[68]

It has been a source of curiosity as to what types of homosexual activities Wilde practised. Certainly kissing, caressing and close bodily contact were routine. According to the testimony of the Crown witnesses, he indulged in mutual masturbation and oral sex. He probably also participated in intercrural intercourse (between the thighs and buttocks), but the question of anal inter-course remains in doubt. Wilde was never charged with it and he himself denied it. (In fact, a sizeable proportion of homosexuals never practise anal sex.) He wrote to Ross: "[T]hough the particular offence required by the law did not find part amongst my perversities of passion, still perversities there were . . ."[69] This statement referred to the possibility of divorce, which was raised late in Oscar's imprisonment, as sodomy was the only ground on which Constance would have been able to divorce him (see page 94). Wilde refused to consider defending a divorce: "If a man gets drunk, whether he does so on white wine or red matters little, and if a man has perversities of passion there is no use his denying particular details in a civil court . . ."[70] What Wilde was implying was that he might not have committed sodomy *stricto sensu* but that he did other things that came close to it. The evidence in his criminal case of the "staining of the sheets" may have explanations apart from anal intercourse, such as the diarrhoea line of defence that was actually advanced by Sir Edward Clarke. There is of course the more likely possibility that digital insertion into the rectum was performed.

Prison did little to douse Wilde's sexual appetite. On the contrary, his post-imprisonment career in France and Italy was spent in vigorous pursuit of a legion of lads and young men with whom he enjoyed an almost continual spell of erotic titillation and sensual pleasures – and without fear of the law. He resumed his relationship with Bosie and for ten weeks they shared a house in Naples. One of the more enduring friendships during his exile was with Maurice Gilbert, who was with Oscar until his death and who took the now famous deathbed photograph (Figure 10, page 110).

A query that is sometimes raised is the stage at which Oscar terminated sexual relations with Constance. It is of course not possible to give a reliable answer to this. Some authors have suggested that Oscar and Constance never resumed sexual intercourse after the birth of the younger son, Vyvyan, in November 1886. The fact that there were no further pregnancies in an other-wise fertile couple who had produced two children in as many years, and in an era when the practice of contraception was in its early stages and not widely practised, does support this contention.[71] When Arthur Ransome published his book *Oscar Wilde: A Critical Study* in February 1912, he made the observation that Constance Wilde was "sentimental, pretty, well-meaning and inefficient" and he proceeded to criticize her for her inadequacy and lack of strength and influence on the marriage. This appraisal annoyed Otho Holland Lloyd, her brother, who promptly riposted with a letter of protest to Ransome in which *inter alia* he noted that Oscar had brought no love to the marriage and that he had in fact "practically divorced" Constance from 1885 onwards.[72] An insight into the state of their marriage in the 1890s is revealed when the Wildes were invited to stay with their wealthy friends Jean and Walter Palmer at their country house in Reading. Oscar ungraciously telegraphed his acceptance of the invitation provided that "you will give us two rooms, one for Mrs Wilde and one for me".73

In conclusion, we return to the notion mooted in the title of this chapter. Was Oscar Wilde a gay martyr? My answer to this is negative. A martyr, according to the standard dictionary definitions, is one who voluntarily suffers death as a penalty for adherence to a belief, faith or principle; or one who suffers and sacrifices his or her life or position or reputation for the sake of an ideology or a cause. It is on the basis of the latter criterion that we have to judge whether Wilde measures up to martyrdom.

It is true that Wilde suffered arduous imprisonment and widespread ostracism as a result of his conviction for homosexual offences. It is true that Section Eleven of the Criminal Law Amendment Act was a thoroughly pernicious piece of legislation. But in order to qualify for the designation of "gay martyr", Wilde would have had to suffer his imprisonment and the destruction of his reputation and career by unquestioningly submitting himself to these privations and penalties in order to uphold and advance the cause of homosexual liberation as articulated by John Addington Symonds, Edward Carpenter and Havelock Ellis.

The most decisive argument against the case for martyrdom is that, far from promoting homosexuality as an alternative and legitimate lifestyle, Wilde actually denounced it. He did so by prosecuting the Marquess of Queensberry for criminal libel. Queensberry accused him of posing as a sodomite and Wilde took him to court on this charge. Wilde therefore regarded the state of being (or posing as) a sodomite as defamatory to his good name and dignity: in effect, he was reinforcing the prevailing view that to be labelled as a sodomite, whether posing or not, was an abomination. Unwittingly he was *harming* the cause and aligning himself with forces of social purity and moralism.

During the Queensberry trial and his two subsequent criminal trials, Oscar steadfastly rejected the evidence that he had had any unnatural or indecent relationships with rent-boys. He was however forced to admit under cross-examination that he was attracted to young males and revelled in their company. And it was in the first criminal trial that Oscar made his celebrated speech from the dock in response to prosecutor Charles Gill's request that he define the "love that dare not speak its name". His reply, impromptu as it was, was brilliant and moving and it evoked a spontaneous outburst of applause from the gallery:

'The love that dare not speak its name' in this century is such a great affection of an elder for a younger man as there was between David and Jonathan, such as Plato made the very basis of his philosophy, and such as you find in the sonnets of Michelangelo and Shakespeare . . . It is in this century misunderstood, so much misunderstood that it may be described as the 'Love that dare not speak its name', and on account of it I am placed where I am now. It is beautiful, it is fine, it is the noblest form of affection. There is nothing unnatural about it. It is intellectual, and it repeatedly exists between an elder and a younger man, when the elder has intellect, and the younger man has all the joy, hope, and glamour of life before him. That it should be so, the world does not understand. The world mocks at it and sometimes puts one in the pillory for it.[74]

The above was the only occasion when Wilde made a quasi-public affirmation of the spiritual nature and noble quality of the ancient Greek ideal of *paiderastia*.

In Chapter 4 I discussed Wilde's petition to the Home Secretary (2 July 1896) in which he prayed for an early release and unrestrainedly depicted his past sexual behaviour in such explicit terms as "sexual monomania of a terrible character", "monstrous sexual perversion", and "the most revolting passions". Admittedly these descriptions were intended to woo the sympathies of the authorities and they were written at a time when Oscar was in a state of depression and anxiety, aggravated by prolonged solitary confinement. Thus the contents of the petition have to be evaluated against this background of isolation and deprivation as well as Wilde's mounting apprehension and desperation. Nevertheless, they categorically rebut any notions of martyrdom; rather they signify a repudiation of homosexuality and an endorsement that homosexual acts are pathological and perverse.

Even after his release from prison Wilde was somewhat tentative and insecure about his homosexuality. He felt slightly ashamed of his previous lifestyle and this sense of embarrassment is conveyed in his communications to heterosexual friends. To Mrs Stannard he wrote: "Still I am conscious that I was leading a life quite unworthy of an artist in every way, and unworthy of a son of my dear mother . . ."[75] To Major Nelson, governor of Reading Prison, to whom he sent a letter of gratitude ten days after his release, he confessed: "I am not a scrap ashamed of having been in prison. I am horribly ashamed of the materialism of the life that brought me there. It was quite unworthy of an artist."[76] To William Rothenstein he was more explanatory about his self-criticism . He was not prepared to say that heterosexual love was better than its homosexual counterpart or that one was all right and the other all wrong. "I know simply that a life of definite and studied materialism . . . and a cult of sensual and senseless ease, are bad things for an artist . . ."[77] Note the consistency with which Wilde measured his previous lifestyle against the standards of the artist.

On the other hand, in reaction to nasty remarks made about him and Bosie Douglas when the two lived together in Naples, Oscar complained to Ross: "To have altered my life would have been to have admitted that Uranian [homosexual] love is ignoble. I hold it to be noble – more noble than other forms."[78] Wilde fully recognized his homosexuality but he seemingly harboured an ambivalent attitude towards it. Moreover, he did not want his role as a homosexual to be overemphasized. He wrote in December 1897 that "there has been more in my life than a love for Narcissus, or a passion for Sporus [male sexual partner]: fascinating though both may be".[79]

A surprising omission is that Wilde did not take up the homosexual cause while he was in exile. He could easily have done so and without any penalty to himself. He could have written one of his characteristically cogent and lucid letters to an English newspaper, denouncing the iniquity and inhumanity of Section Eleven of the Criminal Law Amendment Act and suggesting, as he had done at the Old Bailey, the alternative model of male-male love as practised in Ancient Greece. Such a contribution would have had considerable credibility, coming from one who had enjoyed celebrity status and popularity as an author and dramatist and then fallen foul of the law and suffered imprisonment. It might have had some positive impact on the public and on the authorities, if only to stimulate reflection and discourse and bring the issue into an open forum.

One of the undoubted consequences of the Wilde trials was that homosexuality became an unmentionable subject, and it took another sixty years before it could be debated again in an objective and constructive way. Oscar Wilde had already proved that his opinions produced an effect. His two persuasive letters to the *Daily Chronicle*[80] on the detestable conditions in English prisons had a decided influence in promoting penal reform. His *Ballad of Reading Gaol*, a poignant denunciation of capital punishment, was an instant success and went through five editions within the first month of its first appearance. Wilde was aware of the effectiveness of his input: "I have been able to deal a heavy and fatal blow at the monstrous prison-system of English justice. There is to be no more starvation, nor sleeplessness, nor endless silence, nor eternal solitude, nor brutal floggings".[81] He had the perfect opportunity to strike yet another blow – as an advocate for a tolerant approach towards homosexuals and a recognition of their rights. His studied and wilful silence signalled his indifference in the matter and failed to support the crusade launched by Symonds, Carpenter and Havelock Ellis.

In an ironic sense it was Oscar Wilde himself who, through the prosecution of Queensberry and its aftermath, rocked the boat for British homosexuals. Until then – and despite Section Eleven – the police had generally turned a blind eye to their activities, which they were allowed to pursue without harassment as long as their behaviour was conducted discreetly. But the conviction and sentence of Wilde galvanized British society into what Macaulay called "one of its periodic fits of morality". The case dramatically sensitized people to the horror of same-sex relationships and excited emotions of hate and disgust. The press, with very few exceptions, was vitriolic and vicious and played a major part in crushing Wilde's reputation, sending him and his works into banishment. (Had he not earlier punned, "In the old days men had the rack. Now they have the Press"?) One example was the London evening paper the *Echo*, which on the day of his arrest (5 April 1895) wrote:

> Mr Oscar Wilde is 'damned and done for'. The best thing for everybody now is to forget all about Oscar Wilde, his perpetual posings, his aesthetical teachings and his theatrical productions. Let him go into silence, and be heard no more.

Shortly after Oscar's arrest and weeks before he was actually convicted, the rot had set in. George Alexander was among the first to yield to the pressure of adverse publicity when he removed the name of Oscar Wilde from the posters and programmes of *The Importance of Being Earnest*, which was then playing at his St James's Theatre (Figure 13). This extinction of Wilde's identity became pervasive and prolonged. When Alexander revived the play at the St James's in 1902, he again did so with Wilde's name deleted from the advertising bills and programmes and with "the author of Lady Windermere's Fan" substituted.

A stunning but little known instance of the symbolic annihilation of Oscar Wilde occurred in respect of William Powell Frith's famous painting *The Private View of the Royal Academy (1881)*. This shows a young Wilde in the foreground surrounded by a small group of admirers, and it features among the crowd several eminent personalities of the day including Gladstone, Lord Leighton, Henry Irving, Ellen Terry and Lillie Langtry. The picture was unveiled at the Royal Academy's Summer Exhibition in 1883 and caused a sensation with the public. During Wilde's trials, Frith wrote to the owner of the painting offering to paint over the offending head at no extra cost! "I will do whatever you wish as regards Wilde – it is unfortunate for the picture but what could be so inconceivably unexpected."[82]

Oscar Wilde is being portrayed today as a gay martyr. As I have attempted to show in this chapter, the application of such an epithet to him is unfounded.

Programme of Music.

MARCH	"Tourniquet"	Louis Ganne
FANTASIE	"Pagliacci"	Leoncavallo
BOURREE	"L'auvergnate"	Ganne
MOUVEMENT DE VALSE	"Douce Caresse"	E. Gillet
WALZER	"Minnesinger"	Sobathil

The Furniture by FRANK GILES & CO., High Street, Kensington.

The Wigs by W. CLARKSON.

The Scenery by H. P. HALL and WALTER HANN.

NO FEES. The Theatre is lighted by Electricity. **NO FEES.**

The Attendants are strictly forbidden to accept gratuities, and are liable to instant dismissal should they do so. Visitors to the Theatre are earnestly begged to assist the Management in carrying out a regulation framed for their comfort and convenience.

The Etchings and Engravings in the corridors and vestibule supplied and arranged by I. P. MENDOZA, King Street, St. James's.

The Floral Decorations by REEP & CO., King Street, St. James's.

Photographs of the Artistes appearing at this Theatre, can be obtained of ALFRED ELLIS, 20, Upper Baker Street, N.W.

FIRST MATINEE SATURDAY, FEBRUARY 23rd, at 3.

PRICES:—Private Boxes, £1 11s. 6d. to £4 4s. Stalls, 10s. 6d. Dress Circle, 7s. Upper Boxes, Numbered and Reserved (Bonnets allowed), 4s. Pit, 2s. 6d. Gallery, 1s.

Box Office (Mr. Arnold) open daily from 10 till 5 o'clock, and 8 till 10 p.m.

Seats can be booked one month in advance by Letter or Telegram, or Telephone No. 3908.

ST. JAMES'S THEATRE,

SOLE LESSEE AND PROPRIETOR, MR. GEORGE ALEXANDER.

Thursday, February 14th, 1895,

AND EVERY EVENING AT 8.40.

The Importance of being Earnest,

A TRIVIAL COMEDY FOR SERIOUS PEOPLE.

BY OSCAR WILDE.

John Worthing, J.P. (of the Manor House, Woolton, Hertfordshire)		Mr. GEORGE ALEXANDER
Algernon Moncrieff (his Friend)		Mr. ALLAN AYNESWORTH
Rev. Canon Chasuble, D.D. (Rector of Woolton)		Mr. H. H. VINCENT
Merriman (Butler to Mr. Worthing)		Mr. FRANK DYALL
Lane (Mr. Moncrieff's Man-servant)		Mr. F. KINSEY PEILE
Lady Bracknell		Miss ROSE LECLERCQ (By permission of Mr. J. COMYNS CARR)
Hon. Gwendolen Fairfax (her Daughter)		Miss IRENE VANBRUGH
Cecily Cardew (John Worthing's Ward)		Miss EVELYN MILLARD
Miss Prism (her Governess)		Mrs GEORGE CANNINGE

Time - The Present.

Act I. Algernon Moncrieff's Rooms in Piccadilly (H. P. Hall)

Act II. The Garden at the Manor House, Woolton (H. P. Hall)

Act III. Morning-Room at the Manor House, Woolton (Walter Hann)

Preceded, at 8.20, by a Play in One Act by LANGDON E. MITCHELL, entitled

IN THE SEASON.

Sir Harry Collingwood	Mr. HERBERT WARING
Edward Fairburne	Mr. ARTHUR ROYSTON
Sybil March	Miss ELLIOTT PAGE

Scene - A Room in Sir Harry Collingwood's House   Time - The Present.

ST. JAMES'S THEATRE.

SOLE LESSEE AND PROPRIETOR . . MR. GEORGE ALEXANDER.

PRODUCED THURSDAY, FEBRUARY 14th, 1895.

TO-NIGHT at 9,

(Last Nights of)

The Importance of being Earnest,

A TRIVIAL COMEDY FOR SERIOUS PEOPLE.

John Worthing, J.P.	(of the Manor House, Woolton, Hertfordshire	Mr. GEORGE ALEXANDER
Algernon Moncrieffe	(his Friend)	Mr. ALLAN AYNESWORTH
Rev. Canon Chasuble, D.D.	(Rector of Woolton)	Mr. H. H. VINCENT
Merriman	(Butler to Mr. Worthing)	Mr. FRANK DYALL
Lane	(Mr. Moncrieffe's Man-servant)	Mr. F. KINSEY PEILE
Lady Bracknell		Mrs EDWARD SAKER
Hon. Gwendolen Fairfax	(her Daughter)	Miss IRENE VANBRUGH
Cecily Cardew	(John Worthing's Ward)	Miss EVELYN MILLARD
Miss Prism	(her Governess)	Mrs GEORGE CANNINGE

Time - - The Present.

Act I.	Algernon Moncrieffe's Rooms in Piccadilly (H. P. Hall)
Act II.	The Garden at the Manor House, Woolton (H. P. Hall)
Act III.	Morning-Room at the Manor House, Woolton (Walter Hann)

Preceded, at 8.30, by a Play in One Act, by LANGDON E. MITCHELL, entitled

IN THE SEASON.

Sir Harry Collingwood	Mr. HERBERT WARING
Edward Fairbourne	Mr. ARTHUR ROYSTON
Sybil March	Miss ELLIOTT PAGE

Scene - A Room in Sir Harry Collingwood's House.   Time - The Present.

Programme of Music.

MARCH	"Geradeaus"	C. L. Unrath
INTERMEZZO	"Forget-me-not"	A. Macbeth
VALSE	"Enfin Seuls"	A. M. Fedner
SPANISH BALLET MUSIC		Desormes
VALSE.	"Bravura"	Otto Roeder
SELECTION	"Faust"	Gounod
VALSE	"My Dream of You"	Otto Roeder
MARCH	"Serbischer Parade"	Th. Cursch-Bühren

The Furniture by FRANK GILES & Co., High Street, Kensington,
The Wigs by W. CLARKSON.
The Scenery by H. P. HALL and WALTER HANN.

NO FEES.   The Theatre is lighted by Electricity.   NO FEES.

The Attendants are strictly forbidden to accept gratuities, and are liable to instant dismissal should they do so.
Visitors to the Theatre are earnestly begged to assist the Management in carrying out a regulation framed for their comfort and convenience.

The Etchings and Engravings in the corridors and vestibule supplied and arranged by
L. P. MANSOSA, King Street, St. James's.
The Floral Decorations by RAES & Co., King Street, St. James's.
Photographs of the Artistes appearing at this Theatre, can be obtained of ALFRED ELLIS,
20, Upper Baker Street, N.W.

"THE TRIUMPH OF THE PHILISTINES,"

And How Mr. Jorgan preserved the morals of Market Pewbury under very trying circumstances,

an original Comedy in Three Acts,

By HENRY ARTHUR JONES.

WILL BE PRODUCED SATURDAY MAY 11.

PRICES.—Private Boxes, £1 11s. 6d. to £4 4s.   Stalls, 10s. 6d.   Dress Circle, 7s.
Upper Boxes, Numbered and Reserved (Bonnets allowed), 4s.   Pit, 2s. 6d.   Gallery, 1s
Doors open at 8.   Commence at 8.30.   Carriages at 10.45.
Box Office (Mr. Arnold) open daily from 10 till 5 o'clock, and 8 till 10 p.m.
Seats can be booked one month in advance by Letter or Telegram, or Telephone No. 902.

Figure 13   *Theatre programmes for the first and last nights of "The Importance of Being Earnest". Note that Oscar Wilde's name has been deleted from the later programme owing to the scandal that erupted after the Queensberry libel trial. It is ironic that the play scheduled to replace Wilde's was entitled "The Triumph of the Philistines".*

(Private collection)

155

Oscar had many attributes, but the one that was indubitably absent from his profile was martyrdom. George Bernard Shaw wrote: "Martyrdom is the only way in which a man can become famous without ability." I am certain that Wilde, with his extraordinary ability and hypertrophied egotism, would have heartily agreed.

10

OSCAR AS OTHERS SAW HIM

WHEN Oscar Wilde landed in New York in January 1882 to undertake his lecturing tour of America, he became famous for (reputedly) saying to the customs officer: "I have nothing to declare except my genius." (The astute and not-to-be-outdone official was rumoured to have retorted: "That, sir, is a commodity that does not need protection in the United States.") Wilde was right – he was a genius of a particular kind. His impromptu wit and his extraordinary flair for epigrams and one-liners were hallmarks of his brilliance. He had the ability to turn platitudes into paradoxes, to make the commonplace unusual and even bizarre, and to convert reality into absurdity. He was a magician-wordsmith, a verbal prestidigitator who could juggle ideas and concepts and make them reappear in a slightly different format but with an entirely different meaning. This capacity for nimble mental gymnastics was a very special skill, linked to an exceptional intellect. But Wilde's intellectual prowess was not confined to the sphere of witty aphorisms and humorous remarks; he had been highly proficient academically both at school and university.

At Portora Royal he was a prizeman in the junior school in 1866, and in his last two years there (1869–1871) he distinguished himself in Greek, winning the Carpenter Prize for Greek Testament in 1870. He was one of three pupils to be awarded a Royal School Scholarship to Trinity College Dublin, and in the entrance (matriculation) examination to the College he obtained second place. While at Trinity he proved to be very competent in a wide range of classical studies. In a competitive scholarship examination in 1873 Oscar came sixth out of the ten successful candidates. He continued to excel in Greek, and he ended his career at Trinity in 1874 by winning the Berkeley Gold Medal for Greek (a medal which penury subsequently forced him to pawn from time to time). His performance in Latin was not quite so strong, but the subject in which Oscar consistently struggled and did not make the grade was arithmetic. He scored only two out of ten in the Trinity entrance examination, and he was generally regarded as a dunce in mathematics.[1] Oscar did not complete his degree at Trinity College because in June 1874 he won one of the two demyships (scholarships) in classics at Magdalen College, Oxford, having achieved the highest mark in the qualifying examination.

Wilde's academic record at Oxford was impressive. Admittedly he was about two years older than the average entering undergraduate, and his three-year course of study in classics at Trinity College had given him a definite head start over his fellow students. He obtained a First in Classical Moderations ("Mods") in 1876 and a First in "Greats" in 1878 and was allegedly top in both examinations.[2] It was obvious that Oscar worked hard in order to achieve these distinctions although, according to his contemporaries, he liked to pose as a man who never worked or as a dilettante trifling with his books.[2] It is often remarked that the attainment of a double First in Greats at Oxford was a rare accomplishment and that Oscar was exceptional in this respect. This is not strictly the case. Just over twenty per cent of the candidates who sat Moderations and Greats at the same time as Oscar achieved a First in each examination; and of the eighteen who gained a First in the Greats examination, sixteen had also secured a First in Moderations.[3] Thus Oscar was one of sixteen in his cohort of qualifiers who had scored a double First.

Wilde's crowning glory at Oxford was winning the Newdigate Prize in June 1878 for his poem *Ravenna* and reciting it in the Sheldonian Theatre (Figure 14). He also happened to be the first member of Magdalen College to have won the Newdigate and for this honour he received an additional accolade in the form of a marble bust. "The dons are 'astonied' beyond words," wrote Wilde, "the Bad Boy doing so well in the end!"[4]

Whatever Oscar Wilde's academic, literary or theatrical legacy, the generations that have succeeded him have been deprived of his most astounding talent. He was an outstanding talker, raconteur and conversationalist, and had he lived in the present time he would have cut an extraordinarily appealing figure as a radio personality or as a participant in television talk shows.

The one statement about Wilde that has received unqualified and unanimous endorsement is that his talk and conversation were legendary. To George Bernard Shaw, Wilde was "the greatest *raconteur* in the world" and "the best English speaking talker, of whom we have any record in his time".[5] W.B. Yeats commented as follows: "I never before heard a man talking with perfect sentences, as if he had written them all overnight with labour and yet all spontaneous." To William Rothenstein he was "an unique talker and story-teller ... I have certainly never heard his equal".[7] Wilfred Scaven Blunt wrote: "He was without exception the most brilliant talker I have ever come across, the most ready, the most witty, the most audacious. Nobody could pretend to outshine him, or even to shine at all in his company."[8]

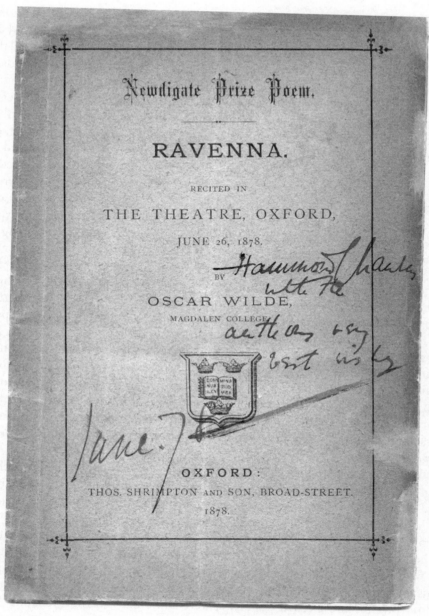

Figure 14 *The earliest recorded presentation copy of a book by Oscar Wilde (June 1878): the Newdigate Prize Poem "Ravenna". It was inscribed to Hammond Chambers, a friend of Wilde's and a fellow undergraduate at Magdalen College, Oxford. One wit quipped that many people had won the Newdigate but never before had the Newdigate won an Oscar!*

(Private collection)

Oscar was an inveterate talker although, as several writers have pointed out, he did not prevent others from speaking. It was just that once he had started on a subject or a story the eloquence of his voice, his mellifluous patter, and the whimsical quality of the content became so enchanting that nobody would dare to interrupt. He was a supreme maestro at the dinner table and was frequently invited to dinner parties specifically to entertain the company. He would begin by conversing with his neighbour, but soon his alluring voice and the rhythm and melody of his talk would catch the ears of the other diners; they would then be drawn into listening until the entire gathering would be held spellbound in what had become a monologue in full flood. Theodore Wratislaw related a weekend visit he made to Wilde at Goring-on-Thames during the summer of 1893. After dinner the two of them returned to the drawing-room where Oscar stretched himself on a settee and talked for some two hours and a half, "an experience which few can have known, and many might envy, to listen for so long to so marvellous a conversationalist".[9]

Wilde's conversational virtuosity was such that even the best of his written work was, as André Gide realized, merely a pale reflection of his brilliant talk. It was said that those who heard him speak found it disappointing to read him. The dialogue of his plays was often an imitation of his own repartee, but it lacked the vibrancy and resonance of Oscar's personal delivery. He recognized at an early stage the effectiveness and attractiveness of his spontaneous wit and humour, and it was with some embarrassment that Robert Ross confided to Adela Schuster, after Wilde's death, that he used to write down what Oscar said during the time he stayed with the Wildes in Tite Street in 1887. He gave Oscar his notes, which were then adapted for one of the later plays that was composed in great haste (probably *The Importance of Being Earnest*).[10]

Wilde was formidable in the cut-and-thrust of a two-way exchange, such as an interview with newspaper reporters. His mental acuity and quick-wittedness were exceptional in this setting and, quite effortlessly, he was capable of squashing his interlocutor with a round of quick-fire replies. The most conspicuous example was his verbal duel with Edward Carson during his cross-examination in the Queensberry trial. Here Oscar was pitted against a highly skilled barrister, who had not only prepared his brief meticulously but also held the trump cards. Wilde's rapid processing of the damning and often unexpected questions, and his prompt and incisive responses, were admirable. Merlin Holland's *Irish Peacock & Scarlet Marquess*[11] has provided a factually accurate, yet spirited, replay of that trial, and it is clear to me that although Oscar lost the case he won the verbal battle against Carson. There was, however, the glaring instance when Wilde's repartee betrayed him. Carson asked whether he had ever kissed the young servant Walter Grainger. "Oh, no, never in my life; he was a peculiarly plain boy . . . very ugly . . . " Carson swiftly pounced on this slip and launched into a merciless bout of interrogation.

Wilde's facility for epigrammatic wit and humour made him perhaps the greatest exponent of this art. He is certainly one of the most quotable persons of all time and his epigrams are as fresh today as they were more than a century ago. In dictionaries of humorous quotations (e.g., the *Oxford Dictionary of Humorous Quotations* (2004) and *The Penguin Dictionary of Modern Humorous Quotations* (2009)), the entries under Oscar Wilde are more abundant than for any other individual. *The Importance of Being Earnest* is the best known and most quoted play in world literature, second only to *Hamlet*. Even when he spoke French he was close to perfect. Gustave Le Rouge wrote: "Oscar Wilde expressed himself in French without trace of an accent and with a purity and correctness that were disconcerting."[12]

Oscar was always in need of an audience even if – as in the case of Theodore Wratislaw – it was an audience of one. He needed approval, applause and acclaim. Without such a milieu he was insecure and frustrated, and this is the reason that his exile on the Continent and his isolation from the public weighed so heavily on him. To a large extent his creativity depended on the availability of a vehicle by which to exhibit it. The writing of plays best suited his tempera-ment because, once these were produced on stage, he was able to revel in the "wave after wave of laughter curling and foaming round the theatre" (in the words of the dramatic critic William Archer). Furthermore, playwriting involved a series of socially-reinforcing encounters preceding the public production of the work, namely, with the director and actors.

Was Oscar Wilde a showman? There is no doubt that he was and that his showmanship contributed significantly to his high visibility. His aim was to be constantly in the public eye. In a questionnaire that he filled in as an Oxford undergraduate in 1877, his response to the question "What is your aim in life?" was "Success: fame or even notoriety".[13] This ambition was already entrenched at the age of twenty-two and it reflects a precocious self-confidence. His consis-tently superior academic record from Portora Royal School onwards had undoubtedly fuelled his belief in his ability and future potential.

His parental background also influenced Oscar's outlook since it was one in which publicity, fame and even a touch of notoriety had featured strongly. His father, Sir William Wilde, was an eccentric and flamboyant character with the reputation of being a philanderer. He had excelled in a number of diverse pursuits: he was not only an acknowledged medical expert in ophthalmology and otology (and the author of a definitive text on aural surgery) but also a clas-sicist, historian, literary scholar and antiquarian. He won several honours and was appointed Surgeon Oculist to the Queen in Ireland. His work as Census Commissioner in Ireland (1851), in which he organized the collection of medical data, earned him a knighthood in 1864.[14] In that same year his name was dragged into a scandalous libel trial in which he was accused of raping a patient.[15]

Oscar's mother, Jane Wilde ("Speranza"), was a larger-than-life woman who, in her younger days (and particularly during the Irish potato famine of 1845–1851), had courageously championed the Irish nationalist cause against the English and did so passionately in the form of militant and inflammatory verse and prose.[15] She had distinct feminist leanings, was adept in several European languages and published several books. She was noted for her salons in Dublin and in London, at which she entertained the literati and *cognoscenti* of the day and over which she presided as a *grand dame*, attired in bizarre costumes and bedecked in ornate headdresses and quaint jewellery. She, like her son Oscar, had sparkling conversational gifts. Oscar was devoted to his mother, and her early bohemian influences on him must have laid the template for some of his future behaviour. Moreover, as a child he and his elder brother were exposed to sophisticated and uninhibited table talk at their parents' dinners, attended by illustrious and highly articulate guests. This rich cultural and intellectual heritage of Oscar's formative years certainly left its imprint; and it is probably true to say that in terms of heredity (from both sides) and environment Oscar Wilde had one of the most extraordinary endowments that any child could have desired.

Wilde's entrée into showmanship began seriously with his advocacy and promotion of the "Aesthetic Movement". His first major inroad into London artistic society was as an undergraduate, when he managed to secure an invitation to the official opening of the Grosvenor Gallery on 1 May 1877. This was a glittering occasion at which luminaries such as the Prince of Wales, Gladstone, John Ruskin, and Henry James were guests. Oscar resolved to make his presence felt and he arrived in a coat that was specially tailored at the back to resemble the outline of a cello.[16] To ensure that he made a more lasting impact, he followed up his visit with an article entitled "The Grosvenor Gallery", which ranked as his first published prose work and appeared in the *Dublin University Magazine* in July 1877.

After his arrival in London from Oxford he cultivated an image of himself as a self-styled "professor of Aesthetics and art critic". He did this by his aesthetic pronouncements, by his association with artistic personalities (for example, Whistler) and by attending art exhibitions and openly stating his opinions. He recognized the importance of permeating the higher echelons of society. When his first volume of poems was published (1881), he sent copies to people like Gladstone, Matthew Arnold and Robert Browning. He sought out glamorous women such as Lillie Langtry and Ellen Terry and captivated them with his verbal skills, wit and flattery. Coupled with these overtures he developed an appropriate appearance with long hair down to his shoulders and a conspicuous but carefully modulated dress sense. It was a sustained process of ostentation, and it succeeded. His daring antics and avant-garde demeanour contrasted sharply with the sombre late Victorian landscape. Wilde was quickly identified and soon portrayed as the prototype of the Aesthetic Movement. George du Maurier of *Punch* incorporated drawings of aesthetic young men into his cartoons and some of his characters bore a physical resemblance to Wilde. It has been argued recently that, rather than *Punch* imitating Oscar, it was Oscar who modelled himself on Du Maurier's caricatures. Indeed there does seem to have been some kind of mutually interactive and self-verifying equilibrium between *Punch*'s Du Maurier and Oscar Wilde so that the journal and the aesthete enhanced their popularity and image, respectively.

William Powell Frith made Wilde a dominant figure in his *A Private View of the Academy (1881)*. But Oscar's greatest publicity coup came towards the end of 1881 with an offer from the D'Oyly Carte Opera Company in New York to "export" him to the United States of America and Canada to lecture on the new aesthetic creed (satirized in Gilbert and Sullivan's *Patience*) of which he was accounted the leading protagonist. For one who had only recently come to London as a virtual nonentity, Wilde's meteoric rise to prominence was attributable only to his exceptional capacity for showmanship and self-advertisement. The Polish actress Helen Modjeska was thoroughly baffled when she tried to fathom what Wilde had actually done: "Oh yes, he talks well, but what has he done? He has written nothing, he does not sing or paint or act – he does nothing but talk. I do not understand."

Wilde's North American tour, which lasted a year, was highly successful, and he travelled the length and breadth of the country giving lectures on art and aestheticism to audiences from all walks of life as well as being interviewed by importunate newspaper reporters at every port of call. He boasted to friends at home how rapturous his reception had been, "more wonderful than even Dickens had".[17] He described the flood of requests for autographs and locks of hair so that the two secretaries delegated to these tasks had developed writer's cramp and baldness respectively! He played the part of the aesthete and dressed accordingly. With his long, straight hair falling on his shoulders, he was fastidiously attired in black velvet jacket, white waistcoat, brilliant blue or green tie, knee breeches, red silk stockings, slippers – and all of these supplemented with a wide-brimmed hat, ivory cane and a bouquet of sunflowers.

It is interesting that once he had exhausted the possibilities of his exaggerated aesthetic attire he discarded it. "The Oscar of the first period is dead," he would say as he transformed himself into the refined dandy with shorter locks of hair, frock coat and buttonhole flower, gloves and shoes of the latest fashion. Arthur Fish, Wilde's assistant editor on *The Woman's World*, described Oscar in his workaday elegance:

> Always well groomed, but without any marked extravagance or eccentricities, he was easily the best dressed man in the establishment. In winter a long fur-lined coat with heavy fur collar and cuffs; in summer a pale-grey frock-coat suit, and always a silk hat of super-glossiness. On his cheerful days there would be a buttonhole of Parma violets.[18]

This capacity of Wilde's to switch roles and change his image was inherent in his personality and he had honed it to a remarkable degree. It characterized him as an accomplished poseur, a superb masquerader, and it is epitomized in his pronouncement that "I love acting – it is so much more real than life".

Posing and posturing became such an essential ingredient of Wilde's behaviour that it became difficult at times to differentiate the real Oscar from the façade or persona; or in conversation with him to know whether he was expressing a genuine opinion or sentiment or merely perplexing his listener with clever paradoxes and verbal ambiguities. He evinced this characteristic when he told a New York reporter that to have walked down Piccadilly with a poppy or a lily was nothing – but to make people think one had done it was a triumph. The paramountcy of "being clever" over "being sincere and honest" was admitted by Wilde himself to Arthur Conan Doyle: "Between me and life there is a mist of words always. I throw probability out of the window for the sake of a phrase, and the chance of an epigram makes me desert the truth."[19]

Wilde's penchant for posing was one of the dominant themes in his life. Robert Ross noted that Oscar, broken as he was in prison, "would hastily assume one of his hundred artificial manners, which he has for every person and every occasion".[20] Arthur Symons crystallized this aspect of Oscar's character:

> His intellect was dramatic, and the whole man was not so much a personality as an attitude. Without being a sage, he maintained the attitude of a sage; without being a poet, he maintained the attitude of a poet; without being an artist, he maintained the attitude of an artist. And it was precisely in his attitudes that he was most sincere.[21]

On the other hand, Arthur Ransome gave a different interpretation:

> Wilde 'posed' as an aesthete. He was an aesthete. He 'posed' as brilliant. He was brilliant. He 'posed' as cultured. He was cultured. The

quality in him to which the word applied was not pretence, though that was willingly suggested, but display.[22]

The upshot of these two perspectives is that whatever poses Wilde chose to adopt were those which he knew he could successfully act out. For example, he could appropriately play the part of the aesthete and the art critic because he had the underlying predisposition and insight for these roles.

It is significant that the Marquess of Queensberry concentrated his attack on Wilde's "posing". He accused him of *posing* as a sodomite not only because this reduced the gravity of the accusation in a legal sense but because Queensberry believed that "posing" had an even more sinister connotation than actually "being a sodomite". In his cross-examination of Oscar during the libel trial, Carson also latched onto the concept. "'Pose' is a favourite word of yours, I think?" To which Wilde answered: "Is it? I have no 'pose' in the matter." And at a later stage Wilde told Carson: "Yes, I don't pose as being ordinary – good heavens! – I don't pose as being ordinary." This was in response to the question as to whether one of Oscar's extravagant letters to Bosie Douglas was "extraordinary".[23]

The irony of the situation was that Wilde was not posing as a homosexual: he was a dyed-in-the-wool homosexual. If he was posing, it was as a happily married heterosexual man. And this was one of his few poses that turned out to be an outright failure and disaster.

Wilde's acknowledged propensity for posing was coupled with serious suggestions that he was a plagiarist. The rejection of his donated volume of *Poems* (1881) by the Oxford Union was argued forcibly by the undergraduate Oliver Elton on the basis that these poems were not by Oscar but by better known and more reputable authors such as Shakespeare, John Donne, Byron and Swinburne. And, of course, James Whistler (famous for his "you will, Oscar, you will" retort when Oscar wished *he* had said something) reproached Wilde who "dines at our tables and picks from our platters the plums for the puddings he peddles in the provinces". Whistler, in fact, wrote a letter to the editor of *Truth* (2 January 1890), openly accusing Wilde of plagiarism.[24] But Oscar had no qualms in admitting that he was party to this practice. "Of course I plagiarize," he told Max Beerbohm. "It is the privilege of the appreciative man."[25] The subject of Wilde's plagiarism (and self-plagiarism) is a study of its own and it has recently been analysed by Guy and Small.[26]

A matter that has been raised by Oscar's friends and acquaintances is whether he was a snob. Shaw regarded him as the Dublin snob of the Merrion Square variety.[27] Oscar had a love for fine names, aristocratic connections, luxury and the height of fashion. He said after his imprisonment: "I have the simplest tastes. I am satisfied with the best." He was a tuft-hunter and one of the elements that probably attracted him to Lord Alfred Douglas was that the latter had a title and the trappings of upper class society.

There is considerable agreement that Wilde had unmistakable traits of snobbishness. Vincent O'Sullivan noted the following:

> It is impossible to avoid speaking of his snobbery, which was very marked. He was often bantered about it during his life-time . . . At times he was wont to talk loftily about 'my class' and to dismiss certain people as not being in his class. And he did not mean his intellectual class but his social class.[28]

This class consciousness of Wilde's was confirmed by Robert Ross, who related to Adela Schuster that, although many people were kind to Oscar during his precarious period of exile, he was too vain or too proud to accept the goodwill of those whom he perceived as his social and intellectual inferiors. "It galled him to have to appear grateful to those whom he did not, or would not have regarded, before the downfall."[29]

Food and restaurants had a particularly strong significance for Wilde. He hated cheap restaurants and despised individuals who ate there: in fact he refused to go out to dinner with people who invited him to those places.[30] A few weeks before the onset of his terminal illness Oscar wrote to George Ives, who was about to visit Paris: "[Y]ou must come to proper, seemly restaurants, not go to dreadful cabarets where *cochers de fiacre* resort. I hope you will never lose the sense of style in life: it keeps the barbarians away."[31]

Theodore Wratislaw was having tea with Oscar at Goring-on-Thames during a weekend visit and was taken aback by Wilde's fit of anger over a plate of biscuits. "So far as I could tell, they seemed excellent biscuits, but it was not until they were removed by his alarmed butler, and others substituted, that he seemed to regain his peace of mind."[9] Wratislaw also remarked that Oscar had asked him if he had brought evening dress for dinner – which he had fortunately done. Dining in ordinary clothes was anathema to Oscar who, as an Oxford undergraduate, had said: "If I were all alone, marooned in some desert island and had my things with me, I should dress for dinner every evening."[32]

Wilde's preoccupation with *haute cuisine* is reiterated in *De Profundis*, where he reminded Douglas of their reckless extravagance at the top restaurants:

> The Savoy dinners – the clear turtle-soup, the luscious ortolans wrapped in their crinkled Sicilian vine-leaves . . . The suppers at Willis's, the special *cuvée* of Perrier-Jouet reserved always for us, the wonderful *pâtés* procured directly from Strasburg, the marvellous *fine champagne* . . .[33]

The cost of these lavish meals featured prominently in Wilde's bankruptcy proceedings, with outstanding debts to the Savoy Hotel and Willis's Restaurant for the year 1893 amounting to a total of £95 (nearly £10,000 in today's money).[34] It is not surprising that he suffered such a gastronomic setback when confronted with prison fare.

Another related characteristic of Wilde's was arrogance. An example of this was given in the previous chapter when Wilde arranged for the American publication of Rennell Rodd's book of poems and, without any reference to Rodd, changed the title and made himself the dedicatee (in effusive terms). During his spell as an Oxford undergraduate there were several occasions when this trait emerged to a singularly ill-mannered extent. One was when Wilde was criticized by his tutor for absence from lectures and unsatisfactory work. "That is hardly the way to treat a gentleman, Mr Wilde," said the president of Magdalen College – to which Oscar rejoined, "But Mr President, Mr Allen is *not* a gentleman." Amazement followed this exchange, which took place in front of the college assembly, and Wilde was instructed to leave the hall.[35]

Louis Farnell, who was a student at the same time as Wilde and later became a distinguished classicist and Vice-Chancellor of Oxford University, described Oscar as a "humorous and objectionable 'freak', who wrote poetry that we rightly judged to be second-rate and second-hand". Farnell described his first and only encounter with Wilde in 1879 at the examination for a fellowship at Trinity College. Wilde objected to the wording of the examination questions and, soon after the paper was handed out, he rose, stretched himself before the hall-fire and then in a lofty but pleasant voice addressed his fellow competitors: "Gentlemen, this paper is really the work of a very uncultured person."[36]

A third instance of arrogance was during his visit to Greece and Rome with John Mahaffy, his former professor at Trinity College Dublin. In the process he missed a month of the summer term without permission, an act that so incensed the College authorities that they fined him half the year's demyship for impudence and rusticated him for the rest of the academic year.

In later life, too, Wilde continued to demonstrate his arrogance and conceit. There was the occasion when he called a rehearsal for *An Ideal Husband* on Christmas Day 1894. Such lack of consideration infuriated the actors, and this was aggravated by Oscar's very late arrival on that bleak morning. When challenged whether he observed Christmas, he replied that Septuagesima was the only Church festival he kept.[38] Charles Brookfield was one of the actors present, and this episode of arrogance and insensitivity contributed to his growing antipathy towards Wilde. It is alleged that afterwards he zealously assisted Queensberry in finding witnesses against Wilde.

But perhaps the most blatant public exhibition of affectation and haughtiness was when he took a curtain call on the opening night of *Lady Windermere's*

Fan. He came on stage smoking a cigarette and made the following extraordinary little speech (recorded in shorthand at the time), with the words that he emphasized in italics:

> Ladies and Gentlemen: I have enjoyed this evening *immensely.* The actors have given us a *charming* rendering of a *delightful* play, and your appreciation has been *most* intelligent. I congratulate you on the *great* success of your performance, which persuades me that you think *almost* as highly of the play as I do myself.[39]

(Compare George Bernard Shaw's curtain call, amid uproarious applause, at the *première* of *Arms and the Man* in 1894. Just before he began his speech there was a solitary hiss from the gallery. "I quite agree with you, sir," exclaimed Shaw, "but what can the two of us do against all of them!")

Wilde's conceited, bombastic and flamboyant demeanour caused antagonism in certain quarters. Men in British society tended to view him with disparagement, as something "foreign", and merely as a entertainer who was sought after by women because of his brilliance.[40] It is pertinent that despite fairly good support for membership of the Savile Club, Wilde's candidature was withdrawn because of strong opposition.[41] Even the more intellectually progressive circles in London such as the "Souls" excluded Oscar.[42] William Rothenstein was surprised to find out that there were plenty of individuals who disliked and mistrusted Wilde.[43] Bosie Douglas described how Oscar was hated by society, yet forced people to listen to him. "This hatred of Oscar on the part of English society was, it must be remembered, long before anything was known against his moral character . . ."[44] This assertion by Douglas is independently corroborated by a letter written to Ross by Rider Haggard, who met up with Oscar in Homburg in July 1892, several years before the tragedy struck:

> Oscar is here, certainly he is an amusing man though I wish he would drop his affectations! It seems from what he tells me that he feels the sneers at and attacks on him . . . Still I must say that if half what one hears is true, he has done a good deal to bring them on his head.[45]

There is a school of thought that attributes Wilde's prosecution of Queensberry to a state of overwhelming pride, which induced in him a sense of invulnerability. In Chapter 1 I argued against this proposition. Wilde's action against the Marquess was virtually forced on him by the latter's continuing harassment and persecution; it was not undertaken primarily as an act of arrogant self-assertiveness but in genuine self-defence against a man who was bent on destroying him. However, once the lawsuit was initiated, Oscar then

Figure 15 *Oscar Wilde in his heyday and shortly before his downfall. His bearing exhibits the haughtiness that characterized him during this period of his life.*

(Photograph courtesy of Sotheby's London)

conducted himself with his customary panache and vanity. He ensured that his appearances at the Marlborough Street Police Court and at the Old Bailey were done in style. On both occasions he drove up with some ceremony in a carriage and pair and was impeccably outfitted. As mentioned above, Oscar was impressive in the manner that he withstood Carson's gruelling cross-examination and, although he was not able to resist occasional flashes of wit, conceit and pretentiousness, he was generally restrained and measured in his responses.

One of the areas in which Oscar's vanity was especially marked was with regard to his age. His mother, Lady Jane Wilde, had stubbornly refused to give her true age until it was to her decided advantage to do so, as an impoverished elderly person, in a grant application in 1888 to the Royal Literary Fund. In *An Ideal Husband* Wilde pointedly discloses his own practice:

Lord Caversham: And it is high time for you to get married. You are thirty-four years of age, sir.

Lord Goring: Yes, father, but I only admit to thirty-two – thirty-one and a half when I have a really good button-hole.

In Oscar's marriage certificate (see Figure 12, p. 141), he gave his age as twenty-eight (he was well over twenty-nine) while Constance's age is correctly stated as twenty-six. It is intriguing to examine the Census returns for April 1881 and April 1891, where Wilde informed the enumerator that he was twenty-four and thirty-five, respectively, shaving off two years at the earlier and one year at the later census. At the Queensberry trial, under oath, he had given his age as thirty-nine whereas he was six months over forty. This little bit of deceit was cunningly exploited by Carson, much to Wilde's embarrassment. ("Yes, I have no intention of posing for a younger man at all," he replied.)[46] In the Bankruptcy Court he testified that his age was forty (not forty-one) and that his mother's was sixty-five (whereas in fact she was just short of seventy-four).[47]

But when it was in his interest to be truthful (as was the case with Lady Wilde), his vanity succumbed. He wrote to Oscar Browning in February 1880 requesting a testimonial for a position with the Education Department. Browning replied that no testimonials could be submitted about anybody who had not reached the age of twenty-five, to which Wilde immediately replied that he *was* twenty-five.[48] He had made it by four months! Yet less than three years before he had send Gladstone his sonnet on the Bulgarian massacres with the comment, "I am little more than a boy."[49]

It has been remarked that Oscar's vanity and ostentation made him highly dependent on a responsive audience. He needed always to be in the limelight. Even when he had outraged the critics and shocked the public by some of his more controversial work, such as *The Picture of Dorian Gray*, he was thoroughly contented. To have created a sensation was an affirmation of his literary or artistic brilliance. But there was another side of the coin that affected him as powerfully in the opposite direction. Once he had fallen from grace and been shamed and ostracized, he became deeply despondent and humiliated. One of the most devastating events of his entire life was the half-hour spent on the centre platform of Clapham Junction, amid a jeering mob, during his transfer from Wandsworth Prison to Reading in November 1895. This episode is poignantly depicted in *De Profundis*:

> Of all possible objects I was the most grotesque. When people saw me they laughed. Each train as it came up swelled the audience. Nothing could exceed their amusement. That was of course before they knew who I was. As soon as they had been informed, they laughed still more . . . For a year after that was done to me I wept every day at the same hour and for the same space of time.[50]

From this account it appears that Wilde developed a minor form of post-traumatic stress disorder (see page 70), in which there was the recurrent experiencing of the traumatic event and the avoidance of situations likely to arouse recollections of it. Oscar was so profoundly distressed by the incident that, several weeks prior to his release, he petitioned the Home Secretary not to transfer him to another prison lest he be subjected again to the terrible ordeal he suffered at Clapham Junction.[51]

In his heyday Wilde had usually been willing to grant interviews to newspapers, but the physical and mental degradation of his imprisonment made him acutely sensitive to any meetings with the press on his release, and this fear was also expressed in the above petition. Similarly, during his exile on the Continent, his sense of disgrace was exacerbated by those English visitors and residents who shunned him (there were even some members of the French literary community who did so); and he developed a strong avoidance to places frequented by such people. What is noteworthy about Wilde's exile is that his erstwhile pride and vanity did nothing to curb his begging and pleading for money, which he did to an inordinate degree.

The other indignity inflicted on Wilde's vanity was the cutting of his hair in prison. The warder whose duty it was to clip Oscar's locks described how the tears rolled down his cheeks as he implored: "Must it be cut? You don't know what it means to me."[52] Interestingly, when Cunninghame Graham was imprisoned in Pentonville for his involvement in the Trafalgar Square Riot in November 1887, Oscar had written: "I hope they won't cut his nice curly hair in prison, or clip that amazing moustache."[53]

In a personal questionnaire that Wilde completed at the age of twenty-two, he was asked what be believed to be his distinguishing characteristics. He first put "humility", struck this out and then wrote "inordinate self-esteem". On the other hand, when asked what trait of character he most detested in others, he answered, "vanity: self-esteem: conceitedness"![13] As the years passed his estimation of his own worth grew exponentially so that he was able to tell Carson at the Queensberry trial: "I have never given admiration to anybody except myself." And he once jokingly bemoaned the fact that "one half of the world does not believe in God, and the other half does not believe in me". With this self-aggrandizement went an insensitivity and hurtfulness which Robert Sherard noted:

> Poor Oscar had a capacity for making enemies because, when there was a *bon mot* to be turned, he did not stop to consider how the person against whom it was directed would appreciate or condone its sting. From the very first days of my acquaintance I noticed this habit of his, of saying bitter things about people, just, perhaps, witty, always, but such as his victims would remember rancorously . . . [54]

Although Oscar was vain and conceited, he could also be charming and generous. As Frank Harris put it: "Like most men of charming manners, Oscar was selfish and self-centred, too convinced of his own importance to spend much thought on others; yet generous to the needy and kind to all."[55] According to Ada Leverson, "Oscar was the most generous man I have ever met, and he showed his kindness always in the most graceful way." She gave the instance of a young solicitor, known then only slightly to Wilde, who needed money to marry his sweetheart. Oscar had just received a large sum for *Lady Windermere's Fan* and he immediately wrote a cheque for £160 and instructed the man to marry at once – which he did.[56] Edgar Saltus related how on one bleak and bitter night an ill-clad man had come up to him and Oscar. Saltus gave him a shilling but Oscar graciously took off his overcoat and wrapped it around the man.[57] Wilde was especially generous to his mother, who had fallen on hard times financially after Sir William Wilde's death. He supported her regularly during her widowhood. And, of course, he was abundantly generous to the rent-boys whom he plied with good food, good wine, silver cigarette cases and money. When he came out of Reading Gaol he felt honour-bound to give financial assistance to about ten fellow prisoners and warders. He expected a peeved Robert Ross to make the payments out of the limited funds that had been contributed by friends and well-wishers and were specifically ear-marked for Oscar's personal use on his release.

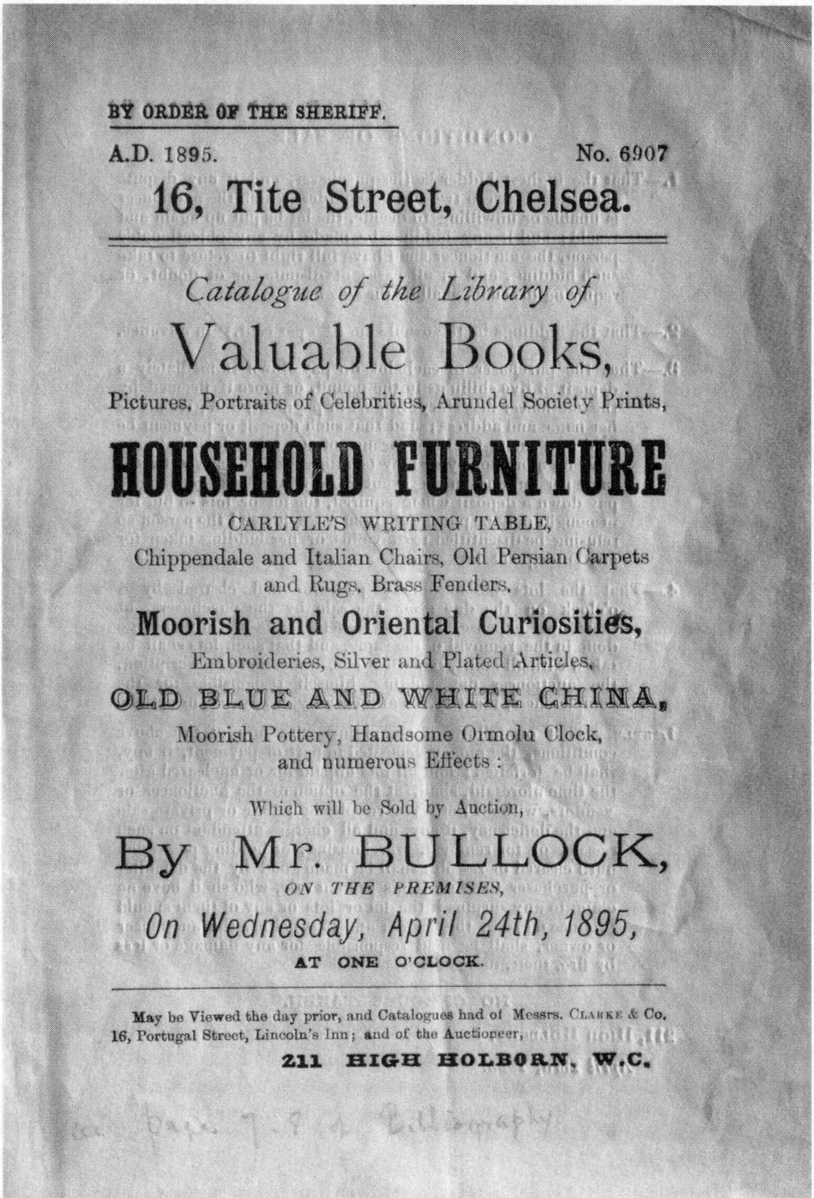

BY ORDER OF THE SHERIFF.

A.D. 1895.   No. 6907

16, Tite Street, Chelsea.

Catalogue of the Library of

Valuable Books,

Pictures, Portraits of Celebrities, Arundel Society Prints,

HOUSEHOLD FURNITURE

CARLYLE'S WRITING TABLE,

Chippendale and Italian Chairs, Old Persian Carpets
and Rugs, Brass Fenders,

Moorish and Oriental Curiosities,

Embroideries, Silver and Plated Articles,

OLD BLUE AND WHITE CHINA,

Moorish Pottery, Handsome Ormolu Clock,
and numerous Effects :

Which will be Sold by Auction,

By Mr. BULLOCK,

ON THE PREMISES,

On Wednesday, April 24th, 1895,

AT ONE O'CLOCK.

May be Viewed the day prior, and Catalogues had of Messrs. CLARKE & Co.
16, Portugal Street, Lincoln's Inn; and of the Auctioneer,

211 HIGH HOLBORN, W.C.

Figure 16 *The devastation by public auction of the precious contents of Wilde's Tite Street home. At the time of the sale, Oscar was detained in Holloway Prison, awaiting the start of his first criminal trial two days later.*

(Photograph courtesy of Sotheby's London)

But the converse of Wilde's lavish lifestyle and uninhibited expenditure was his perverse practice of failing to pay his bills or settle his debts. One of his maxims was: "It is only by not paying one's bills that one can hope to live in the memory of the commercial classes"; and this was a principle that he himself adhered to throughout his life. Spending huge sums of money followed by non-payment became part and parcel of his code of conduct and way of living – "my profligacy, extravagance, and worldly life of fashion and senseless ease," as he described it.[58] This pattern was already present at Oxford, where Oscar was twice summoned before the Vice-Chancellor's Court (on 16 and on 30 November 1877) for long overdue and unpaid accounts. He was ordered to pay the debts plus costs. To give an indication of the extent of his purchases, he had over the course of about thirteen academic months at Oxford incurred a clothing bill (shirts, coats, suits and gloves) in excess of £40 (about £4000 today),[59] this amount being just under half of the annual demyship (£95) awarded to him by Magdalen College.

His mother, Lady Jane Wilde, wrote to Oscar during his American tour in 1882, urging him to pay his bills before he spent all his money, and commenting on his extravagance ("You seem to have lived luxuriously at Tite Street").[60] Theodore Wratislaw has confirmed the flagrantly irresponsible approach that Wilde had to his creditors. He came to visit him at Tite Street in the spring of 1894 and during conversation Oscar placed his hand on a pile of envelopes and exclaimed, "They are all bills – I shall not open one of them."[9]

There were many periods in Oscar's life when he had accumulated enough money to wipe the slate clean of all his debts. For example, midway through his American lecturing tour he had earned $5600, a very substantial amount for a man of twenty-seven.[61] Wilde declared to the High Court in Bankruptcy in November 1895 that his income from royalties received on plays and books was not less that £2000 a year.[7] It has been estimated, partly on the basis of actual theatre receipts, that from the various performances of his four society comedies – during the period February 1892 to his trials in the spring of 1895 – Wilde earned (conservatively) a total of £10,000 (about a million pounds in today's money).[62] Wilde disclosed to his solicitor that his royalties for the *week* preceding his action against Queensberry were £245.[63]

There are some puzzling aspects to Wilde's monetary affairs. According to him, he wanted to leave the Avondale Hotel at the end of February 1895 but the hotel refused to release his luggage until the bill of nearly £140 had been paid.[64] Oscar was unable to do so although earlier in February he had been paid two advances by George Alexander (for *The Importance of Being Earnest*) to the tune of £1000.[65] It is astounding how recklessly – and with such indecent haste – Wilde dissipated huge sums of money and yet left himself incapable of meeting his everyday running expenses. Little wonder that he confessed to his solicitor:

"I am quite incapable of managing my own affairs, and always have been. I don't know what to do with money except throw it away."[63] But his cavalier and persistent obduracy in failing to settle his debts attested to a clearly antisocial trait in his personality. Eventually this behaviour was to sabotage him: first on 24 April 1895 when the Sheriff ordered the sale by public auction of the valuable and treasured contents of his Tite Street house (Figure 16), and then later in the year when he was declared insolvent. Oscar summed it up crisply in a letter to George Alexander: "I am sorry my life is so marred and maimed by extravagance. But I cannot live otherwise. I, at any rate, pay the penalty of suffering."[66]

I I

RELATIONSHIPS WITH FAMILY
AND FRIENDS

T HE previous chapter discussed Oscar Wilde's pronounced personality and behavioural traits as they were perceived by the wider society. In this chapter I discuss Wilde's ability to foster friendships and sustain relationships. George Bernard Shaw was of the view that "Wilde, though he could inspire British friendships of the most devoted kind, was incapable of such friendships himself, though not, on occasion, of noble and generous gestures".[1] In the context of Oscar's supreme egotism ("I have never given adoration to anybody but myself," he informed Carson in the Queensberry libel trial), it is desirable to test Shaw's opinion.

There was a recurrent trend in Wilde's life that played havoc with many of his relationships – namely, his marked predisposition towards boredom. Oscar was strongly extroverted and in need of regular stimulation; without it he became lonely and bored. "*Ennui* is the enemy," he told Frank Harris.[2] Neil McKenna[3] has highlighted this propensity by showing that Wilde began several of his same-sex affairs with passion and delight, but within a relatively short space of time the excitement and novelty had waned, the lust had diminished and usually a new infatuation had begun. This happened *inter alia* with Henry Marillier, Clyde Fitch and Fred Althaus. In the case of John Gray, a relationship of nearly three years' duration was terminated when Oscar met and fell in love with Alfred (Bosie) Douglas. His love affair with Douglas lasted until Oscar's death, although it was punctuated by several stormy episodes and violent fluctuations. It is surprising that Wilde was able to continue the relationship under such torrid circumstances. One reason was that Bosie was not the unstimulating and predictable person that he had come to experience with many of his previous lovers. When Bosie erupted into paroxysms of petulant and unreasonable anger against him, Oscar would meekly react to the outburst with hurt and despair. But, however insufferable Bosie's behaviour was at times, Oscar found him challenging and inspiring. Life with him was anything but dull and pedestrian, and in the pre-imprisonment period there is no doubt that he was deeply in love with Bosie.

While Oscar's affair with Bosie was his most intense and sustained one, it was the quality of his marriage to Constance Lloyd that requires more detailed scrutiny now. In Chapter 9 I argued that, although Wilde embarked on matrimony principally for social and financial reasons, he nevertheless appeared to be in love with Constance at the time of the engagement and marriage. Shortly after the marriage his homosexual impulses reasserted themselves, and after the birth of Vyvyan in November 1886 it is generally assumed that sexual intercourse between the couple ceased while Oscar became increasingly involved in relationships with young men.

Constance in turn was unquestionably in love with Oscar, and it is clear from her remarks and sentiments in the early days (see page 140) that she was fully devoted and committed and foresaw a life of mutual affection, companionship and prosperity. It is difficult to know how she would have responded to the termination of conjugal relations two years after marriage. In the Victorian era the female body and its reproductive functions were regarded with disgust, and women were taught to pretend that there was no place for eroticism. Motherhood was extolled as a noble aspiration but the means of achieving this were beyond discussion. Women learnt to deny their very femininity and to be repelled by their husbands' sexual demands.4 The popular image was of the Victorian bride lying still on her honeymoon night and thinking of England!

Whether Constance Wilde would have conformed to this stereotype is uncertain. If so, then having decided that two healthy children were sufficient for a family, she would have been relieved that it was no longer necessary to submit to the indignity of sex. My belief is that Constance was an emancipated and passionate woman with a more enlightened attitude to sexuality than her contemporaries. Her promise made on her engagement to hold Oscar "fast with chains of love and devotion" was symbolic not only of a spiritual and emotional bond but of a close physical intimacy. Wilde had written in *An Ideal Husband*: "There is one thing worse than an absolutely loveless marriage. A marriage in which there is love, but on one side only."

There is a letter Constance wrote to her brother, Otho, in August 1887 in which she stated: "Oscar and I are very happy together now and Cyril is delightful."5 This gives a hint that there had possibly been some difficulty in the marriage which had then rectified itself. Unfortunately this renewed rapport did not last long. With the passage of time and in parallel with his immersion in numerous homosexual involvements, Oscar progressively detached himself from his wife and children. The drudgeries of everyday family life were beyond his tolerance and patience. And one can imagine that the witty and loquacious Oscar, with his whirl of paradoxes and flights of fancy, would have found in the sober-minded and reality-based Constance an exasperated and worn-out listener. For one who was in a perpetual quest for excitement and titillation 16

Tite Street was not the place to be. By the dawn of the 1890s Wilde had effectively abdicated from his domestic duties and responsibilities. He was the husband and father *in absentia* and it was in this context that he exhibited some of his most selfish and callous characteristics. Notwithstanding his unending succession of extramarital escapades, he was not even willing or considerate enough to attempt to live a double life in which Constance and the children would at least have had some share of him. Oscar admitted while in prison and when the question of divorce arose: "Whether I am married or not is a matter that does not concern me. For years I disregarded the tie . . . She [Constance] could not understand me, and I was bored to death with the married life."[6]

Oscar gradually withdrew physically from the home. At first he would return in the early hours of the morning; later he stayed in hotels on the pretext that it was quieter and more convenient to write his plays there. In fact, from October 1893 until April 1894 Wilde rented rooms at 10 and 11 St James Place,[7] which provided a suitable venue for his sexual pursuits. When he went abroad (not infrequently) it was without Constance, although sometimes the family did spend part of the summer holidays together. On one of the latter occasions at Worthing (August 1894) Oscar commented to Bosie: "A horrid ugly Swiss governess has, I find, been looking after Cyril and Vyvyan *for a year* [my italics]." [8] This may have been facetious but there is more than a little truth in it. Perhaps one of the most pathetic instances of Wilde's dereliction was related by Pierre Louÿs, who was present one morning in the hotel room that Oscar and Bosie were sharing. Constance, who rarely saw her husband, arrived with the post and tearfully pleaded with him to come home. His flippant reply was that he had been away so long that he had forgotten his address.[9]

It was bad enough for Constance that their sexual life had ended, but when she realized too that their domestic life was over it must have been very perplexing for her. From all accounts she was not aware of her husband's homosexuality until the eve of the Queensberry trials. Lady Wilde was distressed at this state of affairs and wrote to Oscar when he had been away on a prolonged visit to Paris in late 1891: "Still I would like you home . . . and Constance would like you back. She is very lonely."[10] With no response from him she reiterated her wish: "*Do* come home. She is very lonely and mourns for you . . ."[11]

It was to no avail. Wilde was incorrigible and by the year 1895 he had abandoned even the veneer of being a husband. He had then decided to keep Constance in the dark over his whereabouts. It was in January of that year that she sustained a serious fall down the staircase at Tite Street. The injury resulted in damage to her cervical (neck) spine from which she never recovered: on the contrary, she subsequently developed progressive weakness of her right arm and leg which disabled her until her untimely death in 1898 at the age of forty. At the time of her accident Oscar had gone with Bosie to Algeria without leaving any contact details. On 28 January 1895 Constance, ill and in a quandary, turned to Ross for assistance. She was due to leave Tite Street the next day to spend a month at Babbacombe Cliff, Torquay, with Lady Mount-Temple. Having overdrawn her account by £38, she needed money from Oscar:

> I am writing this to you as you know what Oscar is about correspondence. He would . . . send me no money. I will send a letter to him on Thursday 'chez vous' as I don't know where he will be . . . and if he wants to come home, tell him he *must* let them [the servants] have a day's notice.[12]

This somewhat despairing letter shows the total lack of communication between the couple at that stage. Oscar was virtually inaccessible to her and she was forced to use Ross as the conduit. From the standpoint of money, Oscar was singularly indifferent to her requirements and obviously made little provision for her household or personal expenses. It is noteworthy that Constance's brother, Otho Holland Lloyd, had informed Arthur Ransome years later that Oscar had brought no love to the marriage, which he had entered on only for money; that he had adopted an attitude of "pitying contempt" for her; and that in his days of prosperity he had neglected her and kept her short of funds.[13]

With regard to finances at the time of the Queensberry trial, Oscar had borrowed £50 from his wife, £50 from her cousin and £100 from her aunt. Constance repaid her cousin the £50 but the aunt's loan was never repaid. Constance herself was left penniless and had to borrow £150 from Burne-Jones. Writing three years later, a bitter Constance protested that "all these things are nothing to Oscar as long as someone supports him!"[14]

In a letter to Ross (dated 12 March 1895) Constance again pleaded ignorance of Oscar's address. He was then about to depart for Monte Carlo with Bosie, having just instituted the prosecution of Queensberry. Constance was moving in with her aunt because she was prohibited from walking owing to her neck condition. "I am going to have an operation (not a serious one!) performed on me next week," she wrote, "and I hope after that to be better."[15] In a further letter three days later, Constance informed Ross that, if Oscar returned from Monte Carlo on Tuesday 19 March and intended to stay in Tite Street, she would probably postpone the operation until the Queensberry case was over; otherwise she would have it done the following week as arranged.[16] Oscar returned only on 24 or 25 March and so it must be presumed that Constance did submit to the operation on the scheduled date. The procedure in question ("not a serious one") was probably traction or manipulation of the cervical spine, presumably in order to correct a suspected misalignment of the vertebrae caused by the fall down the stairs.

In the bankruptcy records there is an outstanding bill for just over £30 owing to Dr Vernon Lamphier Jones of 2 Bennett Street, St James, for medical attention rendered in January, February and March 1895.[17] Dr Jones appears to have been the Wildes' family doctor at that time. (According to the British Medical Register, Constance's previous doctor, Dr Charles de Lacy Lacy, ceased to be registered after 1889.) Jones had qualified at Trinity College Dublin in 1888, practised in Dublin and Leeds, and then settled in London in 1892 where he built up a large practice in the West End.[18] McKenna has made the unwarranted supposition that Wilde contracted gonorrhoea in Algeria and that Jones had treated him for this on his return.[19] Wilde returned only at the beginning of February 1895 and therefore could not have been treated for gonorrhoea during January. The bill is very high (about £3000 today) and it can only have been for the protracted attention and treatment (including operative procedures) necessitated by Constance's injury.

In a communication to Arthur Symons in 1937, Otho Holland Lloyd revealed that Wilde had been unsympathetic to Constance when she tried to describe the unhappiness of her upbringing (her mother had been abusive and cruel to her): he could not be bothered with people who went back to their childhoods for their tragedies.[20] This indifference of Oscar's extended to her ill health, and he was conspicuous by his apparent lack of concern for the post-injury disability that afflicted her in the last three years of her life. When he was informed by Carlos Blacker of the severity of her condition (late July 1897), he cursorily expressed his distress;[21] but there is not a mention or hint of her illness in any of his subsequent correspondence.

Despite the neglectful and uncaring way in which Oscar treated Constance, she remained loyal and kind to him. After the scandal broke in 1895 Constance was utterly devastated: she had lost her husband, her home and her identity. So intense and hostile was feeling against Wilde that even on the Continent, to which she had fled, she was forced to change her surname to Holland to avoid ostracism and to protect the children from humiliation. Yet, through all this turmoil and dislocation, Constance did not renounce Oscar. As discussed in Chapter 6, she had contemplated divorce but never proceeded along this route. She had offered forgiveness and reconciliation to him during his imprisonment but her attitude subsequently soured over the life interest issue. Though ill, she made two trips from abroad to visit him in prison, the second to break the news of his mother's death. Oscar was moved by the "great tenderness and affection" which she displayed on that occasion.[22] Her act of solicitude induced him to allow her to purchase the life interest of the marriage settlement unopposed, a wish that was not honoured by his friends. In a letter to Ross from Reading, he wrote: "And, though it may surprise some of my friends, I am really very fond of my wife and very sorry for her." He admitted that she had some sweet points in her character and "was wonderfully loyal to me".[23]

Constance, who as a child had suffered rejection and hostility from her own mother, was a woman with a need for warmth and kindness. When she failed to get these from Oscar, she developed a close friendship with Arthur Humphreys, a bookseller and publisher with whom she had collaborated in producing *Oscariana*. This was a collection of Wilde's aphorisms, culled from his work by Constance and published in January 1895. Humphreys was an empathetic listener and he allowed Constance to vent her embittered memories of an abused childhood. Although there was probably no physical relationship between them, Constance loved and admired him. In a letter to Humphreys in June 1894, she described him as "an ideal husband" and "not far short of being an ideal man". She added: "I am slow at making friends but those I make are very dear to me, and what is dear to one is sacred."[24] Three months later the friendship was even more passionate, and in a letter addressed to "My Darling Arthur" and signed "Your always devotedly loving Constance" she declared her love for him. "Nothing in my life has ever made me so happy as this love of yours . . . I love you just because you ARE, and because you have come into my life to fill it with love and make it rich."[25]

In later correspondence from Constance to Humphreys the emotional intensity is reduced, and in October 1894 she wrote to him in a slightly peeved tone, having discovered that he had no sympathy with the poverty-stricken of the world – a subject on which she felt strongly but he did not take seriously. She urged that they did not discuss the matter again.[26] During her residence in Italy, Constance continued her contact with Humphreys and he would send her the books she requested.

There is still debate about Constance's attitude to Oscar after his discharge from prison. Some have suggested that, had she allowed Oscar to visit her and see the children shortly after his release, then the marriage might have been resuscitated. On 24 May 1897 Constance wrote to her brother: "O[scar] has written me a letter full of penitence and I have answered it." [27] Thereafter she wrote to her husband every week but no record of that correspondence survives. She sent photographs of the children but without any promise to let Oscar see them. "I want my boys," he wrote to Ross. "It is a terrible punishment, dear Robbie, and oh! how well I deserve it. But it makes me feel disgraced and evil . . ."[27]

Oscar wanted Constance to bring the children to him at Dieppe, but in late July 1897 Carlos Blacker, who was a friend of both his and Constance's and acted as the go-between, wrote that poor health prevented her from making the journey. Oscar then proposed a visit to her within a few weeks, but Blacker again demurred and persuaded him to postpone the meeting until late September or early October when she was settled at Nervi in Italy. This procrastination came as a great blow to Oscar, who was then leading a dreary and lonely life in Berneval and becoming increasingly depressed. "I fear we shall never see each other again," he told Blacker;[21] and a month later (4 September) he informed him that "I have never been so unhappy" and expressed disappointment that Constance had not invited him to meet the children. "I don't suppose now I shall ever see them," he lamented.[28] His words were prophetic for he saw neither Constance nor his sons again.

Four months had elapsed since his release and Oscar could no longer endure his desolation and despondency. In the latter part of September 1897 he left for Naples where he and Bosie Douglas set up house together. "I must remake my maimed life on my own lines," he wrote and added that, had he been allowed to see his boys, his life would probably have been quite different.[29] In the meantime Constance, who was seriously considering the possibility of reconciliation, had invited him and was keenly awaiting the visit although, alas for Oscar, the children had gone back to school. But when she learned that he and Bosie were living together she was stunned and sent Oscar "a very violent letter", forbidding him to see Bosie, forbidding him "to return to your filthy, insane life" and withdrawing her invitation to receive him in Genoa.[30] Oscar was incensed by her blunt interference and her attempt to influence and control his very existence. Any further prospects for a reconciliation were dashed. Worse still, once it became clear that Oscar and Bosie were reunited, Constance took steps through the solicitors to deprive Wilde of his allowance. On 18 November 1897 she wrote to her brother: "I have stopped O's allowance as he is living with Lord Alfred Douglas, so in a short time war will be declared!"[31] She was furious that, contrary to all his previous resolutions, he had resumed his friendship with Douglas, of whom she later commented: "No words will describe my horror of that BEAST, for I will call him nothing else, A.D." [32]

It is necessary to take stock of the situation. What is evident is that Wilde was more interested in seeing the children than in meeting Constance. It is understandable that after two-and-a-half years of absence he should crave contact with his sons. And after the degradation of his trials and imprisonment he had the urgent psychological need to regain affirmation from them ("what I want is the love of my children," he had written[33]). Perhaps Constance's refusal to allow him access to the boys was unreasonable, and in the modern era this may have been a violation of Oscar's paternal rights. But, from the perspective of her times and circumstances, Constance was reluctant to expose Cyril and Vyvyan to their father before first spending time alone with Oscar, re-establishing goodwill, and clarifying and resolving past misunderstandings and differences. She recognized the upheaval that the children had undergone and was wary of imposing any additional emotional burden on them – and certainly not without an initial "debriefing session" with Oscar. But once he had returned to

Bosie she lost faith in his sincerity and, difficult though it was for her, she decided that for her sons' sake she had to keep them apart from him lest he ruin their lives further.

Would the course of events have changed if a family reunion had materialized, say, in July 1897? I do not believe that the eventual outcome would have been different. Oscar would not have been able to reintegrate into married life. It had bored him the first time and a second round would have bored him even more. It is also doubtful whether he would have been capable of participating in marital sex. Furthermore, Wilde's homosexual drive would have kept him from home for long periods (in a repetition of the pre-trial scenario), but this time Constance would not have been the long-suffering wife of earlier years; she would have reacted with ire and recriminations. Finally, her disabling illness would have taxed Oscar's very limited patience and tolerance. Robert Sherard has described Wilde's attitude to pain and suffering:

> At the same time he [Oscar] declared that he had no sympathy with people suffering from physical pain. 'Illness and suffering always inspire me with repulsion. A man with the toothache ought, I know, to have my sympathy, for it is a terrible pain. Well, he fills me with nothing but aversion. He is tedious. He is a bore. I cannot stand him. I cannot look at him. I must get away from him.' That was in 1883.[34]

With all these potential problems, it is perhaps as well that the façade of a marriage was never reconstructed. It is highly likely that it would not have lasted and that the stress would have aggravated Constance's failing health. As it turned out, Constance continued to show interest in Oscar despite her anger at his behaviour. She was greatly moved by *The Ballad of Reading Gaol*; and after he and Bosie had separated she restored his allowance, which continued to be paid after her death. She wrote to Arthur Humphreys in February 1898 that, notwithstanding his treatment of her, she would always care for Oscar and that if she saw him she would probably forgive everything.[35] Just before her death she sent Oscar a very nice letter, and she also wrote to Vyvyan (her last letter to him): "Try not to feel harshly about your father; remember that he is your father and that he loves you . . . and whatever he has done he has suffered bitterly for."[36] These actions exemplify Constance's fairness, unselfishness and compassion.

Constance Wilde died unexpectedly on 7 April 1898, aged forty, at a clinic in Genoa. It was a huge shock to family and friends. Oscar telegraphed his brother-in-law: "Am overwhelmed with grief. It is the most terrible tragedy."[37] To Carlos Blacker he wrote: "It is really awful. I don't know what to do. If we had only met once, and kissed each other."[37] He telegraphed Ross on 12 April: "Constance is dead. Please come tomorrow and stay at my hotel. I'm in great grief." [38] Ross did as requested and his comments, made to Leonard Smithers, contradicted Oscar: "You will have heard of Mrs Wilde's death. Oscar of course did not feel it at all . . . He is in very good spirits and does not consume too many."[38]

I accept Ross's interpretation. Oscar was not in mourning. He had shown true grief on the death of his mother, but with Constance it was merely the superficial expression of grief, and what sadness there was quickly passed. There is no further reference to Constance in the remaining thirty months of his correspondence save for a visit to her grave in Genoa the following year: "It was very tragic," he wrote to Ross, "seeing her name carved on a tomb – her surname, my name, not mentioned of course – just 'Constance Mary, daughter of Horace Lloyd, QC'."[39] This is the typically self-centred Oscar Wilde: the tragedy being the exclusion of *his* name from the tomb rather than Constance's sad life and untimely death. (The words "Wife of Oscar Wilde" were added to the tomb in 1963.)[39] Otho Holland Lloyd had written to Carlos Blacker on his sister's life: "There are lives that are evidently doomed to mistreatment, and hers was one; I doubt if she ever strictly knew what happiness was, at least for any long time together . . . "[40]

What was the quality of Wilde's relationship with his children, Cyril and Vyvyan? There is no doubt that he was very fond of them and they in turn adored him; and, as discussed above, he became thoroughly disillusioned and disheartened when Constance refused him the right to visit them after his release. While in prison he had suffered the humiliation of being stripped of his guardianship by legal process. In happier times he had played with them in the nursery and dining-room, told them his stories in his spell-binding way, and was at his best with them during the summer holidays and at the seaside, where they went sailing or fishing with him or built sand castles on the beach.[41] (Wilde's need for praise was recalled by Vyvyan: Oscar had mended a broken toy one afternoon and then insisted on everyone in the house coming to witness his repair work.)

However, Wilde's frequent absences from home – especially in the early 1890s when Cyril and Vyvyan were in the five to nine age range – must have considerably curtailed the quantity and quality of time he spent with the children. An intimation of this is that in his book *Son of Oscar Wilde* Vyvyan Holland could produce only seven paragraphs of direct personal reminiscences about his father.[41] It also needs to be stated in fairness that, in the upper middle class homes of the period, child care was turned over to nursery maids and nannies so that even mothers spent limited times of the day with their children; fathers

Figure 17 *Oscar's elder and favourite child, Cyril, at the age of twelve, at which stage his surname had been changed to Holland to conceal his paternal identity. Oscar and Cyril never saw each other again after early 1895, when Cyril was nine.*
(Photograph courtesy of Sotheby's London)

could be even more remote.[42] After the birth of Vyvyan, Constance informed her brother that household expenses were growing as she was obliged to have *two* nurses.[43]

Cyril was unquestionably Oscar's favourite child, and it is sometimes disconcerting to read his letters and to note how deliberately he singled out Cyril at the expense of Vyvyan. Cyril was seventeen months older than his brother and, as the first-born son, Oscar had developed a strong and affection-ate bond with him, describing it to Ross as "my idolatrous love of Cyril".[44] Writing from Reading Prison in March 1897, Wilde expressed this preference outrightly: "I sincerely hope I may be . . . allowed to see Cyril from time to time: it would be to me a sorrow beyond words if I were not."[45] In *De Profundis* he extolled the boy's qualities: "I could not bear the idea of being separated from Cyril, that beautiful, loving, loveable child of mine, my friend of all friends, my companion beyond all companions . . . "[46] And in another passage: "I had lost my name, my position, my happiness, my freedom, my wealth . . . But I still had one beautiful thing left, my own eldest son." [47]

As a child Vyvyan was conscious of this favouritism, and the reasons he advanced were that he was less strong and more sensitive that Cyril and more troubled than most by childish complaints, which probably offended his father's aesthetic sense. Also he suspected that his parents had wanted a girl as their second child.[48]

Shortly after his release, Constance sent Oscar photographs of Cyril and Vyvyan while both the boys sent him their remembrances. Oscar had not acknowledged any of these mementoes and Constance had written to him complaining "that he evidently did not care much for his boys".[49] This omission is surprising in the light of Wilde's avowed love for his children. I maintain that this demonstrates that Oscar's craving to see his sons was primarily to appease his own emotional needs for approval and acceptance and not to satisfy or accommodate their wants. In support of this opinion, I have been struck at the apparent lack of concern and sensitivity over his young children's grief and pain on the loss of their mother and the absence of any anxiety on his part as to their future welfare. The Oscar Wilde correspondence in the aftermath of Constance's death makes *no reference whatever* to the plight of Cyril and Vyvyan, who had become virtual orphans at that stage.

It is true, of course, that the children's guardian, Adrian Hope, and Constance's family (the Napiers) made every effort to erase the name of Oscar Wilde from the boys' lives. Had Oscar endeavoured to communicate with his children, either by writing directly to them or through the agency of his own friends, such actions would have been instantly thwarted. Robert Ross, for example, was greatly frustrated by the lack of response from Adrian Hope to news of Wilde's death, and when he did eventually reply it was through Ross's solicitor.[50] Having been a close friend of Oscar's, Ross was mistrusted by Constance's family and barred from any inquiries or business relating to Cyril and Vyvyan. It was only in August 1907 that Vyvyan, then aged nearly twenty-one, met Ross for the first time. Ross was deeply embittered that he had been isolated from the children for all those years because he believed that he could have made their dark and lonely childhood a happier one. Ross told Vyvyan that

Figure 18   *Vyvyan, younger son of Oscar and Constance, aged five.*

(Private collection)

Oscar had asked him to get information about the children's progress and that he had even approached Adrian Hope, through More Adey, to be permitted to write letters for them to read when they came of age. The reply was that such letters would immediately be destroyed.[51]

But despite these reassurances from Ross that Oscar *did* think about his sons, I remain fairly unconvinced. *The Complete Letters of Oscar Wilde*[2] gives an almost complete record of Wilde's correspondence with Robert Ross and More Adey, and yet there is not a single sentence from Oscar concerning Cyril or Vyvyan after Constance's death. He wrote about so many matters pertaining to himself – his financial situation *ad nauseam*, the ever-changing landscape of his romantic and sexual exploits, his trips to Italy and Switzerland, and so on. When Oscar had a cause or a grievance he did not hesitate to champion or air it. This is illustrated by his diatribe against Adey and Ross when his allowance from Constance was stopped (following his cohabitation with Douglas) and by his altercation with Frank Harris over the *Mr and Mrs Daventry* saga (see below). From the perspective of the children he was seemingly silent, except possibly for some casual and superficial inquiries. If Oscar had genuinely sought to determine the fate of his sons and their educational progress, he could have written to the Court of Chancery in London for guidance and information, as he was empowered to do by the guardianship order of March 1897. My conclusion is that once he was prevented from seeing the children, he essentially lost further interest in their lives and development.

The effects of the Oscar Wilde scandal on Cyril and Vyvyan were devastating, as is poignantly related by Vyvyan Holland in his *Son of Oscar Wilde*.[36] Cyril was nine years old when he saw a placard in Baker Street about his father's case and later read newspaper accounts. He realized that something was desperately wrong; he became acutely distressed and never really recovered his equanimity thereafter. Vyvyan never came to learn the truth until years afterwards. He suspected that there was trouble when his surname was changed to "Holland" and his name respelt as "Vivian", and when he and Cyril were instructed to forget that they had ever borne the name of Wilde. He was given the impression by Constance's family that his father was dead. Oscar Wilde became an unmentionable subject and all traces of him in the form of books and letters were destroyed.

Ross did manage to get a letter forwarded to Cyril informing him of Oscar's death. Cyril, aged fifteen, replied: "It is hard for a young mind like mine to realise why all the sorrow should have come on us, especially so young."[52] He recalled the time long ago when they had lived happily in London and when his father had built brick houses for them in the nursery.

Cyril spent the rest of his life proving his masculinity. At school he was a fine athlete, rower and swimmer and became a prefect and head of his house. He joined the British Army and in 1913 got six months' leave in which he undertook, alone, an exceptionally strenuous and hazardous hiking expedition through Tibet to Peking (now Beijing) in dangerous times. He told Vyvyan that his aim was to be a *man* and not an effeminate aesthete or weak-kneed degenerate. He wanted to wipe the stain away and do something himself to retrieve the family name. "I ask nothing better," he wrote, 'than to end in honourable battle for my King and Country."[53] Cyril had his wish fulfilled. His quietus came during the First World War when, fighting for King and Country, he was killed in France by a German sniper on 9 May 1915, a month before his thirtieth birthday.

Vyvyan's life took a different turn. Unlike Cyril, who was brought face to face with the bare facts in his most formative years, Vyvyan's existence was submerged in a nebulous miasma of concealment and repression. The secrecy surrounding his childhood caused him embarrassing shyness, reticence and awkwardness in adulthood with difficulty in making friends.[54] It was fifty-four years after Wilde's death that Vyvyan Holland was first able to declare himself to the world in his remarkable *Son of Oscar Wilde*, written, as he himself put it, "on behalf of those, who, although innocent, suffered in a hurt, uncomprehending way, wondering why they were not treated like other people".[55]

I now examine Oscar's problematic relationship with Willie (William), his elder brother. Willie Wilde was himself a talented individual. He graduated from Trinity College Dublin, then read law and was called to the Bar although he never practised. Like Oscar, he was irresponsible with money and chronically in debt. He became a competent journalist but did not persist with this profession. In 1891 he married Mrs Frank Leslie in New York. She was a wealthy heiress and proprietor of a major publishing firm and Willie hoped to lead an indolent and luxurious life at her expense. But the marriage was a disaster from the start. He was drinking heavily and regularly and this, together with his extreme idleness and constant self-gratification, disgusted Mrs Leslie, who divorced him shortly afterwards. Willie is alleged to have told an acquaintance that he would fight the divorce: "I've never had a client yet, though I've been a barrister a long time. So I'll take advantage of my opportunity and retain myself for my own defence."[56]

Willie's relationship with Oscar was initially satisfactory, but as soon as Oscar became successful in the literary and theatrical world he succumbed to jealousy. Willie was a member of the Lotos Club in New York until he was expelled from it for failing to pay his dues. There was a report that he had hilariously entertained the club members by impersonating Oscar's voice, parodying his poetry and imitating his aesthetic mannerisms.[56] When Oscar read the story he was infuriated at his brother's treachery, although Willie repudiated the article as a pack of lies. Then Oscar's animosity intensified when Willie married again in 1894, this time to a young woman named Lily Lees with whom he had been living as man and wife. Penniless and without employment, he and Lily moved in to live with his mother, Lady Wilde. Oscar was angered by reports that Willie harshly demanded money from Lady Wilde, who could ill afford it, and that he flew into a temper if she hesitated.

Lady Wilde was devoted to both her sons and especially indebted to Oscar for his financial assistance. But she was very distressed at Oscar's hatred towards Willie. "Not a cheering prospect for me to have my two sons at enmity, and unable to meet at my deathbed," she wrote to Oscar.[57] She pleaded with him to forgive Willie for past insults and misdeeds and to show him kindness and friendship; otherwise she would die of grief. She emphasized that there was no reason for Oscar to quarrel with him simply because she had helped him with money. Willie himself wrote affectionately to Oscar begging for forgiveness, but without effect.[58] Oscar was immovable. Much as he adored his mother he was not prepared to reconcile with Willie merely for her sake. But, when out on bail between his first and second criminal trials, Oscar was so harassed in his quest to find accommodation that he was forced to seek shelter with his mother and Willie. The tension between the brothers was so marked and Oscar was so unhappy that Ernest and Ada Leverson offered him sanctuary in their own home.

It appears that Willie's attitude to Oscar, even in spite of the discord, was positive. During the course of the second trial in May 1895 Willie met his mother's friend the Comtesse de Brémont in the gardens of the Middle Temple. "Oscar will need me when the verdict is given," he said with visible emotion. "I must take care of my poor brother – for, one way or another, he will be a wreck after this terrible business."[59] And when Lady Wilde died in February 1896 it was Willie and his wife, Lily, who consulted Ernest Leverson on the best way to break the news to Oscar (then in Reading Gaol).[60] It was Lily who wrote to Constance requesting her to undertake the task. Willie, in a letter to More Adey, paid tribute to Oscar for his generosity to their mother.[60]

One of the other problems was that, at the time of Oscar's trials or imprisonment, certain of his clothes – a fur coat and two trunks – came to Lady Wilde's house in Oakley Street. According to Lily Wilde, Oscar in a fit of generosity told Willie he could have all his things (except his shirts) and do what he liked with them.[61] Willie predictably sold them – for £12 or £13 to a dealer. Oscar was particularly bitter at the loss of his fur coat ("I have had it for twelve years... it was at all my first nights, it knows me perfectly and I really want it"[62]), even though he had apparently donated it to his brother. To illustrate Willie's state in May 1897, Lily Wilde wrote:

> I take no responsibility as regards Willie and that any money from the sale of the clothes I had nothing to do with. Also Willie has not earned *one* farthing for the last ten months and I and my family have had to keep my home over his head. He is a very sick man and I had to pawn my wedding ring yesterday to get food to eat.[61]

When Oscar came out of prison he made no attempt to make contact with Willie. His hostility persisted, undiminished by their mother's death. Willie died on 13 March 1899, at the age of forty-six, from the complications of chronic alcoholism. When Ross telegraphed the news to Oscar, a cool and laconic reply came back: "Between him and me there had been, as you know, wide chasms for many years. *Requiescat in Pace.*" [63]

Oscar's inflexibility towards his brother, in spite of conciliatory overtures from Willie, was another indication of his inflated egotism and his unforgiving and uncompassionate attitude towards an only sibling who had been ill and miserable. It is ironic that one of Oscar's principal reasons for detesting his brother was Willie's "sponging" off Lady Wilde and others. For one who was the master sponger when *he* fell on hard times, this was a remarkably hypocritical stance.

Apart from difficulties that Wilde experienced with his family, there was also friction and dissension with some of his closest friends. It was during his imprisonment that the first signs of intolerance towards them emerged. Understandably, in that situation he was functioning under highly stressful circumstances and yet had to deal with complicated financial and domestic matters. In Chapter 6 the thorny question of the life interest of the marriage settlement was discussed in detail. The matter developed into one of central importance and from it arose issues of guardianship and divorce. Wilde wanted to yield the life interest to Constance, in exchange for a reasonably good financial dispensation, but his friends (particularly More Adey and Robert Ross) acted contrary to his wishes. They bid for and purchased the life interest with the result that Constance retaliated – first by depriving Wilde of his guardianship rights and then by threatening divorce. In the end he was driven to accept a deed of separation in which the life interest was to be surrendered to Constance and she, in turn, was to provide him with an annual allowance of £150. The eventual deal was far less favourable to Wilde's monetary and domestic interests than Constance's original offer, which was made before his friends intervened to acquire the life interest.

In the light of these bungled transactions, Oscar severely reprimanded both Ross and Adey for their incompetence and mismanagement, and he was especially vitriolic and insulting in his comments about Adey (see page 94).[64] Although he may have had some justification for his anger, he was unreasonably severe in his criticism. Ross and Adey had been very kind and dedicated in assisting Oscar and had given up a great deal of personal time to attend to his affairs. Whatever they did was done in what they genuinely believed to be

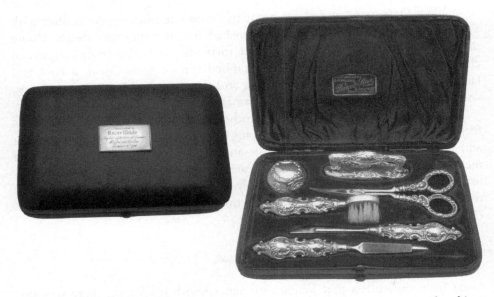

Figure 19   *This manicure set was inscribed to Oscar Wilde and presented to him on his forty-sixth birthday (16 October 1900) by his dear friends Robert Ross and Reginald Turner. At the time he was recuperating from mastoid surgery in his hotel bedroom in Paris, but complications set in and he died six weeks later. The hotel proprietor, Jean Dupoirier, was responsible for laying out Wilde's body and he used this manicure set to assist him in the task.*

(Private collection)

Wilde's best interests. Oscar's attack on these remarkable individuals evoked an emotional response from Reginald Turner, who warned him that he had seriously overstepped the mark with friends of such high calibre. And about Ross he remarked: "I fear, dear Oscar, that you have gone very near to breaking his heart."[65]

One can perhaps ascribe this bitterness and sarcasm to the noxious effect of prolonged imprisonment, although Wilde was then in the more favourable phase of it, under the humane governorship of Major Nelson. But there was yet to be a resurgence of the anger against Adey and Ross long after his release. When Oscar joined Bosie Douglas in Naples, Ross was distraught – possibly out of jealousy and a sense of rejection – and he expressed his strong disapproval to Oscar. There was also a difference in opinion between them over *The Ballad of Reading Gaol*, and by this stage Ross had had enough of Oscar. He wrote to Leonard Smithers, Wilde's publisher, in November 1897: "I regret to inform you that I have ceased to be on intimate terms with Oscar Wilde or to enjoy his confidence in business or any other matter . . ."[66]

The next instalment of Wilde's disaffection was when his allowance from Constance was stopped. He unashamedly blamed Adey and Ross for their lack of protest against such action, even though he and his friends knew perfectly well that this would be the outcome of his reunion with Douglas. Ross and Adey simply had no legitimate basis on which to contest the decision.

The most memorable event of Wilde's imprisonment was the writing of *De Profundis*,[67] an exceptionally long letter addressed to Bosie Douglas and composed during the first quarter of 1897. In this document Wilde blamed Douglas for the disastrous Queensberry case into which he was mercilessly inveigled; dwelt on the way Bosie had exploited and manipulated him to settle old scores with his father and then landed him in prison; accused the Queensberrys of reneging on their promise to meet the legal costs of the lawsuit; censured Bosie for making extravagant demands on him, listing the exorbitant sums of money spent on his food, accommodation and even gambling losses; and denounced Bosie's temper outbursts, the scenes and arguments, and his malicious conduct in Brighton when Oscar was ill. *De Profundis* is a vivid and inexorable catalogue of grievances, recriminations, bitterness and sorrow. In it Wilde achieved his long-overdue catharsis by unburdening himself of the pent-up and cumulative anger and resentment against Bosie. It is a relentless and meticulously structured assault on Douglas, and its mood and tone are diametrically opposed to Oscar's last communication with Bosie, written days before his conviction, which ended as follows: "O sweetest of all boys, most loved of all loves, my soul clings to your soul, my life is your life . . . you are my ideal of admiration and joy."[68]

There is scant acknowledgement in *De Profundis* of the delight and deep-seated love that he had felt for Bosie, and in this sense it is a distorted and misleading portrayal. It paints a persistently bleak picture of a relationship that, although clearly subject to Bosie's mercurial temperament, was nevertheless one full of romantic pleasure and mutual admiration. But there are also elements of insight and self-blame and there are hints of the possibility of future literary work. *De Profundis* suddenly deviates from personal remonstrances against Douglas into a lengthy discourse on the parallels between the life and personality of Christ and the spirituality and creativity of the artist, and on the connection between the sufferings of Christ and the intuitive inspiration and symbolism of the artist. In the end *De Profundis* offers Douglas hope and forgiveness and it concludes self-righteously with: "You came to me to learn the Pleasure of Life and the Pleasure of Art. Perhaps I am chosen to teach you something much more wonderful, the meaning of Sorrow, and its beauty."[69]

What is unambiguous in *De Profundis* is that Wilde had every intention of renewing his relationship with Bosie. As Ross was probably the first person to read the document, he would surely have recognized this and not been so surprised and distressed when the two re-established their relationship.

There is a most revealing letter written by Douglas to W.T. Stead in November 1895, over a year before Wilde launched into *De Profundis*. In this communication Douglas totally rejected the notion that he was an object of pity and the victim of Wilde's greater age and experience. "So far from his leading me astray it was I that (unwittingly) pushed him over the precipice. He lived 36 years without seeing me and then I came and dragged into his life all the influences of our morbid half insane heritage which reaches its highest point in that terrible father of mine . . ."[70] This is a startling admission by Douglas and, ironically, it adumbrates one of the themes elaborated on in *De Profundis*. It was as well that it was not available to the defence in the *Douglas vs. Ransome and the Times Book Club* libel trial in April 1913. The allegation against Douglas was that he was responsible for bringing about Wilde's ruin and disgrace, and this would have been a hugely embarrassing piece of evidence for Douglas to discount. In the event Douglas still lost the case.

There was an unpleasant development in Wilde's relationship with Ernest Leverson, the husband of his good friend Ada Leverson ("the Sphinx"). In March 1895, when Wilde embarked on the prosecution of the Marquess of Queensberry, he asked Leverson to advance him £500 for his legal expenses, undertaking to repay him within a week or ten days.[71] Leverson obliged, and for this Oscar was deeply grateful. He was also generous in buying several items of value at the Tite Street sale in April which he presented to Wilde as a gift on his release from prison. In May 1895 Ernest and Ada thoughtfully invited Oscar to stay at their house (rather than with his mother and brother) while he was out on bail. It was about then that Adela Schuster donated £1000 to Wilde for his personal and family's use, and he handed the money to Leverson to hold in trust for him. According to Leverson, Oscar insisted at the time (May 1895) that he (Leverson) refund himself the balance of £250 that was owing to him.[72] Oscar was infuriated when he later learned that Leverson had done just that. He maintained that Leverson had no right whatever to touch his money for any claim of his own. "It is my money, Reggie!" he wrote to Turner. " . . . Can you conceive such cruelty and fraud as to try to steal it from me?"[73] In a letter to More Adey from prison, he fumed that if Leverson had illegally seized the funds he would never speak to him again or consent to see him, and he would publicly and privately expose his dishonourable conduct.[74]

Wilde was true to his word and he severed his friendship with Ernest Leverson. That was a most unfortunate and unjust step because he had no grounds to accuse him of financial dishonesty. When Oscar needed to borrow the money urgently for the libel case, Leverson lent it to him immediately and in the expectation of a total reimbursement within a week or two. He had been

Figure 20 *A middle-aged Bosie Douglas – a period in his life when he had denounced the memory of Oscar Wilde, describing him publicly in court as "the greatest force for evil that has appeared in Europe in the last 350 years".*

(Photograph courtesy of Sotheby's London)

highly responsible and trustworthy in controlling Oscar's financial affairs (of which he subsequently provided a full account[75]), and he had even visited Wilde at Reading Prison in February 1896. One might argue, again, that Oscar overreacted because of his stressful environment and his understandable financial anxieties. But this explanation does not hold because six months after his release Oscar was still nursing his grievance against Leverson. This break with Ernest affected Wilde's behaviour towards Ada, who sent him many kind letters after his imprisonment which he never answered. Only two written communications are recorded from Wilde to Ada Leverson in the three-and-a-half years of his exile:[76] a querulous one in November 1897, commenting bitterly on Ernest's deceitfulness; and another a year later, which was nothing more than a short message accepting a dinner invitation to him and Bosie during her visit to Paris. He did however retain his affection for Ada by sending her inscribed copies of *The Ballad of Reading Gaol* and *The Importance of Being Earnest* in 1898 and 1899, respectively.[77] Ernest's good-naturedness was such that, despite Oscar's antipathy towards him, he still undertook in June 1898 to make a monetary contribution to a scheme of Robert Ross's to assist Wilde.[78]

Another long-standing and valuable friendship that perished precipitately was the one with Carlos Blacker. Blacker and Wilde had had a close and staunch relationship and Oscar had dedicated *The Happy Prince and Other Tales* (1888) to him. After his release there had been a warm correspondence between the two, with Oscar declaring, "You were always the truest of friends and the most sympathetic of companions."[79] Blacker had rendered considerable assistance and support to Constance and the children, including the offer of accommodation at various times in Freiburg, Germany. His involvement with both parties enabled him to act as a useful mediator between husband and wife in the early post-prison days, when there were plans for a meeting between Oscar and Constance and even suggestions of a possible restitution of the marriage. Blacker had given Wilde substantial sums of money from March to May 1898, and he was probably instrumental in getting Constance to restore his allowance. "Really you have saved my life for me, for a little at any rate . . . ," Wilde wrote to Blacker in his letter of thanks.[80] But that tribute was shortly to signal the abrupt end of their mutual respect and admiration. Blacker became embroiled in a huge public scandal in which he was victimized and forced to leave Paris.

Wilde wrote to Ross (June and July 1898) with a scathing denunciation of Blacker whom he described as behaving "like a hypocritical ass".[81] According to Oscar, Blacker had written him "a coarse, offensive letter" in which he had terminated their friendship.[82] He accused Wilde of attacking his private life in a French newspaper and of disclosing details of past scandals. Wilde replied with vehemence, demanded an apology for the disgraceful accusation and "told him a few truths about himself which he can ponder on in exile". He also described to Ross how he had gloated over the malicious publicity surrounding Blacker: "It amuses me to see Tartuffe in the pillory. I have the most terrible of all pleasures, the pleasure of the spectator . . ."[82]

It is difficult to unravel the dynamics of the vicious exchanges between Wilde and Blacker other than to state that much of the acrimony revolved around the case of Alfred Dreyfus. Dreyfus was the French army officer of Jewish descent who became the focus and victim of the Dreyfus Affair, which split France into two hostile factions at the turn of the twentieth century and heightened anti-Semitism. On manufactured evidence, he was wrongfully convicted in 1894 of selling military secrets to Germany and, in particular, to a Colonel von Schwartzkoppen. He was court-martialled, found guilty and sentenced to life imprisonment on Devil's Island. It emerged later that Commandant Esterhazy had forged the documents that incriminated Dreyfus, and it was only years afterwards that Dreyfus was eventually proven innocent and his sentence quashed.

Carlos Blacker, an ardent Dreyfusard, was an old friend of Alessandro Panizzardi's, the Italian military attaché in Paris, who was actively involved in the espionage business with von Schwartzkoppen. Panizzardi became convinced that Dreyfus was innocent and, in a desperately emotional state about the miscarriage of justice, he confided his evidence to Blacker who, in turn, imparted it in the strictest secrecy to Wilde in an effort to recruit him to the cause. Blacker was planning to expose the entire fraud in the English press. Wilde in the meantime had met Esterhazy himself, who had confessed to him that he had masterminded the forgeries. Wilde, instead of being disgusted that an innocent man should have been so persecuted, expressed mild admiration for Esterhazy's intrigue and machinations. Worse still, he allegedly broke the undertaking he made to Blacker and leaked the secret information gleaned from him to two journalists, thereby pre-empting the English press release. A new wave of public uproar was created in France, with Émile Zola in the forefront. Blacker's name was revealed as the source of the story and he came under fierce attack from the anti-Dreyfusards, who published scandalous material about his past life which, it was presumed, had come from Wilde. The result was that Blacker was forced to flee from Paris. This drama of deceit, fraud and complicity, and the parts played in it by Blacker and Wilde, respectively, are presented in detail elsewhere.[83,84]

The abrupt dissolution of the long-standing Wilde-Blacker friendship was another casualty within Wilde's interpersonal domain. It is usually invidious to apportion blame for the breakdown of a relationship: there are always two sides and each side has its own reasons. But Oscar was not always faithful to the truth and he was verbally skilled in his own advocacy and defence. *De Profundis* is a striking example of his distinctly biased and tendentious account of his affair with Bosie Douglas. When provoked he was capable of writing abusive and damning letters, as demonstrated in his insensitive and unfair treatment of Robert Ross, More Adey and Ernest Leverson. Carlos Blacker had been a compassionate friend in times of need; and if it was true that Wilde had betrayed his secret disclosures to a pair of journalists (probably to create a sensation), then it is understandable that Blacker's trust would have been shattered. After Oscar's death, he recorded his feelings in a letter to Otho Holland Lloyd:

> I had known him for 20 years and for many years up to 1893 saw him daily . . . After 1895 I saw him a counted number of times and then he treated me with gross cruelty and injustice and we parted . . . this final severance under the circumstances has grieved me deeply. When I saw him on his bed [deathbed] and considered the old days, and the sufferings he had endured and caused others to suffer, I broke down and cried as I am almost ashamed to have cried . . .[85]

Wilde had believed (erroneously) that Blacker was a Jew on his father's side. In his angry letter to Ross cited above,[81] he added after mentioning the Jewish origin: "I hope on the day of St Hugh of Lincoln there will be a general massacre, but I don't know when the day occurs. Do you?" St Hugh was a boy of nine whose mutilated body was found at the bottom of a well in Lincoln (*circa* 1255). Legend has it that he had been abducted by Jews and ritually murdered after being scourged and crowned with thorns. In retribution, eighteen Jews were said to have been killed.[86]

This ugly sentiment of Wilde's and his seeming indifference to Dreyfus's fate have raised queries about his possible anti-Semitism. He referred to Lieutenant-Colonel Isaacson, the governor of Reading Prison, as "a 'mulberry-faced Dictator': a great red-faced, bloated Jew"[87] (Isaacson was in fact not Jewish). Christopher Nassaar has drawn attention to the character of Isaacs, a Jewish theatre manager, in *The Picture of Dorian Gray*.[88] Wilde depicts Isaacs as "the horrid old Jew", "a hideous Jew", "the fat Jew manager" and "such a monster". In the story Dorian and Sibyl Vane are repelled by Isaacs, and there is a strong anti-Semitic tone in Wilde's representation of him. As Nassaar comments: "It is difficult to imagine a Jew reading Wilde's novel without being offended by the passages on Isaacs." Indeed, in some recent editions of *The Picture of Dorian Gray* the word "Jew" is removed and replaced by "man" or "manager". There is no suggestion of anti-Semitism in any of Wilde's other works. Wilde had some excellent Jewish friends, notably Ada Leverson and

Adela Schuster, and he had allegedly once proposed marriage to Charlotte Montefiore, who belonged to a renowned and wealthy Jewish family (see page 138).

Oscar Wilde had an unmistakably ambivalent relationship with Frank Harris. Harris was kind and generous to Oscar: he took up the cudgels on his behalf with the Prison Commissioners in an effort to ease his prison conditions (see page 54); he provided him with clothes and money on his release from gaol; he offered to take him on a month's driving-tour of the Pyrenees; and he invited him to spend some months on the Riviera as his guest. But Oscar was a little intimidated by the forcefulness of his personality and by his insistence "on my being always at high intellectual pressure; it is most exhausting".[89] Oscar maintained that when Harris had visited him at Reading in April 1897 he told him that he had made a fortune in South Africa and that he would send him a cheque for £500 before his release. This promise never materialized, and in a bout of anger Wilde wrote: "The Frank Harrises of life are a dreadful type. I hope to see no more of them."[90] Consequently, having accepted the offer of the driving-tour (all expenses paid), Oscar then refused. It was an act which greatly hurt Harris as he had considerably planned it as a special and wholesome treat for Oscar immediately after the rigours of his imprisonment.

This behaviour was consistent with Wilde's pattern of rejecting and denigrating his best friends when they did not meet his unrealistic expectations on a particular occasion. His insensitivity and bluntness induced unnecessary anguish and unhappiness in these friends, and it was only because of their exceptional tolerance and goodwill that some of them persevered in the relationship. Frank Harris was one of these, and he recovered sufficiently from the driving-tour rebuff to resume ties with Oscar and to continue his support and generosity.

But it was with Harris that yet another feud arose. While Oscar was at Worthing in 1894 he quickly outlined the scenario of a play for George Alexander about love between a man and a woman, later to be entitled *Mr and Mrs Daventry*. He was unable to work on it before his imprisonment but after his release he latched onto the idea that the sale of the scenario would bring in a much needed source of income. He proceeded, deceitfully, to sell it to at least six other people, including Frank Harris. With Harris he apparently went further by permitting him to write the full play himself. Harris not only went ahead and completed the play but by the early autumn of 1900 he had organized its production at the Royalty Theatre in London with Mrs Patrick Campbell in the role of Mrs Daventry. On learning this, Wilde demanded more money from Harris on the basis of the royalties. The two met in late September

1900 and Wilde assigned to Harris the entire rights in the plot and scenario for the sum of £175 and a one-quarter share of the profits. Harris made an immediate cash payment of £25 and then sent a further £25. But he withheld the balance of £125 because he soon discovered that Oscar had sold the scenario to several others, who each had to be compensated in the sum of £100 before *Mr and Mrs Daventry* could be staged.[91] The aggrieved Wilde bitterly accused Harris of breaking his contract. This imbroglio occurred after Oscar had undergone major ear surgery that incurred substantial medical expenses; this made it critical for him to recover the money from Harris. It was most unfortunate that his difficult convalescence was complicated by persistent agitation and ruminations over Harris's perceived perfidy. The last five recorded letters that Oscar wrote before his death were repetitious pleas to Frank Harris to honour his pledge. It is not unlikely that the stress of this dispute compromised Oscar's post-operative recovery and predisposed him to the infectious relapse that ended his life. But the wrangle over *Mr and Mrs Daventry* was of Wilde's making. No blame can be laid at Frank Harris's door because ultimately Harris himself became the target of Wilde's wheeling and dealing.

In conclusion, it is worth noting other less glaring instances of Wilde's petulance towards friends or inattentiveness to their needs. In April 1895 Oscar had remarked to Robert Sherard, with whom he had had a close association since 1883: "[Y]our chivalrous friendship – your fine, chivalrous friendship – is worth more than all the money in the world."[92] But in 1897, when Oscar had moved in with Douglas in Naples, the news reached Sherard at the Authors' Club in London. Sherard openly expressed the view that this arrangement was a great mistake and one that would alienate Wilde's sympathizers and be used against him by his enemies. An account of these remarks was conveyed to Wilde, who took umbrage and fired back: "When you wish to talk morality – always an amusement – and to attack me behind my back, don't, like a good fellow, talk so loud, as the reverberation reaches from the Club to Naples."[93] Perhaps Sherard was imprudent in articulating his views on Wilde's lifestyle to members of the Authors' Club. It was a costly indiscretion because thenceforth a once firm and cherished friendship collapsed, and contact between the two men dwindled to almost nothing.

Adela Schuster was extraordinarily generous to Wilde and at the time of his trials she gave him £1000 (£100,000 in today's money) for his own use. As she explained to More Adey: "Personally I have a real affection for Oscar besides any immense admiration for his genius, and I do and always shall feel honoured by any friendship he may show me."[94] She was particularly absorbed by his charming tales and brilliant paradoxes, and she tried to encourage him while he was in prison to write down these stories. In *De Profundis* Oscar expressed deep indebtedness to Miss Schuster, "one of the most beautiful personalities I have ever known", whose exceptional sympathy and kindness "really assisted me . . . to bear the burden of my troubles more than anyone else in the whole world has".95

What is very surprising is that after his imprisonment he did not send her (as far as can be ascertained) a single letter of gratitude or appreciation. He wrote so many letters to so many people that it is astounding that Adela Schuster never received a communication from him. In fact, she wrote to More Adey the year after Oscar's release to ask for information about him and his activities. "I had heard nothing of him since last May [1897]," she replied to Adey, who had by then sent her a detailed and updated account of Wilde's movements and circumstances.96 Five months later she made further inquiries from Adey:

A friend of mine – a lady living in Paris – has written to ask me whether Oscar Wilde is endeavouring to lead a more respectable life, and whether I think she could invite him to her house. Of course I know nothing and therefore find it difficult to answer. She is very sorry for him and wants to be of use to him if possible . . . what happened about the life interest? I never heard how that was settled.97

There is reference to a postcard (dated 21 June 1897) from Wilde to Adey asking whether he had received Oscar's letter addressed to Miss Schuster but sent to Adey's address for forwarding to her. Oscar had not heard from her and was afraid his letter had gone astray. "Otherwise how ungrateful a churl I must seem to that gracious and wonderful personality."98 This is the only mention of a possible letter to Schuster in his entire post-prison correspondence, and it seems obvious that it never reached her.

Wilde was very conscious of his debt to Schuster. He wanted to present her with a copy of *The Ballad of Reading Gaol* in February 1898 but, as he had not communicated with her since his release, he felt too ashamed. He did, however, intend to give her (through Ross) his own Japanese vellum copy of *The Importance of Being Earnest*.99 When Ross published *The Duchess of Padua* in the Collected Edition in 1908 he dedicated it to Adela Schuster and wrote: "A few months before his death Mr Oscar Wilde expressed to me a regret that he had never dedicated any of his works to one from whom he had received such infinite kindness and to whom he was under obligations no flattering dedication could repay."100 And so Miss Schuster did get a belated, posthumous recognition from the one she so greatly admired.

There was another, perhaps even greater, act of generosity that Wilde apparently failed to acknowledge. This was Sir Edward Clarke's munificent gesture of defending him without fee in both criminal trials that followed the Queensberry libel case. Clarke's junior counsel, Humphreys and Matthews, also acted gratuitously. (Nowadays he would have been able to procure legal aid for his defence.) While Wilde may well have thanked Clarke and his team casually during the course of the trials, he never sent a formal letter of gratitude to Sir Edward, not only for waiving his fees but also for the highly skilful way in which he conducted the defence. As *The Law Times* (1 June 1895) commented:

> The devotion of Sir Edward Clarke to the cause of a client who, at his best, was a moral monstrosity, is startling. It has been called heroic. Possibly it was – had it been successful the achievement would have been phenomenal. But it failed, and the worthlessness of the cause which received self-sacrifice of every kind becomes painfully prominent . . .

Robert Ross approached Clarke in March 1897 to seek his intervention with the Home Secretary to get a remission of the last weeks of Wilde's sentence. Clarke was unsuccessful but he told Ross: "[I]t is impossible for me to forget that before I undertook the most painful case that I have ever been engaged in, he gave me his word of honour as a gentleman that there was no foundation for the charges which were afterwards so completely proved."[101] It is significant that Clarke was so embarrassed by the Wilde trials that he omitted any mention of them (sensational as they were) in his published memoirs. But there was gratitude for Sir Edward from another source. On 26 May 1895 (the day after Oscar was convicted) Alfred Douglas wrote from abroad to thank him "from the bottom of my heart for your noble and generous and superb efforts on behalf of my friend".[102]

Finally, there is another individual to whom Wilde owed some act of homage. In 1892 Oscar met and befriended Alfred Taylor, and it was through him that he was introduced to a number of the rent-boys. Taylor was arrested at about the same time as Wilde and both men were committed for trial. At the first criminal trial, Wilde and Taylor were charged jointly under a single indictment. This ended in disagreement among the jury. At the second trial Taylor was tried separately and found guilty; then Wilde was tried and found guilty. The men stood together in the dock while Mr Justice Wills meted out the same sentence to both.

It is noteworthy that Taylor was offered his liberty if he turned Queen's evidence and agreed to testify against Wilde. Commendably he refused, and he accordingly paid the full penalty of two years' imprisonment with hard labour.

Had Wilde not instituted a criminal libel suit against the Marquess, neither he nor Taylor would have been arrested and convicted. Thus it was directly through Wilde's action against Queensberry that Taylor was subsequently identified, charged and sentenced.

I have questioned whether Oscar evinced any guilt or remorse at having effectively (albeit unwittingly) delivered Alfred Taylor into the hands of the law; or, alternatively, whether he expressed any praise for, or recognition of, Taylor's loyalty and courage in declining the Queen's evidence escape route. There is not a word about Taylor (and what he had been made to suffer on Wilde's behalf) in Wilde's abundant correspondence during and after his imprisonment. Oscar was so mawkishly self-pitying throughout the pages of *De Profundis*, bemoaning his fate and blaming Douglas for propelling him into it, that he entirely overlooked any acknowledgement to Taylor, his honourable friend who was enduring equally repulsive conditions. Again Bosie Douglas scored points. He sent £50 to Arthur Newton, Taylor's solicitor: "I felt sorry (not being English) that Taylor should be left as he was: in prison, quite penniless, unfriended and undefended. So I sent Mr Newton a cheque and asked him to do the best he could for Taylor with such a small sum."[103]

I return now to the statement of George Bernard Shaw's, quoted at the beginning of this chapter, namely, that Oscar Wilde was "incapable of friendship". On balance, I maintain that Shaw was correct in this assertion. Constance came to the same conclusion. In a letter written to Arthur Humphreys weeks before her death, she conceded that Oscar seemed to have behaved badly to many of his friends and that his punishment had not taught him the most important lesson – that he was not the only person in the world. "I did think that he was a good friend, but I am afraid I have to change my mind about that as about many other things."[104]

To be a friend of Oscar Wilde's was a mixed blessing and a risky investment. If one humoured him and praised him, and listened attentively and appreciatively to him, then he could be charming and effusive. But if one criticized him or opposed his wishes, he could be abrasive and obnoxious.

Cecily says in *The Importance of Being Earnest*:

It is always painful to part from people whom one has known for a very brief space of time. The absence of old friends one can endure with equanimity. But even a momentary separation from any one to whom one has just been introduced is almost unbearable.

This sums up Oscar's attitude: old, tried and tested friendships were dispensable, exploitable and reproachable; but fresh and new acquaintances were precious and irresistible.

12

HISTRIONIC PERSONALITY DISORDER

IN his petition of 2 July 1896 to the Home Secretary (see page 55), Oscar Wilde cited Professor Max Nordau as an eminent man of science who, in his book *Degeneration*, had devoted part of a chapter to him as a typical example of "the intimate connection between madness and the literary and artistic temperament".[1] This work was originally published in German as *Entartung* (two volumes, 1892–1893), but it was the English translation *(Degeneration)* that blazoned Wilde's name to the British public as a model case in support of Nordau's theory of degeneracy. And the timing was impeccable. *Degeneration* appeared on 22 February 1895, a week before Wilde launched his criminal libel action against Queensberry. By the time the trials were in full swing, the publicity accorded to *Degeneration* (which had already gone through five impressions) was highly prejudicial to Wilde's cause.[2] On 16 June 1895 the *Weekly Sun* published an entire front page review of the book and gave it a very favourable reception.

The following is what Max Nordau wrote about Oscar Wilde, although it is obvious that he was describing him as he presented himself in the "aesthetic mode" of the early 1880s:

> He appears to have abandoned the dress of the present time because it offends his sense of the beautiful; but this is only a pretence in which probably he himself does not believe. What really determines his actions is the hysterical craving to be noticed, to occupy the attention of the world with himself, to get talked about . . . When, therefore, an Oscar Wilde goes about in 'aesthetic costume' among gazing Philistines, exciting either their ridicule or their wrath, it is no indication of independence of character, but rather from a purely anti-social-istic, ego-maniacal recklessness and hysterical longing to make a sensation, justified by no exalted aim; nor is it from a strong desire for beauty, but from a malevolent mania for contradiction.[3]

While Nordau's assessment may sound exaggerated, it is an accurate reflection of Wilde's character traits. What he emphasized were the following descriptions: "hysterical craving to be noticed", "a pretence in which probably he himself does not believe", and an "ego-maniacal recklessness and hysterical longing to make a sensation".

Over sixty years later Macdonald Critchley, the distinguished British neurologist, essentially endorsed Nordau's appraisal, with the following conclusion of his own:

> In seeking to explain Oscar Wilde's conduct and language, it is tempting to invoke the hypothesis of a constitutional hysterical personality . . . This diagnosis would go a long way towards accounting for Wilde's exhibitionism, his histrionic style and behaviour, his flippancy, his shallow emotivity and his lack of awareness of the gravity of a situation.[4]

I believe that Oscar Wilde was a prime example of a hysterical personality. This personality type is characterized by both instability and emotional immaturity. Such individuals show brisk reactions and moods; quick but evanescent enthusiasms and infatuations; easy laughter and tears; and, above all, a superficiality of feelings and responses. The hysterical personality demonstrates marked features of egocentricity and theatricality. Almost everything is valued in superlatives and the events of ordinary life are often dramatized. These personalities show an incapacity for insight that plays havoc with social relationships. They resort easily to self-deception, dishonesty and lying, and their potential for conflict with society is enhanced.[5]

Hysterical personalities behave histrionically in all kinds of situations, whether these are serious or trivial. Their dress is usually vivid and sometimes bizarre; they crave to be in the centre of attention, and if necessary they will manoeuvre themselves into it. Because of their egocentricity, they are demanding and their desires need to be gratified quickly; if not, their low threshold for frustration and delay causes them to react with angry outbursts.

Oscar Wilde had several of the features that would have categorized him as a hysterical personality. However, in order to establish the diagnosis in a more reliable and acceptable manner, I shall apply the criteria of two modern and internationally recognized diagnostic classifications. The first is the *Diagnostic and Statistical Manual of Mental Disorders: Fourth Edition, Text Revision* (2000) of the American Psychiatric Association, Washington DC (hereinafter referred to as the *DSM-IV*). The second is the *International Classification of Diseases: Mental and Behavioural Disorders, Tenth Edition* (1994) of the World Health Organization (hereinafter referred to as the *ICD-10*). Both these systems have discarded the diagnostic term "hysterical personality disorder" in favour of *histrionic personality disorder.*

The problem that immediately arises is that many individuals show some histrionic characteristics in their personalities and yet can hardly be deemed to have a histrionic personality *disorder*. What is it then that distinguishes the "normal" person with histrionic tendencies from the "abnormal" person who qualifies for the diagnosis of histrionic personality disorder? In a nutshell, the diagnosis of a personality disorder (and there are several types other than histrionic) demands that the traits in question are stable and of long duration (i.e., since childhood or adolescence); that they are inflexible and maladaptive and deviate markedly from the culturally accepted norms of behaviour; that they produce distress or harm to the individual and others; and that the deviation cannot be explained on the basis of another psychiatric or medical condition.[6]

Both the DSM-IV and the ICD-10 set out a list of the defining criteria which have to be met in order to satisfy a diagnosis of histrionic personality disorder. The individual being assessed is rated as either positive or negative for each of the criteria. To award a positive rating, one must be certain that that criterion has been a dominant, fixed and enduring feature of the individual's personality and is not merely an occasional or fluctuating occurrence, or one brought on by environmental or situational circumstances. Where there is doubt whether a particular criterion is adequately fulfilled, or where the evidence for it is equivocal, then it is rated as negative.

Let us first judge Wilde against the DSM-IV criteria for histrionic personality disorder.[7] To make such a diagnosis in his case, he would have to be scored positively on at least *five* of the following criteria:

CRITERION 1: *Feels uncomfortable in situations in which he is not the centre of attention.* On this he definitely registers a positive. Oscar's main drive in life, as he himself admitted, was to become famous and, if not famous, then notorious. As described in Chapter 10, he strove for attention and recognition from his Oxford days onwards. His public cultivation of the aesthetic creed, his social ambition to meet with illustrious people, and his success at capturing the focus at dinner parties and similar occasions were all hallmarks of this quest for the limelight. His lecturing tour of North America, in which he paraded as the apostle of aestheticism, was a conspicuous example of self-advertisement.

Throughout his life Wilde's ambition was to be the object of attention, and in his later years, when he was not so flamboyant as he had been in his twenties, he resorted to more subtle methods such as charm, flattery and flirtatiousness. Robert Ross remarked that even in prison "Oscar would hastily assume one of his hundred artificial manners, which he has for every person and every occasion".[8] This chameleon-like propensity was part of Wilde's strategy for fine-tuning his presence in company so as to evoke the desired attention. The sharp reaction from the critics to some of his provocative literary work heightened his self-promotional campaign. After the publication of *The Picture of Dorian Gray* he was able to declare in the *St. James's Gazette* (26 June 1890): "I think I may say without vanity – though I do not wish to appear to run vanity down – that of all men in England I am the one who requires least advertisement." He then added (with a touch of insincerity, I suspect): "I am tired to death of being advertised. I feel no thrill when I see my name in a paper."

Conversely, Wilde found it unbearable to exist in a state of oblivion. When he lived in the small French village of Berneval in the late summer of 1897, amputated from any meaningful community, he became desperate and depressed ("quite suicidal") and soon departed for Naples. With remarkable prescience, Oscar had responded to a questionnaire item ("What is your idea of misery?") *twenty* years before: "Living a poor and respectable life in an obscure village."[9]

CRITERION 2: *In his interactions with others he often behaves in an inappropriate sexually seductive or provocative manner.* I rate him as positive. Oscar was constantly inveigling friends and acquaintances into intimate or romantic relationships. His life, particularly after his marriage, was filled with an almost uninterrupted succession of attempts to seduce young men. His correspondence reveals the extent to which he would use romantic or sexual imagery to flatter others and win over their affections. The practice of exchanging photographs was part of this process. Neil McKenna's *The Secret Life of Oscar Wilde* gives a vivid commentary on Wilde's marathon of seductive and sexually provocative behaviour.[10]

CRITERION 3: *He shows emotions that are rapidly changeable and shallow.* I score him as positive. This trait relates to emotional lability and emotional shallowness. Wilde could wax eloquent and be high-spirited and effusive; and then he could descend into darker and diabolical moods and be full of anger and bitterness. He was very sensitive to loneliness and boredom and in that situation he was unable to maintain emotional stability. He spent much of his time in pursuit of stimulation: "I myself would sacrifice everything for a new experience . . . I would go to the stake for a sensation," he wrote to his young friend Henry Marillier.[11] In a similar vein he likened his exploits with the rent-boys to "feasting with panthers" where "the danger was half the excitement".[12]

The brisk on-and-off vacillations (equally strong in both directions) with Bosie Douglas were characteristic of his ever-changing emotional state. There is a pronounced example of this extreme changeability in his letters. Just after his release from prison he wrote to Robert Ross: "To be with him [Douglas] would be to return to the hell from which I do think I have been released. I hope never to see him again."[13] A few days later he continued: "Bosie can almost ruin me. I earnestly beg that some entreaty be made to him not to do so a second time."[14] Several days after that he confessed to Bosie: "Of course I love you more that anyone else. But our lives are irreparably severed, as far as meeting goes."[15] And barely a week later Oscar was arranging for Bosie to visit him in Berneval.[16]

Wilde's turbulent approach to some of his closest friends, as explored in the previous chapter, was an indication of his emotional reactivity and the alarming shift of his feelings when he perceived opposition or resistance from others. His display of emotions tended to be shallow, superficial and oriented more to the moment or the situation than to any intrinsic sentiments or strongly held convictions. Allied to his emotional shallowness was his capacity for posing and for pretence. He was an undisputed master at acting a part and he did this with aplomb. But he could abandon one role if necessary and speedily assume another and different one. "The Oscar of the first period is dead" had been a slogan of his; this illustrated that when his once aesthetic posture had outgrown its usefulness he could painlessly discard it.

CRITERION 4: *He consistently uses his physical appearance as a means of gaining attention.* There is no doubt that Wilde gets a full mark on this item. For him dress was all-important: it was the vehicle to announce or enhance his presence or to create an effect, and he exploited it to the utmost. He gave fastidious attention to his apparel, as discussed in Chapter 10. His attire changed in accordance with the changing images of himself that he wished to project onto the public – be it aesthete or dandy or man about town. He spent an excessive amount of time and money on clothes, buttonholes and grooming; and in the early days of his marriage he even imposed his dress-sense on Constance and made decisions regarding the style, texture and colour of her garments.

Wilde's arrival at the Marlborough Street Police Court for the preliminary hearing of the Queensberry libel case was newsworthy. As the *Evening News* of 9 March 1895 reported: "[W]hen Oscar Wilde drove up in a carriage and pair, a magnificent turn-out with coachman and cockaded footman . . . he was hardly recognized outside the court." The paramountcy of physical appearance to Oscar was highlighted by his catastrophic reaction to the Clapham Junction incident (see page 171) and by his acute distress at having his hair cut in prison. A month before his discharge from Reading, he petitioned the Home Secretary, in a state almost of panic, to spare him the ordeal of exposure to journalists on his exit from the prison.[17] He wrote to More Adey: "To me I confess the prospect of being pursued by interviewers is horrible, especially considering the terrible change in my appearance."[18] (Ironically, Oscar's appearance on his release was far healthier and trimmer than it had been prior to the trials!)

CRITERION 5: *He has a style of communication that is excessively impressionistic and lacking in detail.* I would give him a positive rating on this trait. His style of speech and writing was "excessively impressionistic and lacking in detail" (to use the words of the DSM-IV). Wilde was often given to expressing himself with dramatic flair and in highly colourful, evocative phrases but without factual detail or supporting evidence. A scrutiny of his correspondence reveals the flowery and extravagant manner in which he wrote, not only to close friends but also to fairly casual acquaintances. To Ellen Terry he began a letter with: "Your love is more wonderful even than a crystal caught in bent reeds of gold . . ."[19] To John Ruskin he gushed forth: "[T]o you the gods gave eloquence . . . so that your message might come to us with the fire of passion, and the marvel of music, making the deaf to hear, and the blind to see."[20] To Aniela Gielgud he expressed delight at the beauty of her name: "Aniela! it has an exquisite forest simplicity about it, and sounds most sweetly out of tune with this fiery-coloured artifical world of ours – rather like a daisy on a railway bank!"[21] Complimenting Richard Le Gallienne on his recently published book, Wilde described it thus: "It is a wonderful book, full of exquisite intuitions, and bright illuminating thought-flashes, and swift, sudden, sure revelations – a book behind which . . . thought shows itself stained by colour and passion, rich and Dionysiac and red-veined . . . "[22]

CRITERION 6: *He engages in self-dramatization, theatricality and an exaggerated display of emotion.* Wilde gets an unquestionably positive score on this item. Much of Chapter 10 deals with Oscar's self-dramatization and theatricality, and numerous examples are given. His tendency towards exaggerated expressions of emotion was evident not only in his exudation of excessive charm and flattery towards people who pleased him but also in his inappropriate anger at, and vituperative criticism of, friends (such as More Adey, Ernest Leverson and Carlos Blacker) who offended him.

CRITERION 7: *He is suggestible, being easily influenced by other people or circumstances.* On this criterion of suggestibility, there is some evidence that Wilde was subject to it. For example, he placed an undue amount of faith in horoscopes[23] and in fortune-tellers (especially Mrs Robinson)[24] whose forecasts, inaccurate as they often turned out to be, were taken seriously by him. He was also decidedly superstitious, as discussed by Coakley.[25] On the other hand, Oscar could often be stubbornly non-suggestible and single-minded, as in his decision to return to Douglas despite the unanimous chorus of his wife and friends. There is doubt about this item and it is therefore scored as negative.

CRITERION 8: *He regards relationships as being more intimate than they really are.* On balance, I would mark him as positive on this criterion. He was very prone to flights into romantic fantasy, and his letters to friends and acquaintances, male and female, were far more intense in their expression of feelings than was justified by the actual nature of the relationship. His series of letters to Ellen Terry highlights his passionate attachment to her:[26] it began in July 1879 with his composing and sending her a sonnet "as a small proof of my great and loyal admiration for your splendid artistic powers, and the noble tenderness and pathos of your acting". His friendship with Rennell Rodd and the improper and effusive dedication of Rodd's book of poems that he gave to himself (see page 134) is another example. He wrote to W. Graham Robertson, the artist and writer: "I am sorry you are going away, but your narcissus keeps you in my memory. What do you allow your friends to call you? 'W'? or 'Graham'? I like my friends to call me Oscar."[27] To Aubrey Richardson Wilde sent a surprisingly suggestive letter: "What a pretty name you have! it is worthy of fiction . . . There is music in its long syllables, and a memory of romance, and a suggestion of wonder."[28] And to Le Gallienne, after he had praised his book, he added: "Friendship and love like ours need not meetings, but they are delightful. I hope your laurels are not too thick across your brow for me to kiss your eyelids".[22]

In summary, Oscar Wilde scores seven out of eight on the list of DSM-IV diagnostic criteria. This establishes beyond doubt the diagnosis of histrionic personality disorder. However, in order to cross-validate the DSM-IV system, it is desirable to evaluate Wilde's personality traits against the other internationally accepted diagnostic classification, namely, the ICD-10. The specific criteria for histrionic personality disorder are shown in the table below, and a diagnosis requires the presence of at least *four* of these characteristics.

ICD-10 Diagnostic Criteria for Histrionic Personality Disorder
At least four of the following must be present:

(1) self-dramatization, theatricality or exaggerated expression of emotion;

(2) suggestibility (the individual is easily influenced by others or by circumstances);

(3) shallow and labile affectivity;

(4) continual seeking for excitement and activities in which the individual is the centre of attention;

(5) inappropriate seductiveness in appearance or behaviour;

(6) overconcern with physical attractiveness.

Table reproduced from *ICD-10 Classification of
Mental and Behavioural Disorders* (1994), World
Health Organization.[29]

To avoid duplication, I shall not repeat the analysis as done for the DSM-IV. But in scoring the ICD-10 list, I would award Wilde a positive rating on five criteria – numbers 1, 3, 4, 5 and 6 – thus confirming the diagnosis of histrionic personality disorder by an alternative diagnostic procedure.

The DSM-IV outlines some of the behavioural features associated with the disorder, and it is noteworthy how these reliably depict Oscar Wilde's temperament:

[T]hese individuals may crave novelty, stimulation, and excitement and have a tendency to become bored with their usual routine . . . [T]heir actions are often directed at obtaining immediate satisfaction . . . Longer-term relationships may be neglected to make way for the excitement of new relationships.[7]

There is a need to reiterate why the constellation of traits possessed by Wilde charaterized him as a histrionic personality disorder. Why is he diagnosed as having a *disorder* and not merely regarded as an individual with histrionic personality features? There are a sizeable number of people in the population with such tendencies, and indeed the presence of one or two histrionic traits may prove advantageous to the person and even enrich her or his life or career. For example, criterion 4 in the DSM-IV ("he consistently uses his physical appearance as a means of gaining attention") may in itself augment an individual's status or success in the community, or enhance the positive perception of that person by others. This benefit is obviously dependent on the role which he or she exercises in society: for instance, it is much more likely to prove useful to an actor or politician than to a laboratory scientist or computer engineer. As shown in Chapter 10, there is no doubt that some of Wilde's histrionic manifestations – his dress and showmanship – catapulted him into the public eye more swiftly than otherwise. Alfred Douglas was correct when he wrote: "He [Wilde] deliberately adopted an eccentric style of dress to get for himself, by a short cut, the audience which otherwise would, for many years, have been denied him."[31]

In the light of the above, why then should Oscar Wilde be labelled as having a histrionic personality disorder? Indeed, instead of constituting an abnormality, his behaviour actually assisted him in becoming a celebrity. This diagnosis, which is more commonly applied to females than males, is given to only a very small percentage of the population (say, two to three per cent); in these persons the multiple characteristics defined in the DSM-IV and ICD-10 represent a virtually lifelong and deviant behaviour pattern that causes impairment, harm or distress to the individual and to others. It is this aspect of *producing harm or damage* to oneself and others that is the litmus test for assigning the notion of a disorder to a specific personality profile.

There is no doubt that Wilde fulfilled the requirements for a diagnosis of histrionic (previously hysterical) personality disorder, thereby confirming the opinions of Max Nordau[3] and Macdonald Critchley.[4] In short, he exhibited a combination of emotional immaturity and instability, egocentricity, and dramatic and florid self-advertisement. All of these attributes were intensified by his extraordinary intelligence, wit and conversation. This blend of flamboyance, vanity and razor-sharp intellect contributed to his unique brand of creative genius and epigrammatic brilliance, and it escalated him into a position of fame.

Thus, at the time of the receipt of Queensberry's card, he was at the zenith of his career, with two plays running to packed houses in the West End – and likely to continue running for a long time. He would have received an excellent income from the royalties, which, if properly managed, would have made him into a wealthy man. But three months later Wilde was in gaol; his marriage and family life had been destroyed; his personal possessions had been sold in execution; and he was *en route* to bankruptcy. His plays had been suspended; his literary works withdrawn from circulation; and he and his reputation had been virtually extinguished. This cataclysmic reversal of fortune on all fronts was a direct consequence of his character and behaviour. This is the rationale for attaching the label of a *disorder* to Wilde's personality. It has been generally assumed that Wilde's ruin and downfall ensued because of his prosecution of Queensberry; and that had he thrown the offensive card into the fire his subsequent life and work would probably have remained intact. In Chapter 1 I argued at length that this was a simplistic and unrealistic notion. Wilde and Queensberry were on a collision course, and had been for about a year. Passivity on Oscar's part would not have appeased the Marquess, who was clearly intent on inciting Wilde into action. Had the card not evoked a reprisal, he would have persevered in his campaign to destroy Wilde – possibly with the risk of physical violence. ("If I were to shoot this hideous monster in the street, I should be perfectly justified," he had written.)

Where Wilde's personality had caused his downfall was *not* in his act of suing Queensberry for criminal libel, but in engineering and orchestrating the prolonged sequence of events that provided the Marquess with the ammunition with which to persecute him.

Individuals with abnormal histrionic personalities are so preoccupied with their own ostentatious behaviour and with the gratification of their need for stimulation and excitement that they lose perspective on the effects of their conduct on society. They lack judgement and have poor insight into the consequences of their activities. Wilde fitted this stereotype precisely. He was so entangled in the fulfilment of his own desires and pleasures that caution and discretion were abandoned. He was fully aware of the Criminal Law Amendment Act and that his liaisons with the rent-boys were an imprisonable offence. Yet he made not a vestige of an attempt to behave clandestinely: on the contrary, he flaunted his associations with his young male companions and was seen openly in intimate and often compromising situations with them. He wined and dined them extravagantly at Kettner's Restaurant and at the Café Royal; he slept with them at the Savoy Hotel and left the evidence for the hotel staff to observe. Even after he had been subjected to blackmail by Wood, Cliburn and Allen for his incriminating letters to Bosie, Oscar did not modify his florid modes of entertainment. He was not prepared to contemplate any dangers – indeed, as he himself admitted, the dangers were half the excitement. Queensberry had heard all the gossip about Wilde's escapades for the past three years and it was a relatively easy task for detectives to track down the witnesses. When Queensberry penned his infamous card he already knew that he had bagged his man.

Wilde also pursued his love affair with Bosie without a whit of circumspection. He realized that he was incurring the wrath of Queensberry – and he had no illusions about the Marquess's aggression and vindictiveness – but he continued to inflame it by his public and indiscreet show of intimacy with Bosie. Of course, Bosie aided and abetted Oscar in this *because* it so enraged his father. Oscar, in spite of his intellectual superiority, entirely failed to anticipate the disastrous course he was taking in defying Queensberry. He was blind to the scandal he was creating and, if not blind to it, he was so contemptuous of it that he ignored it. This disdain was part of his conceit and vanity, and symptomatic of a sense of personal invulnerability. It is alleged that when he launched his case against Queensberry, Oscar naïvely believed that the only evidence the latter had against him derived from some of his so-called "immoral" literary contributions. If that were true, it showed his remarkable lack of contact with reality, a reality that was soon to be revealed to Wilde when he perused Queensberry's Plea of Justification just days before the start of the trial.

Another persistent flaw in his behaviour was his reckless extravagance and profligate expenditure, both of which have been discussed in Chapter 10. "I don't know what to do with money except throw it away," he wrote to his solicitor.[32] Wilde's passion for ostentation and luxurious living outstripped all other more pressing commitments, and he had no conscience whatsoever about squandering enormous sums of money on his self-indulgence. Moreover, he showed from his Oxford days the sociopathic trait of refusing to pay his bills and treating his creditors with utter disregard. These dual tendencies of lavish over-spending and refusal to settle accounts ultimately led to the forced sale of his valuables and then to his bankruptcy. But, again, on account of his personality disorder he was unable or unwilling to foresee the disastrous consequences for his own financial security and that of his family. It was mainly because of Oscar's gross incompetence and irresponsibility in handling money matters that Constance, fearful of the children's welfare in his hands, wrested the guardian-ship from him. It is interesting that she recognized in him the essence of the histrionic personality disorder because, about a fortnight before her death, she confided to Carlos Blacker: "Oscar is so pathetic and *such a born actor* [my italics], and I am hardened when I am away from him."[33]

An aspect of the Queensberry prosecution that is repeatedly raised is that Wilde lied to his legal team about his innocence regarding the Marquess's accu-sation. While it would not be appropriate to describe Oscar Wilde as a liar, there were occasions when he would wilfully resort to untruthfulness. ("If one tells the truth, one is sure, sooner or later, to be found out" was one of his maxims.) He was not truthful about his age, but that was perhaps a relatively trivial fault in the name of vanity – except when he was caught out by Carson at the Old Bailey. But his dishonesty assumed a more ominous nature when he and Douglas in legal interviews "would sit with serious faces telling serious lies to a bald man, till I really groaned and yawned with *ennui*".[34] (It is well recognized that histrionic personalities are prone to dishonesty and deceit.)

When Wilde approached Charles Humphreys, his solicitor, the day after he received Queensberry's card, he was asked if there was any truth in the message written on it. Oscar solemnly declared that is was absolutely untrue. In Chapter 1 I considered that he had probably misread the words as "ponce and sodomite" (and not "posing as sodomite", as clarified by Queensberry in court the next day). Because Wilde was neither a ponce nor had practised sodomy, he was not strictly lying. However, after Queenberry's committal for trial on 9 March 1895, Humphreys briefed the distinguished Sir Edward Clarke Q.C. When Clarke was introduced to Wilde, he demanded from him an assurance that there was not, and never had been, any foundation for the charges levelled against him. Wilde gave that assurance on his honour, knowing then exactly what the Marquess had written and intended; and he continued to perpetuate his pretence of innocence in all subsequent consultations.

If Wilde had thought better of it and confessed that he was not entirely guiltless, Clarke would have refused to act and would have advised withdrawal of the prosecution. But, to reiterate the argument developed in the first chapter, withdrawal of the case *at that stage* was fraught with its own set of potentially adverse legal repercussions. Thus, although lying to Sir Edward Clarke and his colleagues was reprehensible, I doubt that telling them the truth would have rescued Wilde from his ultimate ruin.

There is a point of view that maintains that Wilde sued Queensberry because in part he relished the idea of a court case and the quasi-theatrical opportunities that an appearance at the Old Bailey would offer. On the basis of his histrionic personality, this conjecture has merit. The court scene with judge, jury, lawyers, spectators and press would have afforded him the ideal forum in which to display his wisdom and his wit, and the platform on which to stage one of his impressive dramatic performances. My belief is that, if this was a factor at all, it played a very minor role in Oscar's motivation.

By February 1895 Wilde had achieved exceptional public exposure and acclaim. He had reached the pinnacle of his social and professional success, and his primary agenda then was no longer to promote his self-image but rather to seek sensual gratification and a hedonistic lifestyle. He had also had past experiences of the law and litigation which must have had a detrimental effect on him.

Oscar's parents, Sir William and Lady Wilde, were involved in a sensational, week-long libel case in Dublin in December 1864.[35] The action was brought by Mary Travers, who alleged that Sir William had raped her while she was under chloroform. Lady Wilde staunchly defended her husband's name and claimed that Travers was blackmailing the family and attempting to extort money. Sir William Wilde, much to his discredit, did not go into the witness-box to deny the charges. The jury found in favour of Travers and set damages at the derisory sum of one farthing. Costs of £2000 were awarded against Sir William. Oscar was only ten when the trial took place and, together with his brother Willie, was a boarder at Portora Royal School. It is highly probable that he heard about the case at the time, either through news circulating at school or through his parents.

Oscar Wilde had inherited from his father the Bray houses in County Wicklow, a short distance south of Dublin. In 1876 he employed Battersby & Co to sell the premises by auction, but the reserved price of £2900 was not realized and the sale fell through. Wilde then authorized Battersbys to find a private buyer and he also engaged a second estate agent for the same purpose. The latter found a buyer in a Mr Quain, who offered £2800. Almost simultaneously Battersby & Co managed to secure an offer of £2900 from a Mr Watson and, believing (mistakenly) that they had the authority, they signed a contract of sale on Wilde's behalf. However, unknown to them, Wilde had already finalized the deal with Quain. When Watson came to learn of this, he immediately had the agreement with Battersbys registered in the hope of gaining priority for himself.

Wilde found himself in the untenable position where Quain refused to pay because of the conflict over title, and Watson refused to withdraw his contract with Battersbys. This situation rendered the property unsaleable, and Wilde was forced to bring an action to invalidate Watson's contract and its registration.

The case was heard in Dublin on 11 and 12 July 1878 and judgement delivered on 17 July.[36] During the hearing Oscar wrote in desperation to his Oxford friend William Ward that he was ruined, as the lawsuit was going against him and he would have to pay costs, "which means leaving Oxford and doing some horrid work to earn bread". He added, "The world is too much for me."[37] But his prediction turned out to be wrong. The verdict declared Watson's contract null and void and awarded costs to Wilde. It was an expensive business: each side had engaged three barristers, two of whom were Queen's Counsel. Oscar communicated the news to Ward, but with little joy: "I am so troubled about my law suit, which I have won but find my own costs heavy." [38] He was referring to his untaxed costs; and, worse still, he also had to discharge a mortgage of £1000 on the property, so that eventually his net inheritance had dwindled considerably.

There was another legal incident six or seven years later which dragged Wilde though the processes of the law and almost landed him in court. It has been discussed in detail by Montgomery Hyde.[39] This was a dispute involving a building contractor, a man named Green, who had done work to 16 Tite Street. The work was originally carried out under contract to the landlord, but when Oscar took over the tenancy he wanted additional renovations done for creating "the house beautiful" under the supervision of the architect E.W. Godwin. Although Green allowed Wilde to deduct the amount already contracted for by the landlord, there were disagreements and misunderstandings as to the actual sum owed. Matters came to a head when Green issued a writ against Wilde for the amount of the account. Wilde instructed solicitors to defend the action, and there followed a tiresome series of interviews, affidavits and, of course, fees until a date was set (late May 1885) for the law courts. This was adjourned for a month because of the illness of one of Wilde's witnesses, but the parties settled a day before the adjourned hearing. The details of the settlement are not known but it is assumed that Oscar sustained a financial loss of at least £250.[39] And he was introduced once again to the convoluted and costly machinery of the law.

It was this past exposure to the legal arena that may have made Wilde realize that taking Queensberry to court might not necessarily turn out to be a purely egotistical experience. Furthermore, in terms of his vanity and conceit, the accusation of "posing as a sodomite" was not one which he would have wished to publicize far and wide, even if it gave him the opportunity of defending some of his controversial literary works such as *The Picture of Dorian Gray*. Thus, the suggestion that Oscar was primarily attracted to a court case for reasons of dramatic effect and self-importance is not persuasive. In the solitude of cell C.3.3 at Reading, Wilde showed a glimmer of retrospective insight when he explained to Douglas in *De Profundis*: "Between you both [Douglas and Queensberry] I lost my head. My judgment forsook me. Terror took its place . . . Blindly I staggered as an ox into the shambles. I had made a gigantic psychological error."[40]

It is worthwhile to consider another facet of the Queensberry trial, especially in the context of Wilde's histrionic predisposition. It has long been assumed that, during his evidence as the plaintiff at the Old Bailey, Wilde overplayed his hand and came across as flippant, facetious and arrogant. The recent publication by Merlin Holland of *Irish Peacock & Scarlet Marquess*[41] has provided for the first time a complete transcript of the trial. This has enabled scholars to make a more reliable assessment of Wilde's performance in the witness-box than was previously possible from the more limited versions of the proceedings.

As mentioned before, one of the unnecessary and tactless blunders that Oscar made when questioned by Sir Edward Clarke was in stating his age as thirty-nine and not forty. This little bit of dishonesty was swooped on by Carson in the opening question of his cross-examination. Wilde was clearly embarrassed at his *faux pas* and it must have struck a slightly discordant note with the jury.

But, in all other respects, Oscar did not convey the impression, either during Clarke's examination-in-chief or during Carson's cross-examination, of undue haughtiness or cleverness. If anything, he was relatively restrained during the onslaught by Carson, who relentlessly pursued the same themes, namely, Wilde's love for youth and his association with social inferiors. Oscar rarely lost his composure in the face of such sustained provocation. Not surprisingly, though, he occasionally turned his rising frustrations into a gibe at Carson's expense. But here Holland's book sets the record straight because, prior to its publication, there had been a perception that Wilde had glibly produced a stream of witty ripostes and that a significant portion of his testimony was punctuated by this kind of repartee. The reason was that previous accounts of the court case had selectively culled Oscar's quips and smart retorts, thereby accentuating this aspect. An analysis of the trial clearly demonstrates that most of the Carson–Wilde exchanges were grim and dour – and even monotonous – with Oscar's responses generally concise, relevant and serious. The flashes of levity were certainly memorable, but they were sporadic rather than regular and by no means inappropriate in the context of Carson's stinging line of interrogation.

In conclusion, Oscar Wilde indisputably falls into the diagnostic category of histrionic personality disorder, but it is my contention that that in itself contributed minimally to the actual initiation of the criminal libel lawsuit. What it did contribute to in large measure was the sordid antecedent background which fomented Queensberry's fury and galvanized him into revenge. It is also important to emphasize that the fact that Wilde was overtly homosexual is irrelevant to the diagnosis of histrionic personality disorder. Had he been exclusively heterosexual and lived his life in the same way, *mutatis mutandis*, he would have equally satisfied the diagnostic criteria, which exclude any reference to sexual orientation. Many of Wilde's friends were active, practising homosexuals but nearly all of them were discreet in the conduct of their sexual encounters and provident in the management of their financial affairs. They would not have fallen victim to either the Labouchère Amendment or the bankruptcy court.

Finally, it is germane to this chapter to report on the interesting study of creativity and psychopathology conducted by the British psychiatrist Felix Post.[42] He scrutinized the biographies of 291 world famous men in six occupational groups (scientists, politicians, composers, philosophers, artists and creative writers) and, against the background of their life histories, he evaluated their mental health status according to the *Diagnostic and Statistical Manual* (but using an earlier edition to the one that I had applied). He found that 90 per cent of his group of 50 creative writers (which included Balzac, Dostoevsky, Flaubert, Gide, Ibsen, Joyce, Kafka – and Wilde) exhibited traits of a diverse range of personality disorders, which, in 20 per cent of his sample, had had a seriously negative effect on their relationships or careers. These figures were the highest of any occupational category. In contrast, his group of scientists, composers and politicians showed the lowest proportions: 42, 62 and 63 per cent, respectively, with 2, 12, and 11 per cent, respectively, suffering significant disruption to their lives. Thus, with his diagnosis of histrionic personality disorder, Oscar Wilde was in excellent company – something that he would have greatly appreciated!

13

THE LAST WORDS

THIS book has had a narrow and sombre focus in that it has examined the adversities and misfortunes of Oscar Wilde's life. The title of the book is based on a question that Oscar Wilde put to André Gide: "Would you like to know the great drama of my life? – It's that I've put my genius into my life; I've put only my talent into my work." This declaration was made one evening in Algiers in January 1895, the month before the receipt of the Marquess of Queensberry's fateful card. Wilde was then at the zenith of his professional career – *An Ideal Husband* was playing at the Haymarket and, within a few weeks, *The Importance of Being Earnest* would open at the St James's Theatre to volleys of public acclamation. Little did Wilde realize, when he mischievously and pretentiously broached his favourite subject, namely, himself, that evening in North Africa, what disaster and devastation were to follow his return to London. Essentially what I have written about in this volume is exactly that scenario – hence the subtitle, "How his tragedy reflected his personality". In truth, there was little else to account for his catastrophe but his personality.

It is far too simplistic to point to Section Eleven of the Criminal Law Amendment Act and blame his downfall on that notorious piece of legislation. Of course, it was grossly unfortunate that he fell foul of the law. One wonders how the saga would have unfurled had Wilde lived in an England without the Labouchère Amendment. Would he have been left to continue his way of life unscathed? I doubt it, for the irrefutable reason that he had unwittingly picked as his adversary the paranoid, brutal and redoubtable Marquess of Queensberry. Whether homosexuality was lawful or unlawful, Queensberry had made it his mission to destroy Oscar Wilde. I outlined in the first chapter how, once Oscar had stumbled into Queensberry's trap and launched the prosecution, he had crossed the Rubicon. There was no hope that he would have been able to withdraw the case without dire consequences. The Marquess would surely have countered with charges of criminal libel or malicious prosecution, and it is even possible that Wilde might have been sent to gaol on one of those counts (as Lord Alfred Douglas was, nearly three decades later, when he libelled Winston Churchill). I am fairly certain that, had Queensberry's obnoxious calling card not been the *coup de grâce*, the Marquess would have hatched an even more provocative plan – and probably in a public forum, as he had intended with his foiled scheme to disrupt the opening night of *The Importance of Being Earnest*. Sooner than later Wilde would have been forced to bring a lawsuit against Queensberry, and the whole scandal would have been played out in court and in the press. And if Wilde had managed to avoid imprisonment, he would still have suffered ignominy, ostracism and bankruptcy. Moreover, with Queensberry's aggressive proclivities, there was always the possibility that the feud between the two men might have had a physically violent outcome.

Oscar Wilde's tragedy was not brought about because he was an active homosexual. There were tens of thousands of homosexuals in London in the 1890s, who were left to practise in private without police interference. The Labouchère Amendment was unpopular with the authorities and erratically enforced during that period. But Wilde conducted his intimate affairs with such visibility, and with such a flagrant disregard for social protocol, that he virtually invited retaliation from Victorian society. The histrionic component of his personality, with its flamboyance and self-dramatization, certainly aided his undoing. But these characteristics alone would not have thrown him into danger; it was their combination with a reckless self-indulgence and a brazen repudiation of traditional values that set him up as a target for his enemies.

But it was not only Wilde's enemies who became conscious of his increasingly coarse and egotistical demeanour. Some of his good friends were also affected by it. Max Beerbohm, an astute observer, commented: "But, you know, as Oscar became more and more successful, he became arrogant. He felt himself omnipotent, and he became gross not in body only – he did become that – but in his relations with people. He brushed people aside; he felt he was beyond the ordinary human courtesies that you owe people even if they are, in your opinion, beneath you."[1]

One of the most intriguing aspects of Oscar Wilde was alluded to in a letter by Reginald Turner in June 1938, just before his death: "I don't suppose any book will ever be published on that limitless subject which will be entirely satisfactory to everybody 'in the know' or will be free from inaccuracies . . ."[2] If the subject of Oscar Wilde was "limitless" in 1938, then today it is inexhaustible. The growth in books, articles, films, plays, novels and radio and television documentaries has been phenomenal; and these embrace a wide spectrum of disciplines: biography, literary criticism, gay politics, theatre, criminology, legal history, cultural history, and so on.

What is it about the life of Oscar Wilde that has commanded such prodigious attention and held so many of us, past and present, in its thrall, and will undoubtedly continue to do so without an end in sight? In short, it is the confluence of his extraordinary immaturity with his equally extraordinary intellectual agility and conversational brilliance. These two independent dimensions operated in tandem to produce the person of Oscar Wilde, whose scintillating wit, magical talk and delightful stories and plays went hand-in-hand with his unbridled ostentation, his marked sensuality and his inordinate self-centredness. Within the matrix of an appreciative and admiring society he was able skilfully to exploit his histrionic behaviour to the full, and in this way he established a mutually sustaining balance between himself and his audiences. Once he had lost the ambience of applause and appreciation – as was so evident in his years of exile – he also lost the means to satisfy his quintessentially histrionic temperament. Although he maintained his mental acuity and conversational prowess, he was not able to endure his sense of alienation and disgrace. He overindulged in alcohol and became self-pitying, cloying and demanding. He clearly revealed a lack of those personality resources that would have enabled him to adapt constructively to his altered environment.

Ironically, Oscar Wilde is such a fascinating and perplexing character because of this mix of intellect and personality, both to an exaggerated degree. He was so clever and yet so lacking in insight and judgement; he was so charming and entertaining and yet so irresponsible and negligent; he could be so kind and generous and yet so insensitive and rejecting. He was superficial, emotionally unstable, unpredictable, and full of inconsistencies and contradictions. His identity was not fixed within a single framework and he was in a constant state of flux: hence the description of him as an accomplished poseur who could take on whatever guise was required by the circumstances. These are the ingredients that have fashioned him into such a compelling case study. Literary giants who lacked the histrionic flair (such as Shaw or Yeats) led relatively staid, monochromatic lives compared with the vivid technicolor existence of Oscar Wilde. But for posterity it will be the glamour and the squalor, the spectacular highs and lows, of Wilde's life that will not cease to astound.

It is critical not to overlook the genetic and environmental influences imparted to Oscar by his parents. Both were highly gifted, creative and eccentric individuals. Sir William Wilde was a reputed womanizer who was accused of sexually assaulting one of his female patients. He was renowned for his slovenliness and dirtiness, but he was nevertheless a distinguished surgeon, a meticulous scholar and a prolific author. He appears to have been of the manic-depressive disposition, and in later life he lapsed into a chronic depressive state. Lady Jane Wilde ("Speranza") was in her younger days a doughty Irish nationalist. Afterwards she became a talented linguist, writer and conversationalist but she was vain, bizarre in appearance, and prone to depression. But whatever peculiarities of character and behaviour Wilde's parents displayed, these were in a minor key compared with Oscar's. Their elder son, Willie, was himself burdened with a personality disorder. Intelligent and articulate, he qualified in law and then switched to journalism, at which he showed great promise initially. But he quitted this and spent most of his remaining life in a state of outright indolence, penury and excessive drinking, which eventually killed him. Max Beerbohm described Willie as follows: "Quel monstre! Dark, oily, suspect yet awfully like Oscar: he has Oscar's coy, carnal smile and fatuous giggle and not a little of Oscar's espirit. But he is awful – a veritable tragedy of family-likeness!"[3] Indeed, "a veritable tragedy of family-likeness": Oscar was not only the beneficiary of the family's giftedness and creativity but also the victim of its eccentricity and personality deviation.

Oscar had written in *De Profundis*: "Morality does not help me. I am a born antinomian. I am one of those who are made for exceptions, not for laws." [4] And later he confided to More Adey a rare gem of insight, and one that encapsulates in its two sentences the theme of this book: "I know you all think I am wilful, but it is the result of the nemesis of character, and the bitterness of life. I was a problem for which there was no solution."[5]

In concluding this book, I shall leave it to Oscar's close friends to have the last words – last words, expressed with affection and sincerity at the time of Wilde's death or thereafter.

Once again I turn to the perspicacious Max Beerbohm, who, on the morning that he heard of Oscar's death from Reggie Turner, responded: "I suppose really it was better that Oscar should die. If he had lived to be an old man he would have become unhappy. Those whom the gods, etc. And the gods *did* love Oscar, with all his faults."[6] Turner agreed with Beerbohm: "It is certainly a good thing for Oscar that he is dead, and I confess that I was glad when I saw him quiet on his bed after a week of awful struggle and agony."[7]

Robert Ross shared the following sentiments with William Rothenstein: "I feel poor Oscar's death a great deal more than I should and far more that I expected . . . and he had become for me a sort of adopted prodigal baby. I began to love the very faults which I never would have forgiven in anyone else."[8] And, after giving Adela Schuster a detailed account of Oscar's terminal illness and death, Ross remarked: "Though everyone who knew him well enough to *appreciate* his wonderful power and the sumptuous endowment of his intellect will regret his death, apart from personal affection the terrible commonplace 'it was for the best' is really true in his case."[9]

To George Ives, Wilde's death was "the greatest tragedy of the whole nineteenth century". In his diary four years later, Ives recorded: "He had not the gift of responsibility, he could not estimate consequence, he was all Art, and all

Emotion . . . " Notwithstanding these considerations, Ives reflected: "But he *had* a soul; the sweetest and most lovely that I ever met; not strong, not heroic, not grand, but oh how splendid, how glorious, how consecrated."[10]

And perhaps the final judgement should rest with Frank Harris, a long-standing friend of Oscar's, who had tried to advise him before disaster struck; who had intervened on his behalf with the prison authorities and visited him at Reading; and who was one of the most generous, gracious and attentive of his friends during the exile period, despite Oscar's petulance towards him and his duplicitous behaviour over the *Mr and Mrs Daventry* affair:

I miss no one as I miss Oscar Wilde. I would rather spend an evening with him than with Renan or Carlyle, or Verlaine or Dick Burton or Davidson. I would rather have him back now than almost anyone I have ever met. I have known more heroic souls and some deeper souls; souls much more keenly alive to ideas of duty and generosity; but I have known no more charming, no more quickening, no more delight-ful spirit . . .

But the lovable and joyous things are to me the priceless things, and the most charming man I have ever met was assuredly Oscar Wilde. I do not believe that in all the realms of death there is a more fascinat-ing or delightful companion.[11]

APPENDIX

THE EXPERIMENT:
BIOGRAPHERS SIMULATE
OSCAR WILDE

IN Chapter 12 I used the international diagnostic classifications to establish that Oscar Wilde fulfilled the criteria for histrionic personality disorder. Although I am confident that this is an appropriate diagnosis, it is subjective in the sense that it is based on my own personal rating of Wilde's behaviour. For example, where I allocated a positive score for criterion 5 of the DSM-IV ("has a style of communication that is excessively impressionistic and lacking in detail") – and justified this with explanations – somebody else may have reasons for rating it as negative. One has biases and preconceived ideas and these may influence one's judgement and lead to fallacious conclusions.

I therefore decided on an experimental project in which I would invite a panel of recognized Wilde scholars to complete a personality questionnaire as if they were doing it for Oscar Wilde himself. The outcome of such an exercise would be twofold. The primary objective would be to determine the extent to which these scholars and experts independently agreed in their responses, qua Oscar Wilde, to the questionnaire items. If there happened to be reasonably good concordance, then the secondary aim was to assess whether their consensual view of Wilde's personality corroborated (or refuted) the diagnosis of histrionic personality disorder.

There are tools that psychologists employ to evaluate an individual's personality profile. The commonest method is to administer a questionnaire consisting of a very large number of statements (sometimes up to several hundred). There are clusters of statements distributed within the questionnaire, each of which is linked to a specific personality trait (e.g., outgoing-reserved, suspicious-trusting, assertive-obedient).

The questionnaire selected for this project was the *Sixteen Personality Factor Questionnaire* (16PF),[1] one of the best known and most scientifically validated personality tests available. It was first introduced in 1949 by Raymond Cattell. Since then it has undergone several editions, and it has been applied internationally as a clinical, educational, industrial and research instrument. The 16PF, as its title indicates, identifies sixteen personality factors (traits) and it is therefore able to generate a comprehensive profile of an individual's personality.

The 16PF questionnaire used in this study (Form A, 1967–1968 edition) consisted of over 180 statements. Owing to copyright restraints, I am not able to reproduce specimen items from the test itself, but for the purposes of illustration I am giving five of my own examples of the kinds of statements presented (with the three possible responses):

1. I get bored when I am left to my own devices for long periods:
   (a) true (b) uncertain (c) false.

2. I don't mind discussing my private affairs with friends:
   (a) yes (b) in between (c) no.

3. I become anxious when I am in the midst of a large crowd of people:
   (a) often (b) sometimes (c) never.

4. I support the right of women to have abortions on demand:
   (a) yes (b) in between (c) no.

5. I make every effort to be as punctual as I can in keeping appointments:
   (a) true (b) uncertain (c) false.

Respondents are instructed to make a cross against the response that applies to them personally or, in the case of my project, to mark the response that, in their judgement, Oscar Wilde would have been most likely to make. They are also requested to choose either the *a* or the *c* option and to reserve *b* for instances where they cannot do so, or are genuinely uncertain.

When the questionnaire has been completed, each of the items is scored; then the total score is obtained for the cluster of items that designates a specific personality factor. By reference to a table of population norms, the total score for that personality factor is converted to what is termed a "sten score" (or simply "sten"). This sten score ranges from 1 to 10, and the sten gives one an immediate indication of how that individual, on that particular personality trait, relates to the population as a whole.

Let us take an example. Suppose that on the personality factor assertive-submissive a subject achieves a sten of 10. This would mean that he or she is at the maximum for assertiveness and ranks in the top 2 per cent of the population in terms of this trait. Conversely, if a person were to get a sten of 1, that would place her or him in the bottom 2 per cent of the population and therefore as being exceptionally submissive. Stens of 4 to 7 encompass just over two-thirds of the population; 16 per cent of the population falls into the range 8 to 10 and another 16 per cent in the range 1 to 3.

The next step in the project was to recruit my cohort of participants. I needed to be certain that each one had a high level of understanding and insight into Oscar Wilde's life and character and was in a legitimate position to make judgements on, and give informed responses to, the questionnaire items on Wilde's behalf. To this end, I set as a prerequisite for selection the requirement that each intended participant had to have authored (or edited) and published in his or her personal capacity a work on Oscar Wilde in one of the following categories:

(i)   a book specifically on Oscar Wilde which was either a biographical, literary or academic study or a novel or play; or

(ii) a book on Wilde's family members or very close friends, provided that Oscar Wilde himself featured as a major figure in the book; or

(iii) an edited work such as a book, conference proceedings or a journal specifically relating to the life and works of Oscar Wilde.

The above selection criteria ensured that all my potential respondents had established by publication some authority on the subject of Oscar Wilde.

I dispatched 37 invitation letters, each with an enclosed questionnaire: 28, 6 and 3 to authors/editors in categories (i), (ii) and (iii), respectively. The following was the basic content of the letter, although the actual wording varied slightly from individual to individual, and the tone was more personal in cases where I knew or had previously corresponded with that person:

Dear X,

I am writing a book on the medical and psychological aspects of Oscar Wilde. One of my tasks is to evaluate the personality of Wilde. In order to do this as objectively as possible, I have selected a group of Wilde scholars and experts to complete the enclosed questionnaire. It is my pleasure to invite your participation in this study. I realize that you may well have misgivings about the nature of the project but it is really only an experiment. I also want to determine to what extent Wilde scholars achieve consensus on the questionnaire items.

Kindly fill in each item of the questionnaire *as you think Oscar Wilde would have done*, assuming that he was telling the truth of course. Mark your choice with a cross. Wherever possible, please choose either option (a) or (c) but if you are in doubt or undecided then mark (b).

Your contribution will be acknowledged, although the results of the questionnaire will not be presented in terms of any individual respondent such as yourself but as the outcome of the pooled data.

Your input would be highly valued by me and your time and effort greatly appreciated.

Yours sincerely

Ashley Robins

Where I had received no reply after several weeks, I routinely sent a reminder letter, and, in those cases where I was particularly keen to get the person's contribution, a *second* reminder letter was sent.

I received completed questionnaires from 22 individuals; 5 replied with reasons why they were not willing to participate; and 10 failed to respond at all in spite of at least two mailings. There were no instances where my letters were returned as undeliverable.

As anticipated by me, this exercise evoked a substantial amount of resistance and even anger from some of the group. Of the five who replied but declined to be involved, one gave illness as a reason and the remaining four refused on the following grounds:

1. I am afraid that I am totally incapable of being able to surmise what Oscar Wilde might or might not have thought on the issues you mention.

2. [A postcard]. I am afraid I have no real memory of Oscar Wilde. Apologies.

3. I would not presume to know what Oscar Wilde was thinking in 1890. My answers would all be subjective and in spite of your warning not to answer the questions myself, I would, and that would invalidate your research . . . I am a biographer not a psychologist.

4. I did indeed receive your earlier two letters but assumed they were a joke being played at the expense of either or both of us. [This person, an accomplished Wilde scholar, wrote a more detailed letter than the others. He argued that the project was methodologically invalid and he listed, with reasons, those questionnaire items that he considered inapplicable to Wilde's situation.]

It has to be assumed that most of the ten individuals who entirely ignored my request reacted in a similarly unfavourable way as individual 4 above.

Two of the 22 questionnaires that were returned completed had to be discarded as they were not usable. In one case the respondent wrote:

> You ask me to fill in your form as I think Wilde would have done – if he were telling the truth. But he wasn't interested in telling the truth. And he would have utterly rejected the theories behind your questionnaire. So he would have answered with deliberate falsehoods and paradoxes. I have, therefore, done the same, answering 'truthfully' from time to time to disconcert you.
>
> Yours sincerely
> (and whether that's the right word only you can decide) . . .

In the second case, the respondent had omitted to answer about one-third of the questionnaire items and sent the following:

> I tell you frankly I have only filled it in because I've kept you waiting; the truth is I resisted completing it, as I regard such an exercise as utterly without foundation. In the first place, personality changes: none knew this better than Wilde, who said often that 'personality is a very mysterious thing', and whose own life is a bravura demonstration of the silliness of trying to reduce personality to something static, definable and 'of one essence'. Man is made up of myriad lives and myriad sensations, he says somewhere in *Dorian Gray* . . .
>
> If you refer to my response, kindly include a rider in your article/book that I object to this entire enterprise, and entirely doubt its validity.

Thus, out of the original group of 37 invited participants, I eventually collected 20 completed questionnaires which were judged suitable for analysis. This gave a successful response rate of just under 55 per cent, which I regarded as a satisfactory return considering that the task was not only problematic and unusual but also time-consuming. Moreover, the final sample size of 20 "expert opinions" was an acceptable number from which to draw conclusions. Of the 20 respondents (14 male, 6 female) the numbers falling into categories (i), (ii) and (iii) of the selection criteria were 13, 4 and 3, respectively, with a total of 12 having written full-length biographical studies of Oscar Wilde or his family. Six of these 20 respondents wrote covering letters in which they expressed reservations or made comments about the value and purpose of the project. Their respective views are cited below:

1. At times, I wondered whether I was responding to my own preferences or Wilde's! A lingering doubt remains in my mind as to whether much can be revealed by such a standardized device.

2. The main problem with the questionnaire is having to double-think Oscar. Although he agrees in theory to answer the questions truthfully, I do not necessarily think he would have done. It would also have been significant at which period of his life he filled it in . . .

3. [This respondent replied to me under the name of "Oscar Wilde"!] I have answered the questions as truthfully as I can, bearing in mind that I always had a profound disregard for the truth. If you feel that I have made too many choices from the middle way, do please remember that the Irishman, faced with the option of 'either/or' will invariably declare 'both' – indeed, I believe that a book devoted entirely to this subject has recently appeared . . .
Your disobedient servant
Oscar Wilde

4. I did try to complete them all 'as Oscar might have' remembering all the while that he was nothing if not ambivalent, and that any slight change in mood would change all his answers – and his moods changed frequently; he was always grappling with them . . . He could never agree with himself: 'Whenever people agree with me I feel that I must be wrong,' he quipped. Most of his decisions were forced – 'No man dies for what he knows to be true. Men die from what they want to be true, for what some terror in their hearts tells them is not true.'

5. I had great fun filling in the questionnaire on Oscar Wilde's behalf. I have assumed that he was answering the questions honestly, except for a couple where I just feel sure he would have lied – I've marked them with an exclamation mark. For the rest, I think he is answering 'as truthfully as possible' – though he would have been greatly tempted to reason that since Beauty is Truth, Truth, Beauty, etc, the most beautiful answer must be the most truthful – and sometimes he would have answered a little tongue-in-cheek.

6. Herewith your questionnaire, completed with many of the sort of self-flattering views I think Wilde would have given off the cuff. (I think, also, that he would have declared, 'This is tedious!' about half-way through, and stopped answering!)

I have given an appreciable amount of space to the opinions of my invited participants, whether or not they agreed to cooperate. Their remarks are stimulating and usually appropriate. The recurring strain in most of the commentary is that Wilde's inconstancy of temperament, unpredictability, and non-adherence to the truth made it futile to attempt to respond to the questionnaire as *he* might have done. This aspect of Wilde's personality, expressed independently by the various respondents, is actually supportive of the case argued in the previous chapter, namely, that Wilde conformed to the histrionic personality type.

It was uncanny, but while this questionnaire project was nearing completion, an auction lot came up for sale at Christie's in South Kensington, London (6 June 1997). This was an album, published in New York in 1870 with the title *Mental Photographs, an Album for Confessions of Tastes, Habits and Convictions*, in which Oscar Wilde in 1877 had made an entry as an Oxford undergraduate. He had filled in one of the "Mental Photographs", which was a questionnaire of forty items asking for information both on his cultural tastes and on his own personal characteristics and attitudes. Peter Vernier[2] has analysed every one of Wilde's responses in detail, and it is apparent from Oscar's answers how idiosyncratic and tongue-in-cheek many of them were, thereby confirming the concerns voiced by some of my study subjects.

By and large, the 20 questionnaires that formed the basis of this project were completed according to my instruction that respondents (on the basis of their specialized knowledge of Wilde) should answer in the way they estimated he would have done had he been honest. Although I had originally intended to acknowledge my participants, several of them felt distinctly uncomfortable with the unorthodox nature of the study and insisted on anonymity. I eventually decided that the most prudent course was to withhold all the respondents' names. However, I wish to convey my deep gratitude and appreciation to those who gave their time and serious attention to the questionnaire. They know who they are, and I hope that they will feel some sense of satisfaction that their efforts have at last come to fruition in the publication of this study, and that the results may assist in advancing our understanding and perceptions of Oscar Wilde. I am also grateful to those who chose not to participate but were courteous enough to reply and candid enough to give their reasons.

It must be borne in mind that this questionnaire project was essentially an experiment and one with several inherent flaws. It is obviously ludicrous to expect a present-day biographer or scholar to complete a personal questionnaire on Wilde's behalf about a century after his death. Thus, whatever conclusions emerge, these must be treated with caution. Although they may not necessarily depict an authentic personality profile of Oscar Wilde, they do illustrate how he has been perceived by those who have been devoted (often professionally) to a study of his life and work. I naturally have some expectation that the Wilde perceived by others will bear a reasonably strong resemblance to the "real Oscar Wilde". What this research will certainly demonstrate is the extent to which Wilde scholars and experts agree (or disagree) in their responses to the very large number of statements in the questionnaire. A high degree of concordance would mean that the perception of Wilde by the respondents signified a high measure of consistency (and possibly objectivity); a low concordance would indicate that their perceptions were inconsistent (and possibly subjective) and that Wilde projected an image to which different people reacted differently.

The 16PF displays a subject's personality profile in terms of sixteen personality factors or traits. The 16PF questionnaire used in this project (Form A) consists of 184 items. The thirteen items representing Factor B were deleted from the questionnaire. Factor B relates to intellectual ability and the capacity to think in abstract as opposed to concrete terms. It will be taken for granted that Wilde would have scored the maximum sten of 10 on this factor.

The deletion of the thirteen Factor B items left 171 scorable statements for response by the participants. These statements generated the remaining fifteen personality factors discussed below.

Every item in the questionnaire, as described earlier, was a statement to which *one* of three possible responses had to be marked. In the great majority of instances the form of the three responses was: (*a*) true (*b*) uncertain (*c*) false, or (*a*) yes (*b*) in between (*c*) no. (To repeat, respondents were requested to select either option *a* or *c* and to reserve *b* for statements where there was genuine uncertainty.)

For every one of the 171 statements, the responses of the 20 respondents were counted and recorded as *a*, *b* or *c*. It was necessary to decide which of the three responses for each particular statement would be taken as the final collective verdict. The rule I applied was that if either option *a* or *c* received an absolute majority of the votes, then that option would become the final verdict. If neither *a* nor *c* received an absolute majority, then the final outcome would be deemed to be *b*, which was the intermediate position. Thus, *a* or *c* had to receive at least 55 per cent of the votes (i.e., at least 11 out of the total of 20 responses) to qualify for the final assignment: otherwise the message was that there was no clear direction from the respondents and the final determination was *b* (the "uncertain" or "in between" category). However, I decided that there should also be a more stringent threshold, and for this purpose a final assignment to either *a* or *c* was made only if either of them attracted at least 75 per cent of the votes (i.e., at least 15 out of the 20). If neither *a* nor *c* reached that percentage, then the final allocation would go to *b*. I therefore obtained two sets of results – one based on the 55 per cent threshold (the "standard threshold") and the other based on the 75 per cent threshold (the "stringent threshold").

When the final designation of responses to all 171 questionnaire items had been made on both the standard and the stringent thresholds, the response to each item was scored. In each case an *a* or *c* response received a score of either 2 and 0 or 0 and 2, respectively, while *b* was always scored as 1. Then the sum of the scores for the items associated with a particular factor was obtained, and that total score was converted, by means of a table of population norms for adult males, to a sten score (or sten), as explained in the introductory section of the chapter. As mentioned above, just over two-thirds of the population will have stens ranging from 4 to 7 (inclusive) for any particular personality factor; stens of 8 and above, or 3 and below, therefore indicate that that individual is unusually high or low, respectively, on that trait. A sten of 10 (or 1) is achieved by only 2 per cent of the population.

An analysis of the results shows that all 20 respondents agreed on the response in 10 per cent of the questionnaire items; in 29 per cent of the items 90 per cent and over of respondents agreed (i.e., 18 or more); in 42 per cent of items 80 per cent and over agreed; and in 63 per cent of the items at least 65 per cent agreed on the response. The average agreement rate for an item was 72 per cent. Put in another way, there was, on average, the probability that 72 per cent of the sample of 20 respondents would agree on the response to an item. This is a fairly high figure, which demonstrates that established Wilde scholars and experts show a significant degree of concordance in the way they perceive and interpret Oscar Wilde's attitudes, behaviour and personality attributes. It was in fact both surprising and reassuring that in nearly one-third of the questionnaire items at least 90 per cent of the participants agreed exactly on the response selected.

It would be interesting for readers to know which items elicited 100 per cent concordance and which ones were associated with a lower concordance. As I am not permitted by copyright to reproduce the actual statements on the questionnaire, I have constructed my own statements so as to give some approximation to the original item. I have given an example each of an item which showed (1) a 100 per cent concordance, (2) a 70 per cent concordance, and (3) a 50 per cent concordance (with the figures in parentheses representing the number of responses to the three options):

(1)   100 per cent concordance: "I am regarded as entertaining company by most of the people I meet – (a) true (20), (b) uncertain (0), (c) false (0)."

(2) 70 per cent concordance: "There are times when I feel motivated to undertake some strenuous physical exertion – (a) yes (6), (b) in between (0), (c) no (14)."

(3) 50 per cent concordance: "If I commit an embarrassing social indiscretion, I can easily dismiss it from my mind – (a) yes (10), (b) in between (5), (c) no (5)."

In terms of the final assignment of a response to an item, the first example would be placed in *a* on both the standard and stringent thresholds; the second in *c* on the standard threshold but in *b* on the stringent (less than 75 per cent); and the third in *b* on both the standard and the stringent thresholds (less than 55 per cent).

The hypothetical personality profile (16PF) of Oscar Wilde that was derived from this project is displayed in the graphs (Figure 21). Two graphs are shown: one for the standard threshold (55 per cent) and the other for the stringent threshold (75 per cent). The lightly shaded strip denotes the average band of sten scores (stens 5 and 6), while the range encompassing just over two-thirds of the population (stens 4 to 7) is also shown. The personality factors (or traits) are listed at the side of the graph, with a brief description of the characteristics that are depicted by a high score (8 and above) and a low score (3 and below), respectively.

The initial observation is the obvious one, namely, that the standard threshold graph tends to be more exaggerated than the stringent one, but not markedly so. On six factors (excluding Factor B) there is a complete overlap. The striking feature with both the standard and stringent graphs is that the personality profile shown lies outside the average range on all but two factors. It will be recalled that the sten of 10 on Factor B (intellectual ability) was not based on the questionnaire responses but was awarded independently by myself on what I adjudged to be indisputable evidence of Wilde's brilliant academic, intellectual and literary achievements. This factor will not be discussed further.

Let us now consider the factors (other than B) in which Oscar Wilde was evaluated as lying *outside* the range of sten scores that encompasses just over two-thirds of the population (i.e., stens 4 to 7). I have accordingly taken into account only scores of 8 and above, or of 3 and below. The graph reflecting the standard threshold has been used as the benchmark and, unless otherwise stated, the sten scores cited will refer specifically to that graph. In order to exercise stricter discrimination, though, I have discounted any factor which has not achieved a sten of at least 8, or at most 3, in terms of the *stringent* threshold,

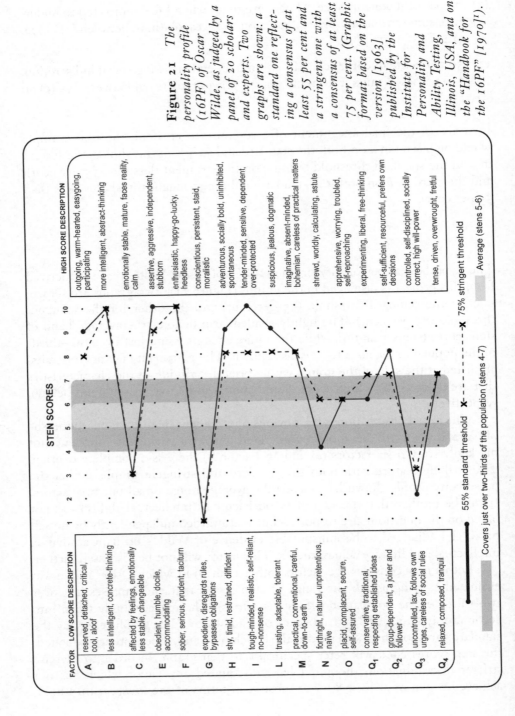

Figure 21 *The personality profile (16PF) of Oscar Wilde, as judged by a panel of 20 scholars and experts. Two graphs are shown: a standard one reflecting a consensus of at least 55 per cent and a stringent one with a consensus of at least 75 per cent. (Graphic format based on the version [1963] published by the Institute for Personality and Ability Testing, Illinois, USA, and on the "Handbook for the 16PF" [1970][1]).*

irrespective of how high or how low, respectively, it has registered on the standard threshold. Thus, I have excluded Factor Q_2 from special mention because, although an 8 on the standard graph, it is rated only as 7 on the stringent threshold. This precaution has ensured that all sten scores which fall towards the extremes, and which will therefore be singled out for discussion, have been endorsed by at least 75 per cent of the respondents.

I shall first identify those factors on which Wilde is represented as being at, or near, the high extreme (i.e. stens of 8 or more). On Factor A he receives a sten of 9: very outgoing, warm-hearted, easygoing and participating. On Factor E he is at the maximum of 10: highly assertive, independent, aggressive and stubborn. On Factor F he is rated as 10: highly enthusiastic, happy-go-lucky and heedless. He is at 9 on Factor H: very adventurous, socially bold, uninhibited and spontaneous. The remarkably high sten scores obtained on these four factors confirm the exceptional degree of extroversion attributed to Wilde. He is perceived not only as thoroughly outgoing, dynamic and ebullient but also as socially dominant, asserting his individuality and flaunting his presence by uninhibited behaviour.

On Factor I he again achieves a maximum sten of 10: excessively tender-minded, sensitive, dependent and over-protected. This factor seems to be linked to a romantic liking for trivial and new experiences; a love of dramatics; and a labile, somewhat unrealistic, aesthetic mind. It also connotes an attention-seeking tendency and a need to seek help and sympathy.[3] (Wilde showed all of these, and the last was especially evident during his exile when he was constantly demanding money and favours.)

On Factor M he scores 8 which reveals him to be imaginative, absent-minded, careless in practical matters and bohemian. These attributes typified his lifestyle and the disorganized management of his affairs.

On Factor L he is scored as 9, which demonstrates a high degree of suspiciousness, jealousy, and dogmatism. This is a somewhat unexpected finding, although on closer scrutiny Wilde did sometimes assume a bearing of self-righteousness and conceit, and his serious disputes with some of his friends towards the end of his life (Leverson, Blacker and Harris) may be explained by this factor.

At the low end of the scale, there are three rankings which appear markedly compatible with Wilde's character. On Factor C he is rated as 3: affected by feelings, emotionally less stable and changeable. On Factor G he is recorded at the minimum of 1: thoroughly expedient, with disregard for rules and obligations. On Factor Q_3 he receives a sten of 2: very uncontrolled, lax, careless of social conventions and self-indulgent.

It is also meaningful to take note of the two factors in which he features in the average range (both at sten 6) – O and Q_1. Thus he is assessed as being well balanced with regard to these two traits: neither too placid and self-assured nor too apprehensive and troubled; and neither too conservative nor too radical.

What is perhaps puzzling is that he does not achieve a higher score on Q_1. One might have expected Wilde to be ranked as more critical, liberal and free-thinking, especially from the standpoint of some of his literary works such as *The Ballad of Reading Gaol* and *The Soul of Man Under Socialism*. But possibly this *is* the correct position for him. There was no political activism or revolutionary fervour in his make-up, as there had been in his mother, Lady Wilde, who in her younger days fiercely championed the cause of Irish nationalism. As discussed in Chapter 9, as an advocate for the reform of the anti-homosexual law he was a failure. Norbert Kohl, who dubbed Wilde "a conformist rebel", put it well: "But these two years of hardship and forced labour [i.e. imprisonment] failed to change the individualistic hedonist into a social fighter . . ."[4] George Bernard Shaw wrote: "Wilde was a conventional man; his unconventionality was the very pedantry of convention; never was there a man less an outlaw than he."[5] And Alfred Douglas added his confirmation: "He [Wilde] never bothered his head about politics. When I knew him he was supposed to be a 'Liberal', but I very much doubt whether he ever took the trouble to vote at an election. He had no interest whatever in social questions."[6]

I believe that my questionnaire project does make a contribution to the study and understanding of Oscar Wilde. The 16PF personality profile that emerges deviates grossly from what one would probably find in more than 95 per cent of the general population. In the case of the Oscar Wilde profile, 14 of the 16 factors lie outside the average range (stens 5 and 6) and, of these, 9 are at the high (stens 9 and 10) or low (stens 1 and 2) extremes. This clearly leads to the conclusion that, from the perspective of present-day scholars and experts, Oscar Wilde was indeed an extraordinary personality – precisely in accordance with his own evaluation of himself!

One would justifiably argue, of course, that Wilde was not an "ordinary" member of society, and that it is patently unfair to measure him against the standards of the man on the Clapham omnibus. If he is to be compared at all, it should be to members of the creative professions. Fortunately, I was able to do this from the findings of a previous study of creative people, also using the 16PF.[7] Figure 22 shows the 16PF profiles of two creative groups,[8] one of writers and another of artists, and superimposed on these is the Oscar Wilde profile generated by my project. Here it is seen that these two groups do show deviations from the average band; and on several factors they even fall outside the 4 to 7 sten range. Creative individuals therefore tend to exhibit specific personality traits that differ significantly from the general population (e.g., high intelligence, assertiveness, expediency, tender-mindedness and imaginativeness). The

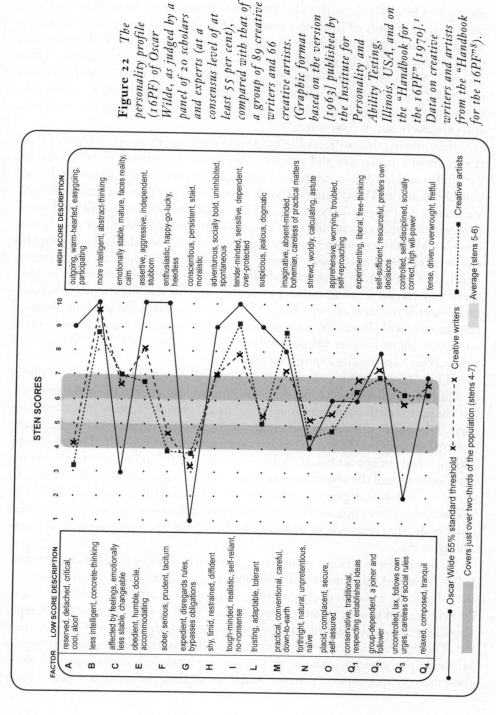

Figure 22 *The personality profile (16PF) of Oscar Wilde, as judged by a panel of 20 scholars and experts (at a consensus level of at least 55 per cent), compared with that of a group of 89 creative writers and 66 creative artists. (Graphic format based on the version [1963] published by the Institute for Personality and Ability Testing, Illinois, USA, and on the "Handbook for the 16PF" [1970].[1] Data on creative writers and artists from the "Handbook for the 16PF".[8]).*

STEN SCORES

FACTOR	LOW SCORE DESCRIPTION	HIGH SCORE DESCRIPTION
A	reserved, detached, critical, cool, aloof	outgoing, warm-hearted, easygoing, participating
B	less intelligent, concrete-thinking	more intelligent, abstract-thinking
C	affected by feelings, emotionally less stable, changeable	emotionally stable, mature, faces reality, calm
E	obedient, humble, docile, accommodating	assertive, aggressive, independent, stubborn
F	sober, serious, prudent, taciturn	enthusiastic, happy-go-lucky, heedless
G	expedient, disregards rules, bypasses obligations	conscientious, persistent, staid, moralistic
H	shy, timid, restrained, diffident	adventurous, socially bold, uninhibited, spontaneous
I	tough-minded, realistic, self-reliant, no-nonsense	tender-minded, sensitive, dependent, over-protected
L	trusting, adaptable, tolerant	suspicious, jealous, dogmatic
M	practical, conventional, careful, down-to-earth	imaginative, absent-minded, bohemian, careless of practical matters
N	forthright, natural, unpretentious, naive	shrewd, worldly, calculating, astute
O	placid, complacent, secure, self-assured	apprehensive, worrying, troubled, self-reproaching
Q1	conservative, traditional, respecting established ideas	experimenting, liberal, free-thinking
Q2	group-dependent, a joiner and follower	self-sufficient, resourceful, prefers own decisions
Q3	uncontrolled, lax, follows own urges, careless of social rules	controlled, self-disciplined, socially correct, high will-power
Q4	relaxed, composed, tranquil	tense, driven, overwrought, fretful

Oscar Wilde 55% standard threshold   x – – – – – x Creative writers

Covers just over two-thirds of the population (stens 4-7)   Creative artists

Average (stens 5-8)

237

profile of Oscar Wilde shares this particular grouping of traits although he is rated as having most of them to a more marked degree. On the other hand, his profile departs from the creative groups in Factors A, C, F and Q_3: his scores on these are located on the *opposite* pole to those of the writers and artists. Thus, whereas the latter are inclined to be reserved, emotionally stable, serious, controlled and self-disciplined, Wilde is represented as emotionally vulnerable, very outgoing, enthusiastic, happy-go-lucky and markedly lax, self-indulgent and careless of social conventions.

In summary, the 16PF profile of Oscar Wilde, constructed vicariously from the input of biographers and scholars, rings true. His strong extroversion, his dynamism and his dominating social interactions, combined with his prodigious conversational and intellectual powers, rocked him to fame, success and virtual stardom – and these without the aid of radio and television. But the other prominent traits in his profile undoubtedly contributed to his tragic fate. These included his rank expediency and carelessness, his neglect of social rules, and his gross disregard of duties and obligations. It was these aspects of his character that led to his inordinate pursuit of pleasure and self-gratification, his reckless spending, his ruthless non-payment of debts, and his dereliction of responsibilities towards his wife and children. They drove him into his publicly flaunted relationship with Bosie Douglas and his open association with the rent-boys, and from there he was swept into his confrontation with the Marquess of Queensberry and its devastating outcome.

This hypothetical personality analysis of Oscar Wilde has no direct bearing on the diagnosis of histrionic personality disorder made in Chapter 12, but these two entirely different approaches are complementary and confirmatory. The 16PF profile, as summarized in the last paragraph, is essentially compatible with the diagnosis of histrionic personality disorder. The attention-seeking and unconventional behaviour, the self-dramatization, the labile emotionality, and the seductiveness portrayed by that diagnosis are revealed, to a greater or lesser degree, by the extremes of the 16PF as depicted for Oscar Wilde. I therefore contend that the diagnosis of histrionic personality disorder independently receives conceptual validation from the outcome of this questionnaire study.

The project described in this chapter was purely of an experimental nature. It has flaws and limitations and it is subject to valid criticism. Its principal aim was to test the hypothesis that a group of people who have a proven record of knowledge and insight into the life of Oscar Wilde are able to reach an acceptable degree of consensus on their perception and interpretation of his personality. The results unequivocally demonstrate that my selected panel of highly informed participants achieve, on average, a 72 per cent concordance in their responses to questionnaire items, filled in as they anticipated Oscar Wilde might have done in honesty. However, the caution to be observed is that the personality profile that has emerged from the pooled questionnaire data (Figure 21) is the collective appraisal of the respondents and it is *not* to be taken as an accurate or true reflection of Wilde's personality – although I have little doubt that it is probably not too wide off the mark on the more conspicuous factors. But on some of the less obvious traits it may have produced an erroneous result. My sample of respondents, expert as they may be in Wilde's life history, have acquired their understanding of him not through first-hand personal experience but by a study of his works and letters and through the voluminous biographical resources that are available. Biographical sources, especially in the case of Oscar Wilde, are biased in that they have a tendency to focus on the more picturesque, dramatic or calamitous occurrences in his life and career. This selective emphasis may produce a distortion in that other less visible, but equally important, events psychologically become blurred or discounted.

There is, for example, very little of real substance about his domestic life in the years before his downfall. There are fragmented comments and scattered opinions (often unreliable) by various of Oscar's friends and acquaintances, but what is blatantly lacking is a well-grounded and cohesive picture of the Wilde family household in its everyday operation. Another gaping lacuna in the Wilde biographies, which has bedevilled my own investigations into his psychological development, is the virtual absence of material on his childhood and adolescence. Apart from records of his academic performance at Portora Royal School and Trinity College Dublin, there is little else of note chronicling this critical and formative period of Oscar's life. One is left in the dark on fundamental matters: his relationship with his parents, his social life with friends, and his behaviour, interests and activities at home and at boarding school. Even Ellmann's definitive biography fails to provide anything more than a relatively short (just over thirty pages) and unsystematic account of Oscar's entire pre-Oxford life,[9] much of which is based on questionable anecdotal memoirs. (Wilde's Oxford period, 1874–1878, covers sixty pages in Ellmann.) One significant piece of information is the twelve-year-old Oscar's grief at the death of his sister, Isola, aged nine, and his regular visits to her grave. He was reported by the attending doctor to be "an affectionate, gentle, retiring, dreamy boy",[10] a description that does not truly presage the subsequent evolution of his character.

There is one certainty about my questionnaire experiment: Oscar would have loathed the idea and looked on the outcome with utter scorn. Who can blame him? He had once written: "However, Psychology is in its infancy, as a science. I hope, in the interests of Art, it will always remain so."[11]

BIBLIOGRAPHY

CHAPTER 1 "PURSUED BY A PUGILIST OF UNSOUND MIND"

1. Holland, M. and Hart-Davis, R. (editors) (2000): *The Complete Letters of Oscar Wilde*. London: Fourth Estate, p. 709.
2. Ibid., p. 780.
3. Mason, S. (1912): *Oscar Wilde Three Times Tried*. London: Ferrestone Press, pp. 94–95.
4. The National Archives, Kew, Surrey: file CRIM 1 41/6.
5. Mason, op. cit., pp. 106–107.
6. *Complete Letters*, p. 598.
7. Hyde, H.M. (1962): *Famous Trials 7: Oscar Wilde*. London: Penguin, p. 72.
8. Roberts, B. (1981): *The Mad Bad Line*. London: Hamish Hamilton, p. 183.
9. McKinstry, L. (2005): *Rosebery: Statesman in Turmoil*. London: John Murray, pp. 349–368.
10. Letter from Queensberry to Alfred Montgomery, 1 November 1894, cited in Ellmann, R. (1987) *Oscar Wilde*. London: Hamish Hamilton, p. 402.
11. Murray, D. (2000): *Bosie: A Biography of Lord Alfred Douglas*. London: Hodder & Stoughton, pp. 65–266.
12. The National Archives, Kew, Surrey: High Court of Justice (Probate, Divorce and Admiralty Division), J77/532/16267.
13. *Complete Letters*, p. 621.
14. Roberts, op. cit., pp. 71–72.
15. Feldman, H.A. *et al.* (1994) Impotence and its medical and psychosocial correlates: results of the Massachusetts Male Aging Study. *Journal of Urology*, 151, 54–61.
16. Roberts, op. cit., p. 270.
17. Ibid., pp. 117–119.
18. *Complete Letters*, pp. 632–633.
19. Ibid., pp. 634–635.
20. Fisher, T. (1997): *Prostitution and the Victorians*. Stroud: Sutton, pp. 148–149.
21. The National Archives, Kew, Surrey: file CRIM 1 41/6, Marlborough Street Police Court proceedings (Wilde versus Queensberry), 2 and 9 March 1895.
22. *Complete Letters*, p. 634 and footnote 2.
23. Letter from Queensberry to Minnie Douglas, 4 March 1895, cited in Queensberry and Percy Colson (1949): *Oscar Wilde and the Black Douglas*. London: Hutchinson, p. 58.
24. Mason, op. cit., pp. 133–134.
25. Letter from Lord Alfred Douglas to James Nichol Dunn, 2 March 1895, Clark Library, cited in McKenna, N. (2003): *The Secret Life of Oscar Wilde*. London: Century, p. 341.
26. *Complete Letters*, p. 759.
27. Ellmann, R. (1987): *Oscar Wilde*. London: Hamish Hamilton, p. 412 and 577, reference 3.

28. Hall, J.G. and Smith, G.D. (2001): *Oscar Wilde: The Tragedy of Being Earnest*. Chichester: Barry Rose, p. 12.
29. *New York Herald*, 3 March 1895, cited in McKenna, op. cit. (reference 25), p. 343.
30. Letter from Queensberry to Minnie Douglas, 26 February 1895, cited in Queensberry and Colson, op. cit. (reference 23), p. 56.
31. *Complete Letters*, p. 708.
32. Douglas, A. (1931): *Autobiography of Lord Alfred Douglas*. London: Martin Secker, p. xiv.

Chapter 2   In Durance Vile: Pentonville

1. Hyde, H.M. (1963): *Oscar Wilde: The Aftermath*. London: Methuen, pp. 1–21.
2. Garland, D. (1985): *Punishment and Welfare: A History of Penal Strategies*. Aldershot: Gower, p. 14.
3. Holland, M. and Hart-Davis, R. (editors) (2000): *The Complete Letters of Oscar Wilde*. London: Fourth Estate, pp. 1045–1049.
4. Harris, F. (1938): *Oscar Wilde*. London: Constable, p. 226.
5. Garland, op. cit., p. 64.
6. Parliamentary papers, House of Commons, Volume 56, pp. 1–773.
7. Garland, op. cit., p. 226.
8. Robin, G.D. (1964). Pioneers in Criminology: William Douglas Morrison (1852–1943). *Journal of Criminal Law, Criminology and Police Science*, 55, 48–58.
9. The National Archives, Kew, Surrey: Home Office (Prison Commission) papers, file HO 45/24514.
10. Ibid., file PCOM 8/432 (13629).
11. Letter from Alfred Douglas to Percy Douglas, 11 July 1895, cited in McKenna N. (2003): *The Secret Life of Oscar Wilde*. London: Century, p. 403.
12. Hyde, op. cit., pp. 26–27.
13. Letter from Max Beerbohm to Reginald Turner, 3 May 1895. In Hart-Davis, R. (editor) (1964): *Max Beerbohm: Letters to Reggie Turner*. London: Rupert Hart-Davis.
14. Letter from Arthur Clifton to Carlos Blacker, 8 October 1895, cited in *Complete Letters*, p. 665, footnote 2.
15. Letter from Robert Ross to Oscar Browning, 13 November 1895. King's College, Cambridge.

Chapter 3   Haldane and Morrison vs. The Home Secretary

1. The National Archives, Kew, Surrey: Home Office (Prison Commission) papers, file PCOM 8/432 (13629).
2. Cohen, E. (1993): *Talk on the Wilde Side*. New York: Routledge, pp. 58–65.
3. *Daily Chronicle*, 27 September 1895.
4. Ibid., 28 September 1895.
5. Rose, G. (1961): *The Struggle for Penal Reform*. London: Stevens & Sons, pp. 62–63.
6. The National Archives, Kew, Surrey: Home Office (Prison Commission) papers, file HO 45/24514 (A56887/12).
7. Harris, F. (1938): *Oscar Wilde*. London: Constable, pp. 230–232.
8. Holland, M. and Hart-Davis, R. (editors) (2000): *The Complete Letters of Oscar Wilde*. London: Fourth Estate, p. 1046.
9. Letter from Lily Wilde to More Adey, 18 October 1895, Clark Library.
10. The National Archives, op. cit., HO 45/24514, pp. 69–71.
11. Report from the Departmental Committee on Prisons (1895): evidence of Dr David Nicolson, 6 December 1894.
12. Obituary, Dr David Nicolson (1932). *Lancet*, 2, 100–101.

13. Winchester, S. (1999): *The Surgeon of Crowthorne: A Tale of Murder, Madness and the Oxford English Dictionary*. London: Penguin.
14. Obituary, Dr. Richard Brayn (1912). *Lancet*, 1, 839 and *British Medical Journal*, 1, 705.
15. The National Archives, op. cit., HO 45/24514, pp. 79–91.
16. Ibid., Home Office (Prison Commission) papers, file PCOM 8/433 (13629/34).
17. Ibid., file PCOM 8/433 (13629/25).
18. Ibid., file PCOM 8/433 (13629/33).

CHAPTER 4 THE BATTLE OF READING GAOL

1. Ellmann, R. (1987): *Oscar Wilde*. London: Hamish Hamilton, p. 465.
2. Beckson, K. (1983). Oscar Wilde and the 'almost inhuman' Governor of Reading. *Notes and Queries*, 30, 315–316.
3. Garland, D. (1985): *Punishment and Welfare*. Aldershot: Gower, p. 23.
4. Letters from Adela Schuster to More Adey, 2 and 4 January 1896, Clark Library.
5. Letter from Adela Schuster to More Adey, 29 February 1896, Clark Library.
6. Holland, M. and Hart-Davis, R. (editors) (2000): *The Complete Letters of Oscar Wilde*. London: Fourth Estate, p. 983.
7. Harris, F. (1938): *Oscar Wilde*. London: Constable, p. 227.
8. The National Archives, Kew, Surrey: Home Office (Prison Commission) papers, file PCOM 8/433 (13629/38).
9. Report from the Departmental Committee on Prisons, 1895.
10. Letter from Constance Wilde to Otho Holland Lloyd, cited in *Complete Letters*, p. 652, footnote 4.
11. *Complete Letters*, p. 721.
12. Ross, M. (1952): *Robert Ross Friend of Friends*. London: Jonathan Cape, pp. 39–43
13. Hyde, H.M. (1963): *Oscar Wilde: The Aftermath*. London: Methuen, pp. 57–61.
14. Robert Sherard to More Adey, as cited in draft letter from Adey to Constance Wilde [undated but probably late May 1896]. Ms. Walpole d.18, Bodleian Library, Oxford.
15. Harris, op. cit., pp. 225–237.
16. The National Archives, op. cit., file PCOM 8/433 (13629/42).
17. Priestley, P. (1985): *Victorian Prison Lives: English Prison Biography (1830–1914)*. London: Methuen, p. 189.
18. *Complete Letters*, pp. 656–660.
19. Gagnier, R. (1986): *Idylls of the Marketplace: Oscar Wilde and the Victorian Public*. Stanford: Stanford University Press, pp. 149–153.
20. Report from Departmental Committee on Prisons, 1895. Evidence from Dr David Nicolson, 4 December 1894.
21. Suedfeld, P., Ramirez, C., Deaton, J. and Baker-Brown, G. (1982). Reactions and attributes of prisoners in solitary confinement. *Criminal Justice and Behaviour*, 9, 303–340.
22. Haney, C. (2003). Mental health issues in long-term solitary and "supermax" confinement. *Crime and Delinquency*, 49, 124–156.
23. *Complete Letters*, p. 942.
24. The National Archives, op. cit., file HO 45/24514, p. 54 (A56887/19).
25. Ibid., p. 50.
26. Showalter, E. (1985): *The Female Malady*. New York: Pantheon, pp. 121–126.
27. The National Archives, op. cit., HO 45/24514, pp. 42–45 (A56887/19).
28. Hyde, op. cit., pp. 77–78.
29. Letter from Robert Ross to Oscar Browning [November 1895], King's College Library, Cambridge.
30. More Adey correspondence (undated), Clark Library.
31. Maudsley, H. (1895). *Journal of Mental Science*, 41, 657–665.

32. *Complete Letters*, p. 862.
33. Ibid., p. 826.
34. Ibid., p. 666.
35. Ibid., p. 754.
36. Draft letter from More Adey to Constance Holland, 30 July [1896], Ms. Walpole d.18, Bodleian Library, Oxford.
37. Letter from More Adey to Constance Holland, 22 September 1896, Clark Library.
38. Letter from More Adey to Adela Schuster, 16 March 1897, Clark Library.
39. Hyde, op. cit., pp. 129–130.

CHAPTER 5   "PASSING FROM ONE PRISON INTO ANOTHER"

1. Leverson, A. (1930): *Letters to the Sphinx from Oscar Wilde, with Reminiscences of the Author.* London: Duckworth, pp. 44–46.
2. Holland, M. and Hart-Davis, R. (editors) (2000): *The Complete Letters of Oscar Wilde.* London: Fourth Estate, p. 842.
3. Sherard, R. (1906): *The Life of Oscar Wilde.* London: T. Werner Laurie, p. 407.
4. Healy, C. (1904): *Confessions of a Journalist.* London: Chatto and Windus, pp. 130–138.
5. The National Archives, Kew, Surrey: Home Office (Prison Commission) papers, file PCOM 8/434.
6. *Complete Letters*, p. 848.
7. Ibid., p. 859.
8. Ibid., p. 873.
9. Ibid., pp. 847–855.
10. Ibid., p. 967.
11. Ibid., p. 935.
12. Ibid., p. 931.
13. Ibid., p. 781.
14. Ibid., pp. 1045–1049.
15. Ibid., p. 1095.
16. Ström, A. (editor) (1968): *Norwegian Concentration Camp Survivors.* Oslo: Universitetsforlaget.
17. Speed, N. et al. (1989). Posttraumatic stress disorder as a consequence of the POW experience. *Journal of Nervous and Mental Diseases*, 177, 147–153.
18. *Complete Letters*, pp. 39–40.
19. Douglas, A. (1940): *Oscar Wilde: A Summing-Up.* London: Duckworth, p. 141.
20. McKenna, N. (2003): *The Secret Life of Oscar Wilde.* London: Century.
21. Rothenstein, W. (1931): *Men and Memories.* London: Faber and Faber, pp. 361–364.
22. *Complete Letters*, pp. 9–40.
23. Fish, A. (1923). Memories of Oscar Wilde: *Cassell's Weekly*, 2 May 1923, pp. 215–216, cited in Mikhail, E.H. (1979): *Oscar Wilde: Interviews and Recollections*, Volume 1. London: Macmillan, pp. 152–154.
24. Robertson, W.G. (1931): *Time Was.* London: Hamish Hamilton, cited in Mikhail, op. cit. (note 23), pp. 209–210.
25. *Complete Letters*, pp. 1095 and 1112.
26. Ibid., p. 1061.
27. Ibid., p. 1141.
28. Ibid., p. 1160.
29. Douglas, op. cit., pp. 136–137.
30. *Complete Letters*, p. 1228.
31. Thornton, B. *Theatre Magazine* (New York), XXVII (June 1918), 370, cited in Mikhail, op. cit. (reference 23), volume 2, pp. 441–443.

CHAPTER 6   THE VEXATIOUS DOMESTIC SAGA

1.   Holcombe, L. (1983): *Wives and Property: Reform of the Married Women's Property Law in Nineteenth Century England.* Toronto: University of Toronto.
2.   Phillips, R. (1988): *Putting Asunder: A History of Divorce in Western Society.* Cambridge: Cambridge University Press.
3.   Holland, M. and Hart-Davis, R. (editors) (2000): *The Complete Letters of Oscar Wilde.* London: Fourth Estate, p. 676.
4.   The National Archives, Kew, Surrey: High Court of Justice in Bankruptcy, file B9/429, 10 August 1895.
5.   Hyde, H.M. (1963): *Oscar Wilde: The Aftermath.* London: Methuen, *passim.*
6.   Robert Ross, "Statement of evidence in his case against Douglas", Clark Library, cited in McKenna, N. (2003): *The Secret Life of Oscar Wilde.* London: Century, p. 426.
7.   Letter from Otho Holland (Lloyd) to Arthur Ransome, 28 February 1912, cited by Brogan, H. (1984): *The Life of Arthur Ransome.* London: Jonathan Cape, p. 79.
8.   Will of Constance Mary Wilde, 29 February 1896, Probate Registry, York.
9.   Letter from Constance Holland to Robert Ross, 21 June 1896, Clark Library.
10. *Complete Letters*, p. 652.
11. Ibid., pp. 671–672.
12. Letter from Robert Ross to Oscar Browning [November 1895], King's College Library, Cambridge.
13. Letter from More Adey to Martin Holman, 6 January 1897, Clark Library.
14. Letter from Adela Schuster to More Adey, 2 December 1895, Clark Library.
15. Ibid., 20 March 1896, Clark Library.
16. Ibid., 19 April 1896, Clark Library.
17. Ibid., 5 December 1895, Clark Library.
18. Ibid., 21 March 1896, Clark Library.
19. Ibid., 1 June 1896, Clark Library.
20. Ibid., 11 June 1896, Clark Library.
21. Draft letter from More Adey to Constance Holland, 30 July 1896, Ms. Walpole d.18, Bodleian Library, Oxford.
22. Letter from Constance Holland to More Adey, 3 August 1896, Clark Library.
23. Letter from Adela Schuster to More Adey, 11 August 1896, Clark Library.
24. Holland, V. (1954): *Son of Oscar Wilde.* London: Rupert Hart-Davis, p. 130.
25. Draft letter from More Adey to Constance Holland [August 1896], Ms. Walpole d.18, Bodleian Library, Oxford.
26. Letter from Adela Schuster to More Adey, 12 August 1896, Clark Library.
27. Ibid., 6 October 1896, Clark Library.
28. Ibid., 3 October 1896, Clark Library.
29. Hyde, op. cit, p. 82.
30. *Complete Letters*, p. 642 footnote 1.
31. Letter from Constance Wilde to Emily Thursfield, 25 June 1895, Clark Library.
32. Hart-Davis, R. (editor)(1962): *The Letters of Oscar Wilde.* New York: Harcourt, Brace & World, pp. 871–872.
33. The National Archives, Kew, Surrey: Home Office (Prison Commission) papers, file PCOM8/432 (13629/26).
34. Letter from Constance Wilde to Emily Thursfield, 12 October 1895, Clark Library.
35. Letter from Constance Wilde to Hannah Whitall Smith, 15 October 1895, cited in Ellmann, R. (1987): *Oscar Wilde.* London: Hamish Hamilton, p. 462.
36. Eversley, W.P. (1896): *The Law of the Domestic Relations* (second edition). London: Stevens and Haynes.
37. *Complete Letters*, p. 783.
38. The National Archives, Kew, Surrey: High Court of Justice, Chancery Division, file J15/2305, no. 1250.

39. *Complete Letters*, p. 823.
40. Ibid., pp. 798–800.
41. Catalogue, Sotheby's, English Literature and History sale, London 22/23 July 1985, Lot 159.
42. Letter from More Adey to Martin Holman, 14 May 1897, Clark Library.
43. *Complete Letters*, p. 1035 footnote 1.

Chapter 7 The Great Syphilis Debate

1. Hayden, D. (2003): *Pox: Genius, Madness and the Mysteries of Syphilis*. New York: Basic Books.
2. O'Shea, J.G. (1990). 'Two minutes with venus, two years with mercury' – mercury as an anti-syphilitic chemotherapeutic agent. *Journal of the Royal Society of Medicine*, 83, 392–395.
3. Holland, M. and Hart-Davis, R. (editors) (2000): *The Complete Letters of Oscar Wilde*. London: Fourth Estate, p. 65.
4. Ibid., p. 533.
5. Ibid. p. 620.
6. Ibid., pp. 697–700.
7. Ibid., p. 1062.
8. Ibid., p. 1176.
9. Ibid., pp. 1173–1174.
10. Harris, F. (1938): *Oscar Wilde*. London: Constable, pp. 230–232.
11. The National Archives, Kew, Surrey: Home Office (Prison Commission) papers, file HO 45/24514, pp. 79–91.
12. *Complete Letters*, p. 659.
13. Obituary, Sir William Dalby. *British Medical Journal* (1919), 1, 60.
14. Douglas, A. (1929): *Autobiography*. London: Martin Secker, p. 108.
15. Harris, op. cit., pp. 232 and 293.
16. *Complete Letters*, p. 659.
17. The National Archives, Kew, Surrey: Home Office (Prison Commission) papers, file HO 45/24514(A56887), p. 54.
18. Ibid., pp. 37 and 38.
19. *Complete Letters*, p. 667.
20. Ibid., pp. 854, 1048–1049.
21. *British Medical Journal* (2001), 322, 1014.
22. *Complete Letters*, p. 1206.
23. Ibid., p. 1200.
24. Ellmann, R. (1987): *Oscar Wilde*. London: Hamish Hamilton, p. 547.
25. Robins, A.H. and Sellars, S.L. (2000): Oscar Wilde's terminal illness: reappraisal after a century. *Lancet*, 356, 1841–1843.
26. Cawthorne, T. (1966). The fatal illness of Oscar Wilde. *Annals of Otology, Rhinology and Laryngology*, 75, 657–666.
27. Critchley, M. (1990). Oscar Wilde's fatal illness: the mystery unshrouded. *Medical Health Annual*, 191–207.
28. Lyons, J.B. (1995). Oscar Wilde's final illness. *Irish Studies Review*, 11, 24–27.
29. Mai, R. and Rutka, J. (2000). The irony of being Oscar: the legendary life and death of Oscar Wilde. *Journal of Otolaryngology*, 29, 239–243.
30. Sellars, S.L. (1974). The origins of mastoid surgery. *South African Medical Journal*, 48, 234–242.
31. Beerbohm, M.: *Letters to Reggie Turner*, edited Hart-Davis, R. (1964). London: Rupert Hart-Davis.
32. Shaw, G.B. Preface to Harris, op. cit., p. xi.
33. *Complete Letters*, p. 1225.
34. Ibid., pp. 1212–1213.
35. Schenker, J. (2000): *Truly Wilde: The Unsettling Story of Dolly Wilde, Oscar's Unusual Niece*. London: Virago, pp. 37–48, 316–325.
36. *Complete Letters*, p. 1178.

37. Ibid., pp. 1174–1175.
38. Harris, op. cit., pp. 355, 358, 365.
39. *Complete Letters*, p. 1182.
40. Ibid., p. 1194.
41. Nater, J.P. (1992). Oscar Wilde's skin disease: allergic contact dermatitis. *Contact Dermatitis*, 27, 47–49.
42. Letter from Dion Boucicault to Oscar Wilde, 22 April 1894 (Harry Ransom Humanities Research Center, University of Texas), cited in Small, I. (1993): *Oscar Wilde Revalued*. University of North Carolina: ELT Press, p. 92.
43. Epigram, Oscar Wilde, cited in Small, I.: *Oscar Wilde Revalued*, op. cit. (see note 42), p. 130.
44. Ransome, A. (1912): *Oscar Wilde: A Critical Study*. London: Martin Secker, p. 199.
45. Sherard, R.H. [1915]: *The Real Oscar Wilde*. London: T. Werner Laurie, p. 385.
46. Letter from Reginald Turner to Robert Sherard, 3 January 1934, University of Reading.
47. Holland, M. (1988). What killed Oscar Wilde? *The Spectator*, 24/31 December, pp. 34–35.
48. Holland, M. (1997). Biography and the art of lying. In Raby, P. (editor): *The Cambridge Companion to Oscar Wilde*. Cambridge: Cambridge University Press, pp. 3–17.
49. Hayden, op. cit., pp. 200–225.
50. Douglas, A. (1940): *Oscar Wilde: A Summing Up*. London: Duckworth, p. 96.
51. Ransome, op. cit., corrected page proofs, p. 199. Catalogue, Sotheby's, London, English Literature and History sale, 13 December 1990, Lot 166.
52. Ellmann, op. cit., pp. 88–90, 545.
53. West, D.J. (1977): *Homosexuality Re-examined*. London: Duckworth, pp. 228–233.
54. Weatherall, D.J. et al. (editors) (1996): *Oxford Textbook of Medicine*. Oxford: Oxford University Press, p. 708.
55. Kaspar, D.L. et al. (editors) (2005): *Harrison's Principles of Internal Medicine* (16th edition). New York: McGraw-Hill, p. 977 (chapter by Lukehart, S.A.).

CHAPTER 8   THE PRECIPITOUS ROAD TO HOMOSEXUAL LAW REFORM

1. Robb, G. (2003). *Strangers: Homosexual Love in the Nineteenth Century*. London: Picador, pp. 272–273.
2. Bell, R. (1999). Homosexual men and women. *British Medical Journal*, 318, 452–455.
3. Cohen, E. (1993): *Talk on the Wilde Side*. New York: Routledge, pp. 9–10, 217.
4. Robb, op. cit., pp. 52–59.
5. Ibid., pp. 80–82.
6. Editorial (1899). *Lancet*, 2, 170–171.
7. The National Archives, Kew, Surrey: file HO 45/24514, pp. 79–91.
8. Holland, M. and Hart-Davis, R. (editors) (2000): *The Complete Letters of Oscar Wilde*. London: Fourth Estate, pp. 656–660.
9. Carpenter, E. (1894): Homogenic love, Lectures, published Manchester Labour Press, January 1895.
10. Ellis, H. (1897): *Studies in the Psychology of Sex*, vol.1 *Sexual Inversion*. Watford: University Press.
11. Calder-Marshall, A. (1972): *Lewd, Blasphemous & Obscene*. London: Hutchinson (Part Five).
12. Editorial (1898). *British Medical Journal*, 2, 1466.
13. Parliamentary Debates (House of Commons), 6 August 1885, columns 1397–1398.
14. Letter from J.A. Symonds to Charles Kains-Jackson, 18 December 1892. Cited by Grosskurth, P. (1964): *John Addington Symonds: A Biography*. London: Longmans, p. 283.
15. Smith, F.B. (1976–1977): Labouchère's Amendment to the Criminal Law Amendment Bill. *Historical Studies*, 17, 165–175.
16. Editorial (1885). *Lancet*, 2, 251–253.
17. Davenport-Hines, R. (1990): *Sex, Death and Punishment*. Glasgow: William Collins, pp. 134–135.
18. Ibid., p. 297.
19. Robb, op. cit., pp. 30–33.

20. Evans.R.J. (2006). *The Third Reich in Power*. London: Penguin, pp. 529–535.
21. Chester, L., Leitch, D. and Simpson, C. (1976): *The Cleveland Street Affair*. London: Weidenfeld and Nicolson.
22. Hyde, M.H. (1976): *The Cleveland Street Scandal*. London: W.H. Allen.
23. Parliamentary Debates (House of Commons), 26 February 1892, columns 1401–1402.
24. Information supplied by Mr Chris Pond, Head of Reference and Reader Services, House of Commons Library, London.
25. Central Criminal Court Sessions Papers (1895), vol. 121, pp. 531–532; vol. 122, pp. 582–583, 625.
26. Parliamentary Debates (House of Lords), 20 March 1896, columns 1434–1451.
27. Editorial (1896). *Lancet*, 1, 932.
28. Parliamentary Debates (House of Lords), 15 August 1921, columns 567–577.
29. Weeks, J. (1981): *Sex, Politics & Society*. London: Longman, p. 117.
30. Parliamentary Debates (House of Lords), 19 May 1954, columns 737–745.
31. Morley, S. (2001): *John G: The Authorised Biography of John Gielgud*. London: Hodder & Stoughton, pp. 231–263.
32. West, D.J. and de Villiers, B. (1992): *Male Prostitution*. London: Duckworth, pp. 22–32.
33. LeVay, S. and Hamer, D.A. (1994). Evidence for a biological influence in male homosexuality. *Scientific American*, May 1994, pp. 20–25.
34. Byre, W. (1994). The biological evidence challenged. *Scientific American*, May 1994, pp. 26–31.
35. Mustanski, B.S., Chivers, M.L. and Bailey, J.M. (2002). A critical review of recent biological research on human sex orientation. *Annual Review of Sexual Research*, 13, 89–140.
36. Langstrom, N., Rahman, Q., Carlstrom, E. and Lichenstein, P. (2010). Genetic and environmental effects on same-sex sexual behavior: a population study of twins in Sweden. *Archives of Sexual Behavior*, 39, 75–80.
37. Smith, G., Bartlett, A. and King, M. (2004). Treatments of homosexuality in Britain since the 1950s – an oral history: the experience of patients. *British Medical Journal*, 328, 427–429.
38. Bayer, R. (1987). Politics, science and the problem of psychiatric nomenclature. In *Scientific Controversies* (edited by Engelhardt, H.T. and Caplan, A.). Cambridge: Cambridge University Press, pp. 381–400.
39. *Complete Letters*, p. 1044.
40. Cretney, S. (2006): *Same Sex Relationships: From 'Odious Crime' to 'Gay Marriage'*. Oxford University Press, pp. 19–42.

CHAPTER 9   GAY SUPERSTAR BUT NOT MARTYR

1. Ellmann, R. (1987): *Oscar Wilde*. London: Hamish Hamilton, p. 261.
2. Croft-Cooke, R. (1972): *The Unrecorded Life of Oscar Wilde*. London: W.H. Allen, p. 25.
3. McKenna, N. (2003): *The Secret Life of Oscar Wilde*. London: Century.
4. Croft-Cooke, op. cit., p. 42.
5. McKenna, op. cit., p. 11
6. Holland, M. and Hart-Davis, R. (editors) (2000): *The Complete Letters of Oscar Wilde*. London: Fourth Estate, pp. 34–35.
7. Ibid., p. 36.
8. Hastings, S. (1985): *Nancy Mitford: A Biography*. London: Hamish Hamilton, p. 80 et seq.
9. Lewis, L. and Smith, H.J. (1967): *Oscar Wilde Discovers America*. New York: Benjamin Blom, p. 158.
10. I acknowledge the research of Ms Abby Yochelson, Reference Specialist, United States Library of Congress, Washington DC.
11. Robb, G. (2003): *Strangers: Homosexual Love in the Nineteenth Century*. London: Picador, p. 105.
12. McKenna, op. cit., pp. 29–30.
13. Dellamora, R. (1990): *Masculine Desire: The Sexual Politics of Victorian Aestheticism*. Chapel Hill: University of North Carolina Press, pp. 158–164.
14. Dowling, L. (1994): *Hellenism and Homosexuality in Victorian Oxford*. Ithaca: Cornell University Press, pp. 112–113.

15. Hyde, H.M. (1976): *Oscar Wilde*. London: Eyre Methuen, p. 35.
16. Ibid, p. 39.
17. Cited in Ellmann, op. cit., p. 141.
18. Dowling, op. cit., pp. 100–103.
19. *Complete Letters*, p. 29.
20. Ibid., p. 47.
21. Ibid., pp. 66–67.
22. Ibid., pp. 71–73.
23. Ibid., pp. 82–83, 82, footnote 2.
24. Cohen, L. [no date]: *Some Reflections of Claude Goldsmith Montefiore (1858–1938)*. London: Faber and Faber, pp. 34–35.
25. Ellmann, op. cit., p. 569, reference 4.
26. Auden, W.H. An improbable life *(The New Yorker,* 9 March 1963) in Ellmann, R. (editor) (1969): *Oscar Wilde: A Collection of Critical Essays*. Englewood Cliffs: Prentice-Hall, p. 121.
27. Ellmann, op.cit., p. 220.
28. *Complete Letters*, p. 794.
29. Melville, J. (1994): *Mother of Oscar*. London: John Murray.
30. Letter from Otho Lloyd to Nellie Hutchinson, cited in Melville, op. cit., p. 179.
31. *Complete Letters*, p. 222.
32. Pearson, H. (1954): *The Life of Oscar Wilde*. London: Methuen, p. 111.
33. *Complete Letters*, pp. 224–225.
34. Amor, A.C. (1983): *Mrs Oscar Wilde: A Woman of Some Importance*. London: Sidgwick and Jackson.
35. *Idem*, "Constantly undervalued: a centenary appreciation of Constance Wilde. *The Wildean*, number 14, January 1999, pp. 8–25.
36. Bentley, J. (1983): *The Importance of Being Constance*. London: Robert Hale.
37. Douglas, A. (1931): *The Autobiography of Lord Alfred Douglas*. London: Martin Secker, pp. 59–60.
38. Robb, op. cit., pp. 126–127.
39. Grosskurth, P. (1964): *John Addington Symonds: A Biography*. London: Longmans.
40. Fryer, J. (1997): *André and Oscar*. London: Constable, pp. 160–179; 226–234.
41. Robb, op. cit., pp. 74 and 131.
42. Wildeblood, P. (1955): *Against the Law*. London: Weidenfeld and Nicolson, p. 33.
43. Sher, A. (2001): *Beside Myself: An Autobiography*. London: Hutchinson, p. 114.
44. Cited in Ellis, Havelock (1900): *Sexual Inversion*. (Studies in the Psychology of Sex, volume 1). Watford: University Press, p. 179.
45. Krafft-Ebing, R. (1892): *Psychopathia Sexualis with Especial Reference to Contrary Sexual Instinct: A Medico-Legal Study*, translated by Charles Chaddock, 7th edition. London: F.J. Rebman.
46. West, D.J. (1977): *Homosexuality Re-examined*. London: Duckworth, p. 20.
47. Friedman, R.C. and Downey, J.I. (1994). Homosexuality. *New England Journal of Medicine*, 331, 923–930.
48. Ross, M.W. (1983): *The Married Homosexual Man: A Psychological Study*. London: Routledge and Kegan Paul, *passim*.
49. Ross, op. cit., pp. 50–53.
50. Sherard, R.H. [1915]: *The Real Oscar Wilde*. London: T. Werner Laurie, p. 318.
51. Gochros, J.S. (1985). Wives' reactions to learning that their husbands are bisexual. *Journal of Homosexuality*, 11, 101–113.
52. *Complete Letters*, p. 642, footnote 1.
53. Harris, F. (1938): *Oscar Wilde*. London: Constable, p. 338.
54. *Complete Letters*, p. 813.
55. Ibid., p. 261.
56. Ibid, p. 262.
57. Ibid., p. 239.
58. Ibid., pp. 266–269, 272–274, 276, 282.
59. Hyde, H.M. (1984): *Lord Alfred Douglas*. London: Methuen.
60. Murray, D. (2000): *Bosie: A Biography of Lord Alfred Douglas*. London: Hodder and Stoughton.

61. Fisher, T. (2002): *Oscar and Bosie: A Fatal Passion*. Stroud: Sutton.
62. *Complete Letters*, p. 544.
63. Ibid., p. 647.
64. Ibid., p. 651.
65. Letter from Alfred Douglas to Frank Harris, 20 March 1925, Douglas manuscripts, Texas, cited by Hyde (1984), op. cit., pp. 27–28.
66. Wildeblood, op. cit., p. 26.
67. Weeks, J. (1981): *Sex, Politics and Society*. London: Longman, p. 113.
68. West, D.J. and de Villiers, B. (1992): *Male Prostitution: Gay Sex Services in London*. London: Duckworth, p. 265.
69. *Complete Letters*, p. 787.
70. Ibid., p. 794.
71. Amor, op. cit., p. 61.
72. Letter from Otho Holland (Lloyd) to Arthur Ransome, 28 February 1912, cited in Brogan, H. (1984): *The Life of Arthur Ransome*. London: Jonathan Cape, p. 79.
73. Frank Liebich, "Oscar Wilde" (unpublished memoir), Clark Library, cited in McKenna, op. cit., p. 162.
74. Hyde, H.M. (1962): *Famous Trials 7: Oscar Wilde*. Harmondsworth: Penguin Books, p. 201.
75. Letter from Oscar Wilde to Mrs Stannard [28 May 1897], Sotheby's English Literature and History sale, London, 15 July 1999, Lot 135.
76. *Complete Letters*, p. 862.
77. Ibid., p. 891.
78. Ibid., p. 1019.
79. Ibid., pp. 1005–6.
80. Ibid., pp. 847–855; 1045–1049.
81. Ibid., p. 1080.
82. Information obtained from Lillie Exhibition, Jersey Museum, St. Helier, 1998.

CHAPTER 10 OSCAR AS OTHERS SAW HIM

1. Sherard, R.H. (1906): *The Life of Oscar Wilde*. London: T. Werner Laurie, pp. 103–121.
2. Mikhail, E.H. (editor) (1979): *Oscar Wilde: Interviews and Recollections* (volume 1). London: Macmillan, pp. 5 and 17.
3. The Historical Record of the University of Oxford (1220–1900).
4. Holland, M. and Hart-Davis, R. (editors)(2000): *The Complete Letters of Oscar Wilde*. London: Fourth Estate, p. 70.
5. Harris, F. (1938): *Oscar Wilde (with a Preface by Bernard Shaw)*. London: Constable, pp. xx, xxxii–xxxiii.
6. Yeats, W.B. (1916): *Autobiography*. London: Macmillan, p. 79.
7. Rothenstein, W. (1931): *Men and Memories: Recollections 1872–1900*. London: Faber and Faber, pp. 7–91.
8. Blunt, W.S. (1932): *My Diaries*, cited in Mikhail, op. cit., volume 2, p. 472.
9. Wratislaw, T. (1979): *Oscar Wilde: A Memoir*. London: The Eighteen Nineties Society.
10. *Complete Letters*, p. 1229.
11. Holland, M. (2003): *Irish Peacock & Scarlet Marquess: The Real Trial of Oscar Wilde*. London: Fourth Estate.
12. Mikhail, op. cit., volume 2, p. 460.
13. Vernier, P. (1998). A 'Mental Photograph' of Oscar Wilde. *The Wildean*, number 13, pp. 28–51.
14. Watts, M.T. (1990). Sir William Wilde: royal ophthalmologist extraordinary. *Journal of the Royal Society of Medicine*, 83, 183–184.
15. Melville, J. (1994): *Mother of Oscar*. London: John Murray.
16. Ellmann, R. (1987): *Oscar Wilde*. London: Hamish Hamilton, pp. 75–76.
17. *Complete Letters*, pp. 126, 158–162.

18. Fish, A. Memories of Oscar Wilde. *Cassell's Weekly*, 2 May 1923, pp. 215–216, cited in Mikhail, op. cit., volume 1, p. 152.
19. Doyle, A.C. (1924): *Memories and Adventures*. London: Hodder and Stoughton, p. 80.
20. Hyde, H.M. (1963): *Oscar Wilde: The Aftermath*. London: Methuen, p. 60.
21. Symonds, A.W. (1901). An artist in attitudes: Oscar Wilde. In Stanford, D. (editor) (1971): *Writing of the 'Nineties from Wilde to Beerbohm*. London: Dent, p. 26.
22. Ransome, A. (1913): *Oscar Wilde: A Critical Study*. London: Methuen, p. 221.
23. Holland, op. cit., pp. 4 and 110.
24. *Complete Letters*, pp. 418–419.
25. Hart-Davis, R. (editor) (1964): *Max Beerbohm: Letters to Reggie Turner*, 15 April 1893. London: Rupert Hart-Davis, p. 36.
26. Guy, J. and Small, I. (2000): *Oscar Wilde's Profession: Writing and the Culture Industry in the Late Nineteenth Century*. Oxford: Oxford University Press, pp. 257–281.
27. Harris, op. cit., p. xlv.
28. O'Sullivan, V. (1936): *Aspects of Wilde*. London: Constable, pp. 80–85.
29. *Complete Letters*, p. 1229.
30. O'Sullivan, V. op. cit., p. 55.
31. *Complete Letters*, p. 1196.
32. Mikhail, op.cit., volume 1, p. 18.
33. *Complete Letters*, pp. 774–775.
34. The National Archives, Kew, Surrey: High Court of Justice in Bankruptcy, file B9/428.
35. Mikhail, op. cit., volume 1, pp. 17–18.
36. Farnell, L.R. (1934): *An Oxonian Looks Back*. London: Martin Hopkinson, pp. 57, 70–71.
37. Ellmann, op. cit., pp. 74–75.
38. Pearson, H. (1954): *The Life of Oscar Wilde*. London: Methuen, p. 247.
39. Ibid., p. 224.
40. O'Sullivan, op. cit., p. 89.
41. Hyde, H.M. (1976): *Oscar Wilde*. London: Eyre Methuen, p. 112.
42. Mikhail, op. cit., volume 2, p. 474 note 1.
43. Rothenstein, op. cit., p. 133.
44. Douglas, A. (1940): *Oscar Wilde: A Summing-Up*. London: Duckworth, p. 53.
45. Letter from Henry Rider Haggard to Robert Ross, 27 July 1892, cited in Ross, M. (editor) (1952): *Robert Ross: Friend of Friends*. London: Jonathan Cape, p. 358.
46. Holland, op. cit., p. 64.
47. The National Archives, op. cit., file B/429.
48. *Complete Letters*, pp. 87–88.
49. Ibid., p. 46.
50. Ibid., pp. 756–757.
51. Ibid., p. 803.
52. Mikhail, op. cit., volume 2, pp. 328–329.
53. *Complete Letters*, p. 340.
54. Sherard, R.H. [1915]: *The Real Oscar Wilde*. London: T. Werner Laurie, p. 256.
55. Harris, op. cit., p. 362.
56. Leverson, A. (1930): *Letters to the Sphinx from Oscar Wilde and Reminiscences of the Author*. London: Duckworth, p. 47.
57. Mikhail, op. cit., volume 2, p. 428.
58. *Complete Letters*, p. 879.
59. *Oscar Wilde at Oxford* (Wilde manuscripts and related items in the Bodleian Library, Oxford). Privately published (Andrew McDonnell), Oxford, 1996, pp. 9–14.
60. Letters from Lady Jane Wilde to Oscar Wilde [1882], cited in Sotheby's Catalogue, English Literature and History sale, London, 13 December 1990, Lot 186.
61. Account book, Arends Collection, New York Public Library, cited in Ellman, op. cit., p. 182.
62. Guy and Small, op. cit., p. 133.
63. *Complete Letters*, p. 799.

64. Ibid., p. 703.
65. *Oscar Wilde at Oxford*, op. cit., p. 7.
66. *Complete Letters*, p. 633.

CHAPTER 11   RELATIONSHIPS WITH FAMILY AND FRIENDS

1. Harris, F. (1938): *Oscar Wilde (with a Preface by George Bernard Shaw)*. London: Constable, p. xlviii.
2. Holland, M. and Hart-Davis, R. (editors) (2000): *The Complete Letters of Oscar Wilde*. London: Fourth Estate, p. 1131.
3. McKenna, N. (2003): *The Secret Life of Oscar Wilde*. London: Century.
4. Harrison, F. (1977): *The Dark Angel: Aspects of Victorian Sexuality*. London: Sheldon Press, p. 55.
5. Letter from Constance Wilde to Otho Holland Lloyd, August 1887, cited in Melville, J. (1994): *Mother of Oscar*. London: John Murray, p. 205.
6. *Complete Letters*, p. 785.
7. Holland, M. (2002): *Irish Peacock & Scarlet Marquess: The Real Trial of Oscar Wilde*. London: Fourth Estate, pp. 66, 172, 176.
8. *Complete Letters*, p. 598.
9. Ellmann, R. (1987): *Oscar Wilde*. London: Hamish Hamilton, p. 371.
10. Letter from Lady Wilde to Oscar Wilde, Clark Library, cited in Melville, op. cit. (see reference 5), p. 226.
11. Letter from Lady Wilde to Oscar Wilde, 3 December 1891, Clark Library, cited in Melville, op. cit. (see reference 5), p. 228.
12. Letter from Constance Wilde to Robert Ross, 28 January 1895, Clark Library.
13. Letter from Otho Holland (Lloyd) to Arthur Ransome, 28 February 1912, cited in Brogan, H. (1984): *The Life of Arthur Ransome*. London: Jonathan Cape, p. 79.
14. *Complete Letters*, p. 1042.
15. Letter from Constance Wilde to Robert Ross, 12 March 1895, Clark Library.
16. Letter from Constance Wilde to Robert Ross, 15 March 1895, Clark Library.
17. The National Archives, Kew, Surrey: High Court of Justice in Bankruptcy, file B9/428.
18. Obituary, Vernon Lamphier Jones. *British Medical Journal*, 1916, 2, 511.
19. McKenna, op. cit., pp. 331–332.
20. Letter from Otho Holland (Lloyd) to A.J.A. Symons, 27 May 1937, Clark Library.
21. *The Complete Letters of Oscar Wilde*, pp. 920–921.
22. Ibid., p. 676.
23. Ibid., p. 785.
24. Letter from Constance Wilde to Arthur Humphreys, 1 June 1894, cited in Sotheby's Catalogue, English Literature and History sale, London, 22 July 1985, Lot 155.
25. Letter from Constance Wilde to Arthur Humphreys, 11 August 1894, ibid., Lot 156.
26. Letter from Constance Wilde to Arthur Humphreys, 22 October 1894, Clark Library.
27. *Complete Letters*, p. 865 and footnote 2.
28. Ibid., p. 935.
29. Ibid., p. 947.
30. Ibid., p. 994.
31. Ibid., p. 982 footnote 1.
32. Ibid., p. 1041.
33. Ibid., p. 952.
34. Sherard, R.H. [1915]: *The Real Oscar Wilde*. London: T. Werner Laurie, p. 163.
35. Letter from Constance Wilde to Arthur Humphreys, 18 February 1898, Eccles Collection, British Library.
36. Holland, V. (1954): *Son of Oscar Wilde*. London: Rupert Hart-Davis, p. 130.
37. *The Complete Letters of Oscar Wilde*, p. 1055.
38. Ibid., p. 1054 and footnote 2.
39. Ibid., p. 1128 and footnote 2.

40. Letter from Otho Holland (Lloyd) to Carlos Blacker, 13 January 1901, cited in Sotheby's Catalogue, English Literature and History sale, London, 10 July 1986, Lot 151.
41. Holland, V., op. cit., pp. 52–56.
42. Davidoff, L. (1990). The family in Britain. In Thompson, F.M.L. (editor): *The Cambridge Social History of Britain*. Cambridge: Cambridge University Press, pp. 71–129.
43. Letter from Constance Wilde to Otho Holland Lloyd, August 1887, cited in Melville, op. cit.(see reference 5), pp. 204–205.
44. *Complete Letters*, p. 821.
45. Ibid., p. 681.
46. Ibid., p. 715.
47. Ibid., p. 744.
48. Holland, V., op. cit., p. 35.
49. *Complete Letters*, p. 955 footnote 1.
50. Ibid., p. 1228.
51. Holland, V., op. cit., p. 200.
52. Ibid., p. 153.
53. Ibid., p. 140.
54. Ibid., p. 201.
55. Ibid., pp. 11–12.
56. *New York Times*, 18 September 1893, p. 5.
57. Letter from Lady Jane Wilde to Oscar Wilde, 29 March 1894, cited in Melville, op. cit.(see reference 5), p. 249.
58. Melville, op. cit. (see reference 5), pp. 241–244.
59. De Brémont, A. (1911): *Oscar Wilde and His Mother*. Lincoln: Everett, pp. 157–158.
60. Letter from Willie Wilde to More Adey, 4 February 1896, Clark Library.
61. Letter from Lily Wilde to More Adey, 8 May 1897, Ms. Walpole d.18, Bodleian Library, Oxford.
62. *Complete Letters*, pp. 785.
63. Ibid., p. 1130.
64. Ibid., p. 823.
65. Ibid., pp. 836–837.
66. Letter from Robert Ross to Leonard Smithers, 25 November 1897, cited in Borland, M. (1990): *Wilde's Devoted Friend: A Life of Robert Ross 1869–1918*. Oxford: Lennard Publishing, pp. 63–64.
67. *Complete Letters*, pp. 683–780.
68. Ibid., p. 652.
69. Ibid., p. 780.
70. Letter from Alfred Douglas to W.T. Stead, 15 November 1895, cited in Sotheby's Catalogue, English Literature, History and Illustration sale, London, 19 July 1994, Lot 150.
71. *Complete Letters*, pp. 635–636.
72. Ibid., p. 827.
73. Ibid., p. 832.
74. Ibid., p. 797.
75. Ibid., pp. 827–828.
76. Ibid., pp. 980–981, 1100.
77. Ibid., p. 981 footnote 2.
78. Letter from Ernest Leverson to Robert Ross, 2 June 1898, Clark Library.
79. *Complete Letters*, p. 911.
80. Ibid., p. 1050.
81. Ibid., pp. 1085–1086.
82. Ibid., pp. 1086–1091.
83. Maguire, J.R. (1997): Oscar Wilde and the Dreyfus Affair. *Victorian Studies*, volume 41, number 1 (Autumn).
84. Hitchens, M. (1999): *Oscar Wilde's Last Chance – the Dreyfus Connection*. Durham: Pentland Press.
85. Letter from Carlos Blacker to Otho Holland (Lloyd), 21 December 1900, cited in Sotheby's

Catalogue, English Literature and History sale, London, 10 July 1986, Lot 151. See introductory account between Lots 121 and 122.

86. Hitchens, op. cit., p. 151 footnote.
87. *Complete Letters*, p. 983.
88. Nassaar, C.S. (2003). The problem of the Jewish manager in *The Picture of Dorian Gray*. *The Wildean*, number 22, pp. 29–36.
89. *Complete Letters*, p. 1110.
90. Ibid., pp. 812–813.
91. Hyde, M.H. (1976): *Oscar Wilde*. London: Eyre Methuen, pp. 367–368.
92. *Complete Letters*, p. 644.
93. Ibid., p. 962 footnote 3 and p. 963.
94. Letter from Adela Schuster to More Adey, 13 August 1896, Clark Library.
95. *Complete Letters*, p. 738.
96. Letter from Adela Schuster to More Adey, 16 March 1898, Clark Library.
97. Letter from Adela Schuster to More Adey, 9 August 1898, Clark Library.
98. *Complete Letters*, p. 904.
99. Ibid., p. 1136.
100. Ibid., p. 1091 footnote 1.
101. Letter from Sir Edward Clarke to Robert Ross, cited in Ross, M. (1952): *Robert Ross Friend of Friends*. London: Jonathan Cape, p. 46.
102. Hyde, H.M. (1984): *Lord Alfred Douglas: A Biography*. London: Methuen, pp. 90–91.
103. Douglas, A. (1931): *Autobiography of Lord Alfred Douglas*. London: Martin Secker, p. 110.
104. Letter from Constance Holland to Arthur Humphreys, 27 February 1898, cited in Pryor, F. (1988): *The Faber Book of Letters*. London: Faber and Faber, pp. 218–219.

CHAPTER 12   HISTRIONIC PERSONALITY DISORDER

1.   Holland, M. and Hart-Davis, R. (editors) (2000): *The Complete Letters of Oscar Wilde*. London: Fourth Estate, p. 656.
2.   Bridgwater, P. (2002). Some German Oscar Wildes. In Böker, U. et al. (editors): *The Importance of Reinventing Oscar*. Amsterdam: Rodopi, pp. 237–247.
3.   Nordau, M. (1895): *Degeneration* (Book 3, Chapter 1). London: William Heinemann, pp. 317–319.
4.   Critchley, M. (1957). Oscar Wilde: a medical appreciation. *Medical History*, 1, 199–210.
5.   Slater, E. and Ross, M. (1969): *Clinical Psychiatry* (third edition). London: Ballière, Tindall and Cassell, pp. 110–111.
6.   *ICD–10 Classification of Mental and Behavioural Disorders*, World Health Organization (1994). Edinburgh: Churchill Livingstone, pp. 222–223.
7.   *Diagnostic and Statistical Manual of Mental Disorders*, Fourth Edition, Text Revision (2000). American Psychiatric Association, Washington DC, pp. 711–714.
8.   Hyde, H.M. (1963): *Oscar Wilde: The Aftermath*. London: Methuen, p. 60.
9.   Vernier, P. (1998). A 'Mental Photograph' of Oscar Wilde, *The Wildean*, number 13, 28–51.
10. McKenna, N. (2003): *The Secret Life of Oscar Wilde*. London: Century.
11. *Complete Letters*, p. 272.
12. Ibid., p. 758.
13. Ibid., p. 858.
14. Ibid., p. 865.
15. Ibid., p. 880.
16. Ibid., pp. 898–899.
17. Ibid., pp. 802–803.
18. Ibid., p. 805.
19. Ibid., p. 310.
20. Ibid., p. 349.
21. Ibid., p. 113.

22. Ibid., pp. 456–457.
23. Ibid., p. 262.
24. Ibid., pp. 594–595, 636.
25. Coakley, D. (1994): *Oscar Wilde: The Importance of Being Irish.* Dublin: Town House, pp. 100–104.
26. *Complete Letters*, pp. 81, 96, 107 and 310.
27. Ibid., p. 347.
28. Ibid., p. 418.
29. *ICD–10 Classification of Mental and Behavioural Disorders*, op. cit., p. 230.
30. *Diagnostic and Statistical Manual of Mental Disorders*, op. cit., pp. 714–717.
31. Douglas, A. (1940): *Oscar Wilde: A Summing-Up.* London: Duckworth, p. 53.
32. *Complete Letters*, p. 69.
33. Ibid., p. 1041.
34. Ibid., p. 759.
35. Melville, J. (1994): *Mother of Oscar.* London: John Murray, pp. 88–106.
36. Law Reports: Ireland (1878), volume 1, pp. 402–412.
37. *Complete Letters*, p. 69.
38. Ibid., p. 70.
39. Hyde, H.M. (1976): *Oscar Wilde.* London: Eyre Methuen, pp. 98–101.
40. *Complete Letters*, p. 690.
41. Holland, M. (2003): *Irish Peacock & Scarlet Marquess: The Real Trial of Oscar Wilde.* London: Fourth Estate.
42. Post, F. (1994). Creativity and psychopathology: a study of 291 world famous men. *British Journal of Psychiatry*, 165, 22–34.

Chapter 13 The Last Words

1. Behrman, S.N. (1960): *Conversation with Max.* London: Quality Book Club, p. 68.
2. Letter from Reginald Turner to Robert Sherard, 21 June 1938. Manuscripts, Reading University.
3. Cecil, D. (1964): *Max: A Biography.* London: Constable, p. 85.
4. Holland, M. and Hart-Davis, R. (2000) (editors): *The Complete Letters of Oscar Wilde.* London: Fourth Estate, p. 732.
5. Ibid., p. 995.
6. Letter from Max Beerbohm to Reginald Turner, 1 December 1900. In Hart-Davis, R. (editor) (1964): *Max Beerbohm: Letters to Reggie Turner.* London: Rupert Hart-Davis.
7. Letter from Reginald Turner to Max Beerbohm, 8 December 1900. In *Complete Letters*, p. 1225.
8. Letter from Robert Ross to William Rothenstein, 11 December 1900, cited in Rothenstein, W. (1931): *Men and Memories.* London: Faber and Faber.
9. Letter from Robert Ross to Adela Schuster, 23 December 1900. In *Complete Letters*, p. 1229.
10. Stokes, J. (1996). Wilde at bay: the diary of George Ives. In Stokes, J.: *Oscar Wilde: Myths, Miracles and Imitations.* Cambridge: Cambridge University Press, pp. 83–84.
11. Harris, F. (1938): *Oscar Wilde.* London: Constable, p. 371.

Appendix

1. *Handbook for the Sixteen Personality Factor Questionnaire (16PF)* (1970 edition), by Cattell, R.B., Eber, H.W. and Tatsuoka, M.M. Institute for Personality and Ability Testing Inc., Champaign, Illinois (1992).
2. Vernier, P. (1998). A 'Mental Photograph' of Oscar Wilde. *The Wildean*, number 13, 28–51.
3. *Handbook for the Sixteen Personality Factor Questionnaire (16PF)*, op. cit., p. 93.
4. Kohl, N. (1989): *Oscar Wilde: The Works of a Conformist Rebel* (translated by Wilson, D.H.), Cambridge: Cambridge University Press, p. 323.

5.   Shaw, G.B. My memories of Oscar Wilde. In Harris, F: *Oscar Wilde*, new edition (1989). New York: Dorset Press, p. 340.

6.   Douglas, A. (1940): *Oscar Wilde: A Summing-Up*. London: Duckworth, p. 90.

7.   Drevdahl, J.E. and Cattell, R.B. (1958). Personality and creativity in artists and writers. *Journal of Clinical Psychology*, 14, 107–111.

8.   *Handbook for the Sixteen Personality Factor Questionnaire (16PF)*, op. cit., pp. 192 and 227.

9.   Ellmann, R. (1987): *Oscar Wilde*. London: Hamish Hamilton, pp. 3–35.

10. Ibid., p. 24.

11. Holland, M. and Hart-Davis, R. (2000) (editors): *The Complete Letters of Oscar Wilde*. London: Fourth Estate, p. 969.

INDEX

B = Douglas, Lord Alfred ("Bosie")
C = Wilde, Constance Mary (née Lloyd)
O = Wilde, Oscar Fingal O'Flahertie Wills
Q = Queensberry, Lord John Sholto Douglas, ninth Marquess of